Toxic Voices

Northwestern University Press
Studies in Russian Literature and Theory

Toxic Voices

THE VILLAIN FROM EARLY SOVIET LITERATURE
TO SOCIALIST REALISM

Eric Laursen

NORTHWESTERN UNIVERSITY PRESS / EVANSTON, ILLINOIS

Northwestern University Press
www.nupress.northwestern.edu

This book has been published with the support of the Andrew W. Mellon Foundation.

Printed in the United States of America

10 9 8 7 6 5 4 3 2 1

Library of Congress Cataloging-in-Publication Data

Laursen, Eric, 1957–
Toxic voices : the villain from early Soviet literature to Socialist realism / Eric Laursen.
p. cm. — (Northwestern University Press studies in Russian literature and theory)
Includes bibliographical references and index.
ISBN 978-0-8101-2865-1 (cloth : alk. paper)
1. Russian literature—20th century—History and criticism. 2. Socialist realism in literature. 3. Villains in literature. I. Title. II. Series: Studies in Russian literature and theory.
PG3026.S58L38 2013
891.7093580904—dc23

2012022488

♾ The paper used in this publication meets the minimum requirements of the American National Standard for Information Sciences—Permanence of Paper for Printed Library Materials, ANSI Z39.48-1992.

For Mary Lou Vaughan and for Sarah and Emma Laursen—my mother, who gave me books, and my daughters, who opened them up again

In other times a young poet would have found inspiration in his bent figure wandering through the clouds of snow with his billowing muffler. But now the times were different: it was not blizzards which transported poets, nor stars, nor countries beyond the clouds, but the sound of hammers all over the country, the whine of saws, the hiss of sickles, the whistle of scythes, happy, mundane songs.

—Aleksey Tolstoy, *Aelita, or the Decline of Mars* (1922)

Contents

Acknowledgments

This project received the generous support of the Tanner Humanities Center, where I was a Virgil D. Aldrich Fellow in fall 2000, and the University of Utah, which awarded me a faculty fellowship in spring 2001; this year of leave was crucial to beginning my work on this manuscript, and I am most grateful. And in the firm belief that every public thank-you should include a teacher or two, I would also like to thank Harry Weber, who worked with me on a master's thesis on Gladkov's *Cement* many years ago at the University of Iowa. A wonderful teacher and caring mentor, Harry passed away recently, and I will always remember his kindness and belief in me. He taught me to read and to trust my instincts, lessons I have returned to many times in the course of this book. I would also like to thank Judith Kornblatt for a wonderful seminar on the Soviet 1920s at the University of Wisconsin-Madison, where my interest in the questions addressed in this book was piqued; much later, her encouragement gave me the impetus to push forward at a crucial time in the project. I would also like to thank Jane Hacking and Rimma Garn for their unwavering support and for picking up the slack in the Russian program more times than I can count in the final stages of this project. Most important, a huge debt of gratitude is owed to Christine Jones, who read every page of this book many times. Her challenging questions, steady encouragement, and the example of her intellectual daring continually pushed me to say what I needed to say. It was a wild ride. Finally, I want to thank my daughters, Sarah and Emma, and my wife Carolyn for their constant support and patience, and once again, I thank my mom, Mary Lou Vaughan, who gave me the gift of books.

Note on Transliteration

All texts are translated into English. When I have indicated the original Russian, I have used the Library of Congress system of transliteration. Surnames and the names of some institutions have been left in their most popular forms (e.g., Gorky, Proletkult).

Toxic Voices

Introduction

Scrounging in the Soviet Garbage Pit

> The millennia are like some garbage pit. The pit is littered with machines, bits of scrap iron, tin, screws, springs. It's a dark gloomy hole. But there's a glow from the rotting wood, the phosphorescent fungi, the mold. Those are our feelings! That's all there is left of our feelings, the flowering of our souls. The New Man comes up to the pit, scrounges around, crawls into it, picks out what he needs—some machine part that's still got some good in it, a wrench maybe—but he crushes the rotting wood under his foot and stamps out its glow.
> —Yury Olesha, *Envy* (1927)

SOCIALIST REALISM, like Olesha's "new man," seems to have had little use for the past except as scrap metal and spare parts for its literary factories and collective farms where the Communist future was always under construction. However, the villains who play such an important part in the socialist realist plot—the kulaks and obstructionists, bourgeois throwbacks and wreckers, saboteurs and Nazis—are creatures constructed *entirely* of the past, cobbled together from scraps of luminous rotting wood found in the literary garbage pit. Despite the intriguing presence of their toxic glow, most studies of the Soviet era overlook the recycled villains of socialist realism in favor of its freshly minted heroes and their reflection of the Communist future. Focusing on the villain, however, reveals that far from abandoning the poisonous toxins of the past, socialist realism was intentionally designed to deploy them as psychic chemotherapy for the Soviet reader, a literary treatment for the cancers caused by a class society: selfishness, escapist dreaming, and the desire to exploit others. This book explores the development of this therapy in the period leading up the official adoption of socialist realism in 1934.

After the 1917 Revolution, there were loud calls for an entirely new literature and an unprecedented hero, but most Soviet protagonists were still written with the weak wills and self-centered angst of prerevolutionary heroes.[1] In this book I argue that these trashy antiheroes of the early Soviet period were not crushed underfoot when the hero strode out of the garbage pit and into the socialist realist factory. Instead they became the villains of socialist realism, important components of a hygienic literary strategy that developed from a variety of influences in the early Soviet period. I explore a diversity of texts, from banned books to Soviet classics, with a view from the garbage pit as well as from the factory floor, to show that if the hero accomplishes the great deed that moves Soviet society closer to Communism, the villain's example transforms the hero so that he can imagine this bright future and act to bring it about. It was none other than the toxins glowing in the literary garbage pit that fed the bright light of socialist realism.

A NEW PARADIGM

Scholars posit a model of human development in socialist realism that is very similar to that of Marxism-Leninism, an evolution ever upward toward the perfected human being imagined by Communism, the "New Person" (*Novyi Chelovek*). Leon Trotsky in *Literature and Revolution* (1924) describes this New Person as a higher type of human being, in whom the intellectual and the emotional would no longer be at odds:

> Man will make it his purpose to master his own feelings, to raise his instincts to the heights of consciousness, to make them transparent, to extend the wires of his will into hidden recesses, and thereby to raise himself to a new plane, to create a higher social biologic type, or, if you please, a superman. . . . Man will become immeasurably stronger, wiser and subtler; his body will become more harmonized, his movements more rhythmic, his voice more musical.[2]

Motivating forces that reside in the lower regions of the body—gut, groin, heart—would now all be controlled by the conscious mind: feelings would be mastered by intellect and instincts would be elevated "to the heights of consciousness." The result would be a biochemical symphony, with every cell united in "harmony" and "rhythm" and every thought, every word "more musical," tuned to the key of Communist principles.

Bronze and stone avatars of this future New Person once towered above all the sacred places of Soviet achievement, their glowing faces reflecting the light of the bright future of Communism, and their steadfast gaze directing lesser, flesh-and-blood comrades forward. With the onset of socialist realism every art form from opera to propaganda posters emulated their metallic heroism. Scholarly studies of the Soviet period have devoted considerable energies to excavating these larger-than-life heroes. Nowhere is this truer than in literary scholarship, where the hero is rightly seen as integral to the transformative mission of socialist realism and frequently compared to invincible heroes of past literature such as those found in formulaic saints' lives or folk epics.[3] Diverse and often contradictory studies have found a common denominator in these men and women constructed from stainless steel and party conferences, and the present study owes much to them.[4] However, this book turns its lens away from the hero's mesmerizing face and onto the villain, who can always be seen lurking at the foot of his pedestal, eager to pull him back into the garbage pit. By turning from the hero to the villain, I show that the vision of the Soviet New Person that informs socialist realism is not in fact Trotsky's harmonized superman but instead an unstable psyche in constant need of maintenance by "engineers of the human soul."

The vision of a precariously balanced psyche put forth in the present study departs significantly from the spontaneity-consciousness paradigm that dominates scholarship on the Soviet period. Under this paradigm, the New Person sheds the darkness and chaos of spontaneity (*stikhiinost'*) for the light of consciousness (*soznatel'nost'*) or awareness of the truth of Marxism-Leninism, handed down by an already conscious vanguard (the Bolsheviks).[5] It is a model of human evolution as one of steady progress forward. The dominance of the spontaneity-consciousness paradigm rests on the priority given in studies of Soviet culture to Lenin's 1902 essay *What Is to Be Done? Burning Questions of Our Movement*, in which he argues that "the task of Social Democracy is *to combat spontaneity, to divert* the working-class movement from this spontaneous, trade-unionist striving to come under the wing of the bourgeoisie, and to bring it under the wing of revolutionary Social Democracy."[6] Lenin's mistrust of the proletariat's spontaneity became the definitive statement on the Bolshevik vision of human transformation.[7] The depiction of the positive heroes of socialist realism, in control of their actions, their emotions, and even the people around them, would seem to support this fear of the spontaneous. However, the figure of the villain reveals that the total suppression of the extra-conscious is no more desired than its unharnessed expression. The New Person must maintain a precarious balance between unharnessed desire and cold intellect, a balance engineered and maintained by Soviet writers.

This literary reevaluation of the spontaneity-consciousness paradigm finds inspiration in recent work by historians who have challenged the critical commonplace that spontaneity was viewed as negative by the early Soviets.[8] Lars Lih, in his study of spontaneity and consciousness, asserts: "[the idea] that the essence of Leninism is pessimism about the workers simply did not occur to the people most informed about Lenin's life and outlook."[9] Anna Krylova has taken this observation a step further, revealing that early Soviets viewed "the extra-conscious (that is, the 'spontaneous,' the instinctual, and the emotional)" as a positive force inherent in the proletariat and as necessary to the revolution as the vanguard's consciousness.[10] This positive view of the extra-conscious as a necessary if volatile aspect of the human psyche is omnipresent in literature of the early Soviet period. The New Person may need to acquire an intellectual understanding of Communism in order to consistently direct the extra-conscious to the needs of the group, but he or she must not lose the connection to the physical world and to other people that allows ideas to be put into action.

Concern about the imbalance of the extra-conscious and the intellect drives the texts treated here, all of which embody the problem in two familiar antagonists. The animalistic "beast," a frequent target of early Soviet satire, follows the dictates of the body, motivated by greed and selfish desire. The dissociative "alien," central to the early Soviet fantastic, lives a life of the mind, building castles in the air and dreaming dreams that are never fulfilled. I examine both of these character types to show that the socialist realist villain was formed from these denizens of satire and the fantastic, and that a strategy evolves in texts of the early Soviet period that galvanizes even as it rejects the energies of the villain: in order to overcome the mind-body disconnect, the beast and the alien are silenced and their individualistic desires translated into collective desire. The hero must learn to harness—that is, in a sense, to embrace—the forces they represent for the good of the group and to maintain a balance at the center of a continuum with the beast on one end and the alien on the other. This strategy was already formed by the end of the First Five-Year Plan (1928–32), but the period of socialist realism witnesses an escalating panic about the difficulty of controlling reader response, which is essential to this strategy, and as the Stalinist period moves forward, the alien and the beast become increasingly distanced from the hero and by his influence from the reader, seen more and more as hostile outside forces intent on knocking the Soviet reader from a precarious psychic balance.

RECYCLING TOXIC HEROES

Literary scholars have long searched for the origins of socialist realism, finding the scrap metal for its bronze heroes in the prototypes mentioned at the First Congress of the Soviet Writers' Union in 1934 and in the theories of avant-garde and proletarian literary groups.[11] This study casts a wider net to suggest that socialist realism is the culmination of debates in the early Soviet period about character, genre, and language that began before the Bolshevik

Revolution and intensified in the latter half of the 1920s. These discussions were conducted not only by the militant avant-garde and proletarian groups, but also by the "fellow travelers" (*poputchiki*), a term coined by Trotsky to describe non-Communist writers who supported the general goals of the revolution. In the early Soviet period these fellow travelers created antiheroes, weak-willed, self-centered characters filled with longing for the past and doubt about the future. When socialist realism was officially adopted, the antiheroes of the early Soviet period were resoundingly trashed, not only by Communist critics, but also by their own creators.[12] Scholars therefore view the transition to socialist realism as an abrupt break in literary history—the creatures of the 1920s are expelled from the pages of Soviet literature and replaced with wholesome models of virtue. This book rests on an alternate vision in which antiheroes of the early Soviet period are neither discarded nor made into positive heroes but instead become radical extremes of their former selves. The two negative qualities of 1920s antiheroes that were most criticized—selfishness and doubt—become super-concentrated in the villain and paradoxically serve as a catalyst for transforming the positive hero and through him the Soviet reader. Socialist realist plots transfigure the dangerous radioactive "glow" from the garbage pit into radiation therapy.

Prior to the First Five-Year Plan, genres that gave birth to stock characters—satire (the beast) and the fantastic (the alien)—challenged the literary status quo by directing doubt at the textual world.[13] If they dominate this period as revolutionary weapons in the writer's arsenal, it is because satire and the fantastic targeted enemies and pointed the way to social reform. When revolution gave way to reconstruction, these volatile genres and characters were modified with the intention of turning them into useful tools of social stability. By looking at texts that represent key moments or tendencies of early Soviet literature, this book traces the evolution of an increasing anxiety over the toxic voices of the antihero turned villain and the increasingly urgent response to this anxiety. Over the course of the 1920s writers, critics, editors, literary groups, and censors put their collective hand into a campaign of literary eugenics, picking and celebrating those texts that passed muster and censoring and vilifying those that did not. Through this campaign, there arose a series of narrative strategies that writers were led to use to contain the fear of toxic voices: introducing the villain as possible hero, exposing the villain as anti-Soviet, and then translating the villains' and the heroes' beastly selfishness or alien dreaming into collective desire. Writers individually enacted this plot and advanced or challenged the development of these literary strategies. Thus, it was not only top-down legislation that informed socialist realism when it was adopted. The many recastings of genres by the early Soviet period's best writers helped illuminate what worked politically and what did not.

To track the evolution of these strategies across Soviet literature, I have chosen to examine texts that are disparate in type but united by their concentration on human transformation. Each chapter focuses on one genre—utopia (chapter 1), satire (chapter 2), the fantastic (chapter 3), and the production novel (chapter 4)—and pairs close readings of two texts, one of which uses but fails to complete a generic strategy and one that attempts to address this failure. Each of the genres discussed is informed by early Soviet anxieties not only concerning the transformation of society, but more important to this study, the transformation of literature itself. The banned novels and Soviet classics discussed in this book together reveal the development in early Soviet culture of a profound conflict about the role of art in society that informs literary production in the age of socialist realism.

Chapter 1 outlines the conflict at the heart of the Soviet literary project through readings of the first Bolshevik utopia, Aleksandr Bogdanov's *Red Star* (1908), which had a profound impact on literature of the 1920s, and Evgeny Zamyatin's dystopia *We* (1920), which interrogates the devices of Bogdanov's novel. Both utopia and dystopia are written in the form of diaries and are united in their focus on the writer and his power to transform himself and others. They divide, however, on what that power entails. Bogdanov's novel speaks to the proletarian writers' efforts to "organize the human psyche" with the written word, while Zamyatin's novel argues for the written word as an instrument of eternal revolution, designed to *disorganize* the human psyche. Together they show a central conflict in the early Soviet period between writers who viewed themselves and their work as tools for building the Communist utopia, and writers who viewed themselves and their work as conforming to the long tradition of the Russian intelligentsia to challenge authority and nurture societal change through literature. Despite this conflict, both *We* and *Red Star* accomplish their goals in the same way: by the revolutionary act of exposing the alien and beast. Zamyatin's novel stops there, arguing that revolution should be an eternal process fostered by heretical writers. Bogdanov's novel, on the other hand, creates a balance between the alien and the beast through the narrator's act of writing about them—the dystopian novel is made utopian by bringing its writer-narrator to a psychic equilibrium.

Although the happy endings of socialist realism might seem like replicas of Bogdanov's writing-induced utopia, they also contain a dystopian echo, a distrust of stasis, an insistence that this balance is precarious and must be fiercely protected from enemies lurking in the darkness, ready to topple the organized psyche of the Soviet reader. Chapters 2 through 4 examine the evolution of this uneasy coexistence of the utopian mission of socialist realism and its pervasive dystopian fear. I argue that the two visions of literature outlined in chapter 1 merge to make socialist realism a hybrid of utopian and revolutionary literature in which an idealized and unstable reality is under constant threat of outside attack. As Soviet literature becomes increasingly focused on its utopian mission, it also becomes increasingly informed by an anxiety concerning the danger of the villain to socialist realism's command to depict "reality in its revolutionary development," that is, to show the present and past as moving toward Communism. The resulting dystopian fear leads to ever more rigid attempts to control reader response. Paradoxically, the only way to protect the reader from the villain is to depict fiercely anti-Soviet characters in high relief.

Chapter 2 examines two satires of the early Soviet period that expose the dangers of selfishness in the context of campaigns to change people into Communists by changing language. Exposing characters who use Soviet words for selfish and exploitative purposes, Mikhail Bulgakov's novella *Heart of a Dog* (1925) reveals that everyone is a beast—despite the new words they speak, no one has been transformed into a New Person. Vladimir Mayakovsky's play *Bedbug* (1929), on the other hand, exposes the beast and his pseudo-Soviet speech against a backdrop of utopian collective speech, pointing the way toward socialist realism but also illuminating with its own devices the dystopian fear that would reside there. Including a villainous voice in a utopian text introduces a danger that would be trumpeted by writers, editors, and critics as Soviet literature moved toward socialist realism. In increasingly virulent attacks on satire in the late 1920s and early 1930s we see a rising anxiety concerning the control of satirical exposure. How does one design a villain who effectively and predictably repulses the reader?

In the First Five-Year Plan (1928–32), this question came to the fore, as Soviet literature turned from diagnosis of society's problems to cure, and in chapter 3 I examine two texts that bookend the plan and illustrate the increasingly strident call for a narrator who would not only expose the villain but also translate his selfish desire into collective desire. Yury Olesha's *Envy* (1927) exposes the alien dreamer in an unreliable narrator who holds the potential to lead the reader astray. Like *Heart of a Dog* and *We*, Olesha's novel ends with exposure but fails to show transformation, to translate alien dreaming into "reality in its revolutionary development," that is, to show the present and past as moving toward Communism. Critical attacks on *Envy* during the First Five-Year Plan manifest a newly minted intolerance for satirical exposure without translation. Lev Kassil's *Shvambraniia* (1932) attempts to meet this criticism with a narrator who chronicles for the reader his own conversion from useless alien dreamer to Soviet writer. This strategy anticipates the hygienic impulse of later socialist realism, a specialized use of the fantastic that introduces doubt so that it can be dramatically cleansed from the text for the benefit of the reader.

Chapter 4 explores how the strategies discussed in previous chapters become formal plot devices in the early Soviet production novel, one of the mainstays of later socialist realism. In Fedor Gladkov's *Cement* (1925), one of the novels mentioned as a model for socialist realism at the First Writers' Congress in 1934, aliens and beasts inspire heroes to eradicate inner doubt by translating their own beastly desire and alien dreaming into collective desire. The successful transformation of heroes is signaled by the acquisition of a new, unifying language that is representative of a mounting pressure to create in Soviet literature a collective voice emanating from a collective hero emptied of self. Valentin Kataev's *Time Forward!* (1932), a production novel published at the conclusion of the First Five-Year Plan, brings this hero to fruition in its depiction of a series of writers at a five-year-plan construction site, who must either embrace the emptying of self and channeling of the collective voice required of the Soviet writer or must become a silenced villain.

Leon Trotsky proposed the creation of a New Person with a "voice more musical," a harmonious expression of an organized psyche. This study traces the evolution not of this musical voice but of the toxic voice that ensured its harmony. When socialist realism was officially adopted in 1934, these two voices would occupy center stage. In counterpoint to the voice more musical, the villain's voice would rise up in each successive performance, destined to a dramatic fade-out, as doubt and selfishness were overpowered by crescendos of optimism and collective achievement. Inevitably, the villain's cry threatened to upstage the melodious voice of the hero and to turn harmony into uncontrolled dissonance even as it faded to assure triumphant finales. Soviet literature, seemingly designed to engineer musical voices, was in fact organized entirely around the anxiety over controlling doubt and selfishness, expressed by the toxic voices of its villains.

Chapter One

Writing a Precarious Balance

> Our friend Robinson . . . having rescued a watch, ledger, and pen and ink from the wreck, commences, like a true-born Briton, to keep a set of books.
>
> —Karl Marx, *Capital,* volume 1 (1867)

IN ILYA ILF AND EVGENY PETROV'S "How Robinson Was Created" ("Kak sozdavalsia Robinson," 1933), a writer is assigned the task of composing a "Soviet Robinson Crusoe." He obediently drafts the story of a sole shipwreck survivor, fighting the elements and bravely battling a hostile environment with only his wit and resourcefulness to aid him in the struggle. Remarkably, his manuscript is rejected on the basis that there is nothing *Soviet* about the Soviet Robinson. The editor then suggests a series of changes to *make* it Soviet: now, among the things that must wash up on shore with the hero are a committee to conduct party meetings, a woman activist to collect dues, a safe for the dues, a meeting table, and a pitcher of water, a bottle of ink, and a bell to call meetings to order. Conscious of the writer's fragile ego, the editor concludes his detailed directives with the caveat: "The tablecloth can be of any kind—red, green. I'm not one to interfere with the work of the creative artist."[1] The table washed up on the shore of Robinson's island is intended to draw a laugh, but countless such tables were quite seriously described in later socialist realist novels, each representing the link of the individual collective to the overarching universal consciousness. Robinson's table is analogous to Mircea Eliade's "axis mundi," the symbolic place at religious sites where heaven and earth meet.[2] It may be decorated with a tablecloth of the author's choosing, but, underneath, the table is the same in each work of Soviet literature; it is the collective consciousness informing the individual writer's creative imagination. Under socialist realism, no writer is a creative island; he or she is linked to the mainland by such a table and by an editor who ensures that a bottle of ink and a set of stock symbols are placed upon it. By sitting at the collective table and obeying the instructions of the collective editor, the writer will transform the individualist Robinsons of the past into collectively conscious Robinsons.

The comical changes suggested by the editor in Ilf and Petrov's 1933 story provide an outline of the all-too-serious requirements that would soon exist when socialist realism was officially adopted in 1934. First of all, the editor forbids a romance, "cheap vulgarity and unwholesome eroticism,"[3] between Robinson and the female activist: the beast must be harnessed and desire controlled. Second, the editor suggests that the wave wash up "the masses, the broad strata of the laboring people,"[4] and that the island be changed to a peninsula: the alien must be directed away from his individual imagination and linked with the collective imagination. The Soviet Robinson therefore exists in a precarious balance. He must be a heroic leader yet not at all separate from the masses. And he must be passionate yet in control of his passions. These editorial commands rule out traditional conflicts found in Western literature—the hero in conflict with society and the hero in conflict with himself. And the editor's final command reveals that the Soviet Robinson must be written entirely without Robinson: "Throw him out altogether. A preposterous, totally indefensible figure of a whining pessimist."[5] The editor's dismissal of the novel's main character and central conflict points to a problem that lies at the heart of Soviet literature: the writer must create a hero as intriguing as the Onegins, Pechorins, and Levins of prerevolutionary Russian literature, but the Soviet novel must be emptied of the conflicted "whining pessimists" at the heart of literary history.

Ilf and Petrov's satire on the Soviet writer seems prophetic. It was published in the year between the founding of the Soviet Writers' Union and its First Congress, when Soviet writers were given their one and only assignment: change readers into New People with the written word. "How Robinson Was Created" can in this context be read as a disturbing prophecy of the literary future, where no writer's hero would be safe from revision. It can also be seen as a final comment on the tumultuous early Soviet period, on the long journey to expel the whining pessimists from Soviet literature. It is the thesis of this book, however, that whining pessimists did not simply disappear beneath the tsunami of positive heroes that inundated the socialist realist peninsula. They remained, but even when seated at the standard, albeit sandy, meeting table, the Soviet Robinson can be seen only as a villain.

ORGANIZING THE HUMAN PSYCHE

Immediately after the revolution, the Proletkult (Proletarian Cultural and Educational Organization) promoted the production of cultural products that would not only reflect the ideas of the ruling class—now the proletariat—but also cure the person viewing or reading them of the crippling infection of bourgeois ideology.[6] Proletkult was founded by Aleksandr Bogdanov, the Bolshevik physician, philosopher, and science fiction writer, who returned to Russia in 1917 with plans to build a new proletarian culture.[7] Bogdanov calls for an art that would appeal not only to the intellect but also to feelings: "By means of living images art organizes social experience, not only in the sphere of cognition but also in the sphere of feelings and desires. Therefore, it is the mightiest weapon in the organization of collective forces, in a class society of class forces."[8] Affecting the extra-conscious, "the sphere of feelings and desires," would be vitally important to creating the organized psyche of the Soviet New Person. Heart and mind would need to be co-ordinated into a single organized entity and individual organized psyches brought together into a single worldwide collective. Bogdanov argues that any remaining aesthetic value from past art, music, and literature lies in the human being's instinctual response to this organizing power—the Venus de Milo served to organize the religious community of the ancient world, and modern viewers appreciate its beauty because something of that power draws them to the statue.[9] Art not only reflects the "ruling ideas of the ruling class," but also unites people in action—or inaction—according to the dictates of its ideals.[10] Accordingly, religious art draws people into "submission, humility, and blind faith," and bourgeois art nurtures "individualism." In Bogdanov's view, proletarian art would for the first time nourish something completely positive: "deep solidarity, comradely cooperation, a close brotherhood of warriors and builders, united by a common ideal."[11]

Bogdanov gives little instruction on the literary strategies that would produce this "deep solidarity," but his own creative writing, which had a profound impact on literature of the 1920s, provides insight. After the Bolshevik Revolution, his science fiction novel *Red Star: Novel-Utopia* (*Krasnaia zvezda: Roman-utopiia,* 1908) had a second life. New editions of this highly influential book came out in 1918, 1922, and again after Bogdanov's death in 1928, and it was produced as a play by the Proletkult in 1920. In *Red Star* the Earthling Leonid visits a futuristic communist society on the planet Mars, goes insane, and returns to Earth, where he regains sanity by writing about his experiences (the novel is in the form of Leonid's journal). The first half of this chapter examines Bogdanov's literary prescription for organizing the human psyche as presented in *Red Star.* The second half turns to Evgeny Zamyatin's *We* (*My,* 1920), which was written at the height of the Proletkult and which engages critically with Bogdanov's novel and with his cure for the fractured psyche. Zamyatin's response to Bogdanov's utopia is a dystopian vision of a communist future often held up as an anti-Soviet anthem of individuality and protest. As Phillip E. Wegner notes, however, reading the novel primarily as an anti-Soviet anti-utopia limits our understanding of the book, because Zamyatin, like the Bolsheviks, argued for "total transformation of both society and the subjects that inhabit it."[12] Indeed, a comparison with Bogdanov's novel reveals that *We* is not so much anti-Soviet as anti-Proletkult.[13] Zamyatin's criticism of Bogdanov and the Proletkult is not an uncommon one, especially among "fellow travelers" (*poputchiki*), Leon Trotsky's term for those writers who were not Communists but who more or less supported the revolution. Comparing the first Bolshevik utopia and the first banned novel reveals a key divide in early Soviet debates over the transformation of heroes into villains, and, more important, over the dedication of literature to transforming Soviet readers.

SUPERFLUOUS MEN IN UTOPIA: ALEKSANDR BOGDANOV'S *RED STAR: NOVEL-UTOPIA* (1908)

Utopias of the late nineteenth and early twentieth centuries often transport a well-educated man to a future society, where humankind lives in perfect harmony, freed from the injustices of the past. The naive time-traveler is taken on a grand tour of utopia, with obligatory stops at egalitarian government institutions, innovative schools, and clean, well-lit workplaces, where fulfilled people create beautiful things with marvelous technology. In this brand of utopian narrative, the traveler's excursion to the future constitutes a brightly lit realization of his own theories about society, religion, and family, filled with shiny, glass-and-metal extrapolations of contemporary science and technology.[14] Bogdanov's "novel-utopia" is no exception; the Bolshevik revolutionary Leonid is brought to Mars and escorted around the hospitals, museums, factories, and schools of his Martian hosts, where he is treated to a wondrous vision of a communist future complete with flying cars and 3D color movies. As the Bolsheviks predicted, archaic institutions such as government and family have withered away, and Leonid is confronted with all his fondly held principles of equality and community come to life, fulfilled in each and every Martian activity, from raising children to piloting spaceships.

There is, however, an undercurrent of dystopia in Bogdanov's utopia. The Bolshevik revolutionary who fights for the communist future is driven insane when he has to live in it, and the Martians who have built the communist future have either lost the will to live or the desire to share their utopia with others. Whether on Earth or Mars the inhabitants of Bogdanov's solar system are unbalanced—Martian men are rational but cold and unfeeling, while Leonid, the novel's earthly hero, is passionate but self-centered and irrational. Both the natives of Mars and their earthly visitor are superfluous men in a communist utopia, who demonstrate that simply intellectualizing the ideas of communism or feeling the solidarity of the collective is not enough. One must be able to combine intellect with feeling in order to achieve the organized psyche that Bogdanov proposed, and literature is the tool that would create and then continually calibrate this equilibrium. Accordingly, after going insane on Mars, Leonid returns to Earth and restores equilibrium by writing about his experiences in utopia. He organizes his own fragmented psyche and thereby becomes a New Person, able to use the passion of the beast for effective action and yet control it with the cool intellect of the alien. Yet the ease with which Leonid transforms himself into a suitable citizen of utopia belies the fragility of the New Person envisioned by *Red Star,* which only the writer's pen keeps in its precarious balance.

The Superfluous Man as Alien

Ellen Chances, in her study of the "superfluous man" (*lishnii chelovek*), the ubiquitous hero of nineteenth-century Russian literature, defines this character as one who cannot or will not conform to the status quo.[15] In the communist society of Bogdanov's Mars, nonconformity to the status quo signals a character at odds with the principles of communism. And as Andrey Sinyavsky writes in his underground essay "On Socialist Realism" (1960), such a character occupies an unacceptable gray area in Soviet morality and therefore has no place in a literature of clearly defined heroes and villains: "To the positive hero of the new era he was strange and incomprehensible. The superfluous man seemed to him much more dangerous than the openly negative enemy."[16] Indeed, in *Red Star,* the coldly calculating men of Mars have become detached from the principle of the "Whole" that supposedly governs their entire society, and in their nonconformity, they are capable of contemplating the liquidation of Earth's entire population. The Martian men Leonid observes have lost the capacity to feel, and therefore they have become superfluous men in a communist utopia, alien to the very world they inhabit.

Bogdanov's Mars is a dying planet, and Martians must colonize either Venus or Earth in order to survive. At the conference to decide Earth's fate, there is a distinct emotional coldness to the Martian men Sterni and Menni, who calmly and rationally discuss liquidating the Earthlings. Sterni speaks in a "mathematical, businesslike tone"[17] which reflects the rational morality that he uses to measure the value of lives quantitatively. Since Mars needs Earth's resources and since there are only a few "embryonic human beings" (116) on Earth (the revolutionaries), he argues that it is justified to exterminate them in favor of the much greater number of fully human Martians. Sterni lacks an organized psyche, which would view the universe as an indivisible whole, where every component is indispensable. His decision-making process is cut off from feeling, and therefore he cannot connect with this Whole: "Sterni has a very strong but cold and for the most part analytical mind. He lays out everything inexorably and logically, and his conclusions are often one-sided, sometimes extremely severe, because an analysis of the parts gives you not the whole but less than the whole" (32). Because he is disconnected from his emotions and instincts, Sterni cannot see the value that Earthlings, who operate primarily from the extra-conscious, might have. On the contrary, Sterni fears that the more rational Martians might be infected by Earthlings' negative emotions and instincts, were they to colonize an inhabited Earth: "Little by little, our life would be penetrated by suspicion, mistrust and an egoistic greed for self-preservation and the brutality that comes with it" (112). Contact with Earthlings would cause a degeneration of Martians into primitive pre-socialist beasts.

In a society that claims to love life more than anything, suicide is common on Mars, and assisted-suicide centers have been set up for those who have lost the will to live. Those who choose suicide seem to do so because they have failed to develop the emotional coldness of Sterni or Menni; they have retained their connection to the extra-conscious, and because of their passion or emotional sensitivity they are unable to continue living in a rational utopia. Letta has an "especially gentle and sensitive nature" (36) and Enno has an "ardent, youthful imagination" (66), and therefore they are unable to thrive on Mars, where the cold, dying planet reflects the passionless intellects of many of their fellow citizens. Letta and Enno postpone their suicide plans only because they have been chosen for the mission to Earth, and reason that duty to the collective calls them; but going to Earth and meeting Leonid awakens within them passion and purpose. The elderly Letta still dies on the journey, but his death now has meaning; he sacrifices himself in order to save Leonid when a wall of the spaceship ruptures. The beautiful Enno abandons her suicide plans when she meets Leonid—she returns to Mars with a renewed desire to live. Leonid is brought to Mars in order to decide whether Earthlings are necessary to the cosmic "whole"; Enno's rebirth and Letta's sacrifice on the journey back proves early in his journey that Mars is sorely in need of the passion found on its more primitive neighbor.

Again at the conference to decide whether to colonize Venus or Earth, Menni speaks at length, but his only argument for settling Venus rather than Earth concerns the ease of finding radioactive fuel there. A life of the mind has weakened his empathy for the Earthlings, among whom he has spent so much time. As a consequence, his wife Enno is not only intellectually attracted to Leonid but also sexually aroused by him, partially because Menni has been unable to satisfy her either mentally or physically: "Menni matured from boy to man too late and began to live the extremely intense life of a scientist and thinker too early. Owing to its extreme development, his brain activity sapped and suppressed his reproductive vitality" (98). Menni's doctor recommends that he focus all energy on intellectual production and therefore advises him to avoid physical activity, including sex. With this modification, Menni's work as a psychologist flourishes. The use he makes of psychology, however, demonstrates what happens to the psyche when it is disconnected from the extra-conscious; Menni uses his professional expertise not to cure the mentally ill but to manipulate the sane; while visiting Earth he starts a series of arguments between Leonid and his Earthling wife so that she leaves him, freeing him to go to Mars.

The Whole that the Martians so value is symbolized in *Red Star* by the union of men and women, but on Mars this union is sterile; Sterni and Menni, the two cold Martian men, have passionate, imaginative wives who are unsatisfied spiritually or sexually by their husbands. Netti, Sterni's wife, has the organized psyche envisioned by Bogdanov and the Proletkult; she therefore filters all choices, all decisions through the Whole, which is a collective version of her own organized psyche. But without a suitable mate, Netti exists in perpetual longing to merge with that Whole. She can sense a lack of passion on Mars, which is manifested in her former husband's approach to the world: "Netti began to be repulsed by Sterni's cold, analytical mind. He systematically and stubbornly demolished all of her castles in the air, her intellectual and emotional fantasies, which she so needed in order to live" (102). She has spent her life studying Earth from afar, and at the conference Netti makes an impassioned plea to save the Earthlings, which stands in direct opposition to her former husband's cold, rational analysis of the situation. Because of their more intense struggle to survive, Netti argues, Earthlings have developed more intense emotions: "energy and passion, with such a strong capacity for heroism and martyrdom" (119). Sterni fears these emotions, but Netti believes that joining forces with the Earthlings would create a new collective psyche, in which intellect and emotion would be organized into a seamless whole: "our two worlds . . . will be united into a single uniquely beautiful and harmonious entity" (139). Unlike Sterni, who sees the most advanced form of humanity as one that is cleansed of all emotion, Netti argues that the "highest form of reason" is possible only with emotion: "The unity of life is the highest goal, and love is the highest form of reason" (120). In order for the Martians to advance to a higher stage of evolution, all they need is love.

The Superfluous Man as Beast

The mismatch of cold Martian men and passionate Martian women is mirrored at the beginning of *Red Star* by the romantic partners Leonid, the passionate Bolshevik, and Anna Nikolaevna, the cold, intellectual Menshevik.[18] In Leonid's words:

> Gradually a deep ideological disparity was revealed both in our approach to revolutionary work and in the understanding of our own relationship. She had entered the revolution under the banner of duty and sacrifice and I of my own free will. She joined the great movement of the proletariat as a moralist, finding satisfaction in its highest morality, I as an amoralist, simply love life and desire its highest flowering . . . For Anna Nikolaevna, proletarian ethics were sacred in and of themselves; I thought them to be a useful device, necessary to the working class in its battle but transitory like the battle itself and the way of life born from it. In Anna Nikolaevna's opinion, in a socialist society the transformation of proletarian morality into a universal morality was the only possibility, whereas I found that the proletariat was even now beginning to destroy all moral codes, replacing them with a social feeling that was transforming people into comrades united in labor and joy and suffering, a state of being that could evolve freely and fully only when the fetishistic shell of morality was discarded. (8)

Leonid operates solely from gut feeling, unable to tolerate any intellectual overlay to his emotions. Anna Nikolaevna operates solely from principle, relying on an intellectual interpretation even of love. She accuses him of attempting "to cover a coarsely sensual outlook with an ideological wrapper" (9), and his jealousy proves her right—he wants "free love," but only for himself. When writing about his experiences Leonid asks: "Was it that I did not know how to *feel* as I *thought*?" (103). Indeed, Leonid's Communist ideals are abstract. He does not allow them to affect his emotional life and consequently remains individualistic and proprietary, and he is drawn to difference and hierarchy, not only in his personal relationships with Martians, but also in his vision of history. The individualism surfaces when he is told that Martians honor only collective achievements but nevertheless recommends a monument for one whom he considers especially heroic. Until he matches feeling to thought, his union with Netti, which promises the harmony missing on both planets, is impossible. Although attracted to him, Netti finds Leonid's desire for her aggressive and frightening: "It seemed to me that in your arms I felt your entire youthful world. Its despotism, its egoism, its desperate thirst for happiness—all of this was in your caresses. Your love is like murder" (89). If the cold Martian men lie at the alien end of the human continuum, unable to feel, then Leonid lies at the beastly end, with no intellectual harness for his desires. Like the cold Martian men, he is a superfluous man in a communist utopia.

Throughout the novel, Leonid's primitive state of being—and that of most Earthlings—is compared to the psyche of a child: "It seems to me that the two humanities are like brothers. The elder one has a calm and balanced nature, while the younger one is stormy and impetuous" (46).[19] According to the Martians' "general law of life" (62), children pass through earlier stages of societal development as they mature.[20] Individuality, aggression, and the desire for private property, atavistic remnants of the pre-socialist human, are often manifested by Martian children. When Leonid visits the Children's Home, he witnesses several such acts of selfishness, among them a child's claim that a toy belongs solely to him. Like the boy, Leonid continues to express feelings that are throwbacks to a more primitive time. He was chosen for the trip to Mars because he is a socialist, the most advanced form of Earthling known to Martian scientists. Yet on Mars he demonstrates that even the most evolved life form on Earth is merely an atavistic child, ruled by primitive desire and instinct.

One of the Martians tells Leonid that "unnecessary, excessive violence" (76) is only possible on Mars among the mentally ill: "a reasoning and conscious person is of course incapable of it" (77). Children, however, have not yet become conscious, and without consciousness they are like the insane. At the Children's Home one little Martian boy breaks a frog's leg to punish the animal for not obeying him. A teacher then strikes the boy in order to demonstrate the frog's pain. As the teacher's action shows, violence has not been banished among the adults on Mars. However, it is now used only for the greater good, to instill in the boy a heightened sense that all creatures feel pain. Later, while watching a film on Venus, the boy begins to cry when a dinosaur is killed: "I feel sorry for the monster" (65). Although demonstrating a newfound and necessary empathy for other living creatures, his reaction is nevertheless a sign of immaturity. Whereas the boy's violent act against the frog is cruel and pointless, the Martians' destruction of the dinosaur is necessary in order to obtain natural resources. The boy's act is performed to benefit the individual; the dinosaur's death benefits the Whole. This ability to balance empathy for the individual and empathy for the Whole is a delicate state of being. If the boy feels no empathy for living creatures, he may become cold and unfeeling like Sterni, who sees the extermination of all human beings as a mathematically sound solution to the Martians' troubles. But if he does not filter his empathy through the idea of the Whole, he will become like Leonid, violent, overly emotional, and unable to understand the greater good—trapped forever in childhood and never able to mature.

Leonid's childlike state is manifested in his difficulties with the Martian language. Communist ideas are reflected in grammar and lexicon, and Leonid has yet to mature enough to assimilate these concepts. Although there are no exceptions to the grammatical rules of the Martian language, Leonid continually seeks them—especially exceptions to those rules that reflect the ideas of communism. Since the Martians have achieved equality, the hierarchy implicit in language etiquette is missing, and therefore titles, greetings, and expressions of gratitude are noticeably absent. The Martians have also achieved equality between the sexes, and therefore gender has vanished from the Martian language. Most important, since the Martians have gained a conscious understanding of all of history—past, present, and future—their nouns are declined "temporally" (35). These grammatical traits all signal a transformed mindset that refuses to separate the individual from the whole, whether on the basis of hierarchy, gender, or historical significance. Leonid's immature mind is unable to acclimate to this linguistic egalitarianism. On the journey to Mars, as he struggles to learn the Martian language, Leonid spends much time trying to distinguish differences among his fellow passengers—which of the Martians is in charge, which are men (Martian men and women have evolved to look very similar) and which are deserving of history's nod. Although Leonid is supposedly a conscious revolutionary, he is stuck in a pre-socialist stage of linguistic development.

Leonid's educational process is fraught with difficulty. On Mars he cannot grow up, and, rather than becoming increasingly integrated, his psyche instead becomes increasingly fragmented. Unable to acquire the Martian concept of time, he gradually loses any sense of time and place or of the difference between reality and fantasy. Fragmentary visions of fairy tales, landscapes, and people from childhood and youth appear to him as vivid hallucinations. Netti nurses him back to health but must leave on a scouting trip to Venus, after which Leonid begins to descend into insanity once again. When she leaves, Netti writes a note to Leonid declaring: "I love you not only as a wife, I love you as a mother who guides her child into a new and alien life full of hardships and dangers" (104). This revelation and her departure initiates an Oedipal drama that ends in the murder of Netti's ex-husband, the emotionally cold, threatening Sterni, by the jealous and paranoid child-Earthling. But in order to regress to the primitive state where this can happen, Leonid must withdraw even further from the Whole. He works at a Martian factory and soon becomes alienated from the others, operating from pre-socialist feelings and instincts: "As a person from an individualistic world, it was I who unwillingly and unconsciously separated myself from the rest, and in my sickness I perceived their kindness and comradely services as something—so it seemed to me, a person from a capitalist world—for which I had nothing to repay them" (97). When he gains access to the proceedings of the Martian conference and learns of Sterni's proposal to exterminate Earthlings, he quits work and isolates himself even further, regressing into a more primitive stage of development: "There arose in me an irrepressible desire to throw myself at everything around me, living and dead, to hit, to smash, to destroy everything without a trace. But I still realized that this was senseless and childish" (124). In this violent, atavistic, childish state, "time stopped" (124).

Shortly before he commits murder, Leonid learns that the plan to exterminate Earthlings has been abandoned; nevertheless he strikes Sterni with a tripod and kills him. Like the Martian boy's injury of the frog, this murder is pointless and cruel. His violent act goes against all rational thought and drives him even further into insanity, now compounded by his guilt over the thought that he may have sealed Earth's fate by convincing the Martians that Earthlings are unredeemable. Despite their need for Leonid's passion, his atavistic violence has no place in Martian society; therefore, the Martians return Leonid to Earth, where he is placed in an asylum. However, the asylum's resident psychiatrist provides no real help for Leonid. Instead, writing itself serves as a form of therapy for him, as he interrogates both the alien Martian men and his own beastly self and finds the balance between both extremes that he needs to become a citizen of the communist future. Through writing about his experiences, the superfluous man is cured.

The Writing Cure

According to Bogdanov, the organization of readers' psyches is the goal of Soviet literature—by reading about transformation, Soviet citizens would be transformed into New People. Leonid's trip to Mars does not, however, transform him into a harmonized New Person, at one with the universal Whole. On the contrary, although Leonid is told by the Martians that he will serve as a "living link" (19) between their planets, when he is returned to Earth he feels that he has instead severed all links. He could not adapt to life on Mars, and on Earth he no longer feels that he fits in "either with my intellect or with my feeling" (139). He has become a space-age superfluous man, unable to conform to life on any planet in the solar system. Ending the novel with Leonid's failure would signal a deep and seemingly unbridgeable divide between Earth's past and the Martian bright future.[21] However, since he writes his experiences down, Leonid finds a cure for his own superfluousness and the novel finds its positive ending. As proletarian literary groups promised, writing organizes his psyche, and Leonid's disconnect between mind and body is cured.

One chapter, set in the insane asylum on Earth, is entitled "Did It Happen or Not" ("Bylo—ne bylo," 129), and, as Leonid writes, he is torn between these two possibilities, locked in a liminal world of doubt, an internal battle between reason and feeling. His gut feeling tells him that the trip was real, but his psychiatrist Dr. Werner repeatedly tells him that the trip must be fantasy. Under Werner's guidance, Leonid begins to view his trip to the communist future as "delirium" (130) and "false memories" (130). Guilt-ridden over the murder of Sterni, Leonid welcomes these "calming doubts"

(131): "And although somewhere in the depths of my soul I knew that it was a lie, I stubbornly abandoned myself to it as to a joyful dream" (131). Immersed in this "joyful dream," Leonid now suppresses every aspect of the extra-conscious, becoming disconnected from his instinctual desire for revolution and for the collective. At the asylum, he moves from one end of the continuum to the other, from unharnessed beast to dissociative alien. This state of being may seem less dangerous than his murderous former self or even the cold calculation of the aliens Menni and Sterni, but if Leonid and other Earthlings accept such an existence, the revolution will never happen on Earth—his denial of the trip to Mars is a denial of the communist future.

In the depiction of Dr. Werner, we see a rejection of nineteenth-century psychological realism, which diagnosed the superfluous man and his generation but which offered no cure. Werner shares his name with a character from Mikhail Lermontov's *Hero of Our Time* (1841), a doctor who took the pulse of Grigory Pechorin, Russian literature's most notorious superfluous man.[22] Bogdanov's Dr. Werner, like Lermontov's, fails to cure his patient. In fact, Werner further harms Leonid by forbidding any contact with other revolutionaries, since he believes that revolutionary activities have led to his patient's insanity. Under Werner's care Leonid becomes increasingly isolated and immersed in his "joyful dream" and retreats further and further from any type of positive action. Psychology in Werner's hands is like love for Anna Nikolaevna, Leonid's former Menshevik romantic partner: a principled and unemotional explanation of human emotions, detached from passion and instinct. It is removed from revolution and therefore invokes nothing but empty fantasy, not positive action.

Leonid's writing breaks him out of the reality/fantasy divide and serves as a means of merging the revolutionary present and the communist future. He organizes his emotions through the intellectual act of describing them: "As I wrote these memoirs, the past became clear before me, chaos gave way to definition, and my role and my situation took shape before my consciousness" (137). While writing he explains his instinctual reactions to Martian culture, his confused feelings, and the disconnect between his socialist theories and his gut reactions to the world around him. By identifying the reasons for his own mental breakdown and the horror he found when faced with the coldness of the Martian men, Leonid creates literary characters out of the Martians and himself; he becomes the narrator of his own experiences, choosing and weighing the feelings and thoughts that guided him in his irrational choices and the Martians in their overly rational arguments. The characters he creates from his journey serve as clear literary examples of existence on the far ends of the continuum. The beast (Leonid on Mars) and the alien (the cold, unfeeling Martian men) become negative warnings to maintain a balance at the center.

As a sign of his resulting maturity, Leonid now begins to see the Earthlings around him as "embryonic human beings, children of a youthful humanity" (135). He then turns utopian thought to revolutionary action and leaves the mental hospital to fight in the 1905 uprisings. Later, when Leonid lies wounded in a makeshift hospital, the mother-figure Netti returns and forgives him for his violent act, just as the little Martian boy is forgiven by his teacher for hurting the frog. They both disappear, leaving behind an empty apartment and a large open window, implying that she has taken him back to Mars, where he and Netti can now contribute the integrated psyche so essential to saving the Martians from cold spiritual death. In setting pen to paper, Leonid gains clarity by reflecting on his experience and by examining the reasons behind his reactions, and he finds a solution to the extremes of the beast and the alien in Netti's universal Whole, symbolized by the marriage of Earthling and Martian. If we accept Leonid's account, he has organized his own psyche through writing, and his departure from Werner's clinic with the mother-figure Netti assures the final stage of his maturation, wherein he returns to the communist future and becomes a valuable member of the Martian utopia, offering Earthly passion to the universal Whole.

Through this writing cure, *Red Star* treats the mainstays of Russian realism, the psychological novel and the superfluous man. According to the devices of the "first Bolshevik utopia," the Soviet novel could no longer serve as a psychological analysis of the superfluous man and his failure to conform, and heroes could no longer serve merely as diagnostic tools for a society gone wrong. Under Bogdanov's vision of Soviet literature, the superfluous man must not only be diagnosed but also cured—transformed from a superfluous *Hero of Our Time* into a positive hero of a future time. The villain is crucial to this transformational process. In Leonid's account of his trip to Mars the villainized alien and beast are silenced and their cold calculation and selfish desire transmuted into love of the universal "Whole," a process that enables Leonid to become a New Person. Only by doing so can he achieve the balance between intellect and desire that is needed to transform him into a full-fledged citizen of communist utopia.

AN IMPOSSIBLE EQUILIBRIUM: EVGENY ZAMYATIN'S *WE* (1920)

One thousand years into Earth's future, the communist One State instructs its citizens to write "treatises, poems, manifestos, odes, or other compositions about the beauty and greatness of the One State."[23] These writings are intended to convince primitive beings on other planets to embrace the One State's "mathematically infallible happiness" (10). D-503, the designer of the spaceship that will carry this happiness to the stars, obediently sets out to write a journal in celebration of their strictly regimented life. Thus the end to Leonid's tortured journey provides the beginning for Zamyatin's novel. D-503's plan soon goes awry, however, as his journal becomes a record not of a happy, orderly life but of chaos and confusion. As he writes, the "we" of his journal's title loses its hold on him as he leaves behind his former friends, joins with revolutionaries, and becomes a criminal in the eyes of his beloved One State. Where Leonid was incarcerated but left to his own devices and self-cure, D-503 is lobotomized to assure his obedience and eternal happiness. Predictably, *We*—an inspiration for George Orwell's *Nineteen Eighty-Four*—is often read as a forecast of Stalinist oppression, forced conformity of thought, and loss of individuality.[24]

I argue here that *We* is not a prophetic depiction of things to come but rather a polemic with the image of the writer put forth by the Proletkult, which was at its most powerful when Zamyatin wrote *We.* It is specifically aimed at Bogdanov's *Red Star,* which was at that time achieving a renewed popular success. Scholars have previously noted that Zamyatin's novel satirizes some of the setting and plot devices of *Red Star* but have failed to notice its satirical treatment of the proletarian writer and his role as organizer of the human psyche.[25] Through writing, Leonid of Bogdanov's *Red Star* cures his own insanity and gains acceptance in a futuristic communist utopia; writing cures the superfluous man, organizes the disorganized psyche. D-503, on the other hand, starts *We* as an accepted member of such a utopia and through the act of writing goes insane—writing creates the superfluous man, *disorganizes* the human psyche. Only through a lobotomy can the One State impose on D-503 the psychic organization that Leonid achieves merely by writing—the organized psyche proposed by Bogdanov and the Proletkult is thereby revealed as a chimeric state of being. The nonconforming, ever-questioning madman is for Zamyatin the necessary and therefore natural citizen, always fighting the tendency of society to suppress change and strive for stasis. For Bogdanov, the ideal writer is the creator of equilibrium and for Zamyatin he is its eternal enemy, writing life-giving "revolution" rather than static "entropy."

Revolution and Entropy

In his most famous statement on the nature of writing, "On Literature, Revolution, Entropy, and Other Matters" (1923), Evgeny Zamyatin argues that literature always serves one of two opposing forces. Revolution, the "cosmic, universal law," is described as the explosive destruction necessary to renewal: "Two dead, dark stars collide with an inaudible, deafening crash and light a new star: this is revolution."[26] It is always and inevitably followed by entropy, a cooling down of molten rock to cold, petrified stone. Ideas like planets have a life span, born in fire and gradually cooling from "magma" into "dogma."[27] The opposition of revolution and entropy constitutes the philosophical foundation of Zamyatin's essays and fiction, and scholars have used it to analyze many aspects of his most famous novel, *We*.[28] The following pages take up an aspect of revolution and entropy that has been neglected by scholarship: their relationship to writing. *We* abounds with references to literary production and to its role in the revolutionary pattern.

When D-503, the hero and narrator of *We*, sets out to write a description of his society, he embraces the One State's quest for an eternal state of entropic stasis: "The ideal (it's clear) is in that place where nothing happens" (23). He wants desperately to be as rational and unemotional as Bogdanov's Martian men, and initially he does behave like the cold entropic Sterni, who cannot satisfy his passionate wife Netti—he ignores O-90's love for him and her desire to have his child, which both conflict with the One State's attempts to control love and sexual desire, revolutionary forces that inhibit the development of entropy. And he fervently believes that he can write "useful" literature, supporting the entropic goals of the One State to spread stasis throughout the universe. D-503 intends to express the "mathematically infallible happiness" that he attributes to the *We* of his journal's title, but by recording his observations about the world around him, D-503 instead falls away from the "we." He becomes a superfluous man, charged with emotion, at odds with society and a danger to himself and those around him. Nevertheless, throughout his journal, he longs to become the sort of writer that the One State envisions him to be—obedient, clear, rational, and sane. Entropy is comfortable. Revolution is painful. Only in the end, when he is lobotomized by the One State and thereby freed of "fantasy," is he able to become an entropic writer. By means of neurosurgery, D-503 is cured, and his final entry shows that without fantasy he has become the writer he hoped to be at the beginning of the novel: "No delirium, no absurd metaphors, no feelings; just the facts" (142). He cannot stop smiling, having achieved the "mathematically infallible happiness" promised by the One State at the beginning of the novel. The lobotomized D-503 sends a powerful message: the writer must lose his imagination in order to write the literature of entropy.

D-503's descent into madness and revolution is often attributed to the influence of I-330, a leader of the underground revolutionary movement.[29] However, it is evident in the few pages written before meeting I-330 that no outside force is needed to induce in D-503 "the insanity of thoughts" (12) that he asserts is missing in One State citizens.[30] Before meeting I-330, D-503 records a series of "insane" thoughts, all conflicting with the One State's entropic values of equality, interchangeability, and erasure of the past.

He refers to O-90 with the ancient word "mine" (12) and imagines himself to be the creator of all he surveys. Moreover, he envisions a multicolored chaotic city of the twentieth century superimposed onto the rigidly ordered glass streets of the One State, a confluence of revolution and entropy that should be impossible in the mind of the One State's most valued citizen.

Since his goal in writing is to convince others to embrace the One State, D-503 begins his journal by describing a series of images that for him epitomize the seductive beauty of its entropy. However, his writing infuses each of these images with revolution. He begins with a rapturous description of the clear blue sky: "I love—I'm sure I'm not mistaken if I say we love—only such a sterile, impeccable sky" (11). In order to write this line, he must ignore his earlier description of wind-borne pollen drifting over the city's glass walls, interfering "somewhat with logical thinking" (11). The clear blue sky and D-503's narrative are far from the "sterile" entropy he claims them to be, as evidenced by the parenthetical comment that follows: "(how wild were the tastes of the ancients, if their poets could take inspiration from these absurd, disorderly, stupidly rushing piles of vapor)" (11). D-503 obediently walls off these ancient clouds in parentheses from his description of the sterile blue sky, just as the chaos of nature is walled off from the transparent glass buildings and streets of the One State. Nevertheless the cloudy inspiration of the ancients, just like the invisible pollen of the present, drifts over these parenthetical walls and "keeps one from completely thinking logically" (11).

In the pages written before meeting I-330, D-503's narrative contains many such cloudy, pollen-filled intrusions on entropic thought. He works to contain them through logical explanations of his increasingly illogical assertions or through parentheses: for example, his parenthetical observation that O-90 needs the modifier "mine." Moreover, as he becomes increasingly frustrated with the inconsistency of his own narrative, he fills his journal with ellipses. These markers of irrational thought are accompanied by an unconscious revolutionary use of figurative expressions that cloud his description. A key example is his description of the machine, his second metaphor for the entropic perfection of the One State.[31] Although D-503 expresses regret that he is not a poet, his description of the machine, like poetry, is filled with metaphor. He describes its movement as a "grandiose mechanical ballet" (11). And parts of the machine are personified in his description, dancing to "the beat of silent music" (11). D-503 concludes by asking the question once posed by the cloud-inspired ancient poets: "Why is this beautiful?" (11). He asserts that the answer is "unfree motion" (11). However, his description implies something else. Within his mechanical ballet one part singles itself out: "the balance wheel proudly rocked its shoulders" (11). His conscious mind fills the narrative with entropic images; his unconscious mind modifies them with revolutionary words.

After describing the machine, D-503 proceeds to a lengthy description of the human equivalent of sterile "unfree motion": the daily march, when citizens parade in straight lines and rows, moving uniformly down the glass streets of the glass city. In his narration, D-503 tries to make these marching, seemingly identical citizens conform to an entropic ideal, but just as in his descriptions of the clear blue sky and the "unfree motion" of the machine, D-503 fails: revolutionary ideas and images enter against his intention. In D-503's description of the marching citizens, just as in his description of the machine components, people differentiate themselves as "proud." I-330, with whom D-503 becomes fascinated in the course of the novel, asserts her power over the timetable, the most sacred institution of the One State, claiming the ability to foretell where D-503 will be assigned on the following day. And O-90, in her declaration to I-330 that D-503 is registered to her, expresses the proprietary love that supposedly vanished when the state regulated sexual desire with pink tickets, issued in accordance with scientifically determined hormonal levels. Like the components of the machine, both women are "proud" and as disturbing to D-503 as the wind-borne pollen. Each will later reveal that she harbors revolutionary thoughts: O-90 of having D-503's child without the sanction of the One State and I-330 of overthrowing the One State itself.

Despite overwhelming evidence to the contrary recorded in his notebooks, D-503 continues to assert that his fellow citizens have achieved entropy. He concludes the second entry of his journal by finding a comforting reflection of the sterile sky in O-90's eyes: "I kissed her wonderful blue eyes, unspoiled by a single cloud" (15).[32] Yet throughout the second entry O-90 has shown a cloudiness of thought that continually disturbs him. When D-503 tells her about the clear blue sky at the beginning of the second entry, he believes that he has imparted a "formula" delivered with the "flywheel of logic" (12), but his mechanically logical description produces an unexpected reaction: "'Yes, wonderful. It's spring,' O-90 smiled rosily at me. Well, what can you do: spring . . . She talks about spring. Women . . . I fell silent" (12). Later, when she reads his journal, a tear drops from her clear blue eye onto its page and creates a disturbing ink blot in his narrative. D-503 tries to rewrite O-90's love for him, walling it off from his "rational" text, but words cannot contain her irrational emotion, and the best he can do is "fall silent"; language fails him in harnessing the irrational world he describes. In fact, he is repeatedly astonished and dismayed by the words that flow from his own hand.

D-503's lack of control over his own words plagues the journal from the very start. Already at the beginning, as D-503 vows to write for the "we," the title of his journal, he preconditions its impossibility by figuring himself in the first-person subject pronoun.[33] In the first entry alone D-503 uses "I" thirteen times and "we" only three (one of these is the title he gives his journal). When he tries to paint himself as only one of many, he instead emphasizes his individuality: "I, D-503, builder of the Integral, am only one of the mathematicians of the One State" (10). Not only does he not use "we" in his assertion that he is "only one" of many; he follows the pronoun "I" with two modifications, his name and his status as builder of the spaceship Integral. By the time we reach the modest declaration of his status as "one of," he has made himself decidedly singular. D-503's problem with using "we" is, however, more than an assertion of individuality. Ultimately, his grammar exposes that he finds it next to impossible to understand the people who constitute that "we." And the person D-503 understands least of all is himself. He is continually surprised at and puzzled by his own disobedience against the One State. The pronoun "I" is as impossible for him to fill as the pronoun "we." Filtered through his pen, D-503's thoughts become something alien to him: "[The journal] is I, and at the same time, not I" (11). In *We* the writer is not capable of shaping his prose to transform himself and others—Proletkult's vision of the writer. Writing is continual revolution, continual death and rebirth, composed of unreliable words written by an unreliable narrator, who can understand neither his own motivations nor those of the characters he creates. The journal intended as an entropic reproduction of the One State becomes instead a liminal, uncanny, and thoroughly revolutionary creature; with horror he realizes that the intended "mathematical poem" (68) has become "some kind of fantastic adventure novel" (68).

The Questioning Muse

D-503 writes that the faces of his fellow citizens are "unclouded by the insanity of thoughts" (12). Yet it is one of D-503's "insane" thoughts that first attracts I-330's attention. When D-503 imagines a chaotic ancient city superimposed on the perfect glass streets and even columns of people, he laughs out loud, and I-330 comments: "'You looked at everything in such an inspired way—like some mythological god on the seventh day of creation. It seems to me that you were sure that you, and no one else, had created even me" (13). In the original Russian, her name is represented by the English letter "I," which can stand not only as a mathematical term for the "irrational" or "imaginary," but also as the English first-person pronoun. She represents a previously unrecognized "I," a side of him formerly unspoken, except, as he himself notes, on the pages of his journal: "It was a striking intersection of thoughts: she used almost the same words that I wrote down before my walk" (13). As with his journal, he has little control over her, and his conversations with her, like his journal entries, constitute a dialogue between two irreconcilable extremes of his own psyche, D-503 the entropic One State writer (the alien), and D-503 the revolutionary (the beast). The entropic D-503 is repulsed by the same quality in I-330 that attracts the revolutionary D-503: "in her eyes or on her brow some sort of strange irritating 'x'" (13). When he is faced with the unknown "x" signaled by her quizzical look, he is also faced with that part of himself that cannot be solved "logically" with the One State's simple math.

Throughout the book she continues to challenge him and to question his long-standing entropic assumptions. When he claims that everyone is alike, she asks him, "Are you sure?" (13), and his vision of the world immediately seems to change; he suddenly becomes acutely aware of the physical differences in his marching neighbors. The questions she evokes in him expel him from the safe entropic self-image that the One State has fostered: "Homo sapiens—is only a human being in the full sense of this word when in his grammar there are absolutely no question marks, only exclamation points, commas, and periods" (77). I-330's words have the same effect on him that the pollen does, interfering with logical thought: "For some reason I was embarrassed" (13) and "again for some reason I was confused" (13). During the march, when he uses one of his favorite expressions, "it is clear," she asks him the question "Are you sure?" (13). And suddenly nothing is clear. Later, when they visit the museum-house, she repeatedly taunts him by applying this expression to a series of subjects: individuality, irrational love, and originality. All of these sins of the past have supposedly been vanquished by the One State—clearly—and yet he finds each of these things in I-330 and on the pages of his journal. Because of her challenging, sarcastic repetitions of his own "clear" assertions, by the end of their exchange, he becomes almost incapable of making a declarative sentence: "'It's clear . . . that is . . . I wanted . . . (that cursed 'it's clear!')" (26).

I-330 is responsible for D-503's reassignment to an auditorium where she herself is demonstrating ancient music. Before she comes on stage, an announcer praises the "musicometer," a machine that can compose three sonatas an hour; by applying mathematical formulas to music, this machine contains artistic energy in entropy. The announcer compares this entropic art with that of the ancients: "They could create only by inducing in themselves attacks of 'inspiration'—an unknown form of epilepsy" (19). The concert is intended to show that the controlled music of the musicometer is more beautiful than the unhealthy creation of the ancients, but when I-330 begins to play the ancient composition, D-503 is drawn to it, even though he finds it disturbing, primitive, and undisciplined. D-503's fellow numbers laugh uproariously, just as he laughed in the opening march when he pictured the motley ancient city streets, but he now unexpectedly finds pleasure in the ancient music: "Yes, epilepsy, a spiritual sickness, pain . . . Slow, sweet pain—a bite—and you want it still deeper, still more painful. Then, slowly, the sun. Not ours, not that bluish-crystal, even light through glass bricks, no—a wild, rushing, scorching sun—and off with everything, tear everything to shreds" (19). The revolutionary fire of the ancient music invokes a primitive desire for destruction and for nudity, for the removal of the uniform identity assigned by the One State.

Through his depictions of it, the reader is made aware that any art created by human beings cannot help but be infused with revolution. A poem written in honor of the execution of a One State poet who has declared himself a genius is intended to celebrate entropy, but it roars with energy that D-503 cannot ignore:

> . . . A fire. In the iambs the buildings rock, liquid gold splashes up from them, and they crash down. Green trees are contorted, sap drips—already they are only black skeletal crosses. But Prometheus has appeared (that of course is us): "And suddenly fire becomes machine, steel, / And chaos is shackled with law." And everything is new, steel: steel sun, steel trees, steel people. Suddenly some madman "lets fire loose from its chains" and again everything perishes . . . I have, unfortunately, a poor memory for poetry, but one thing I remember: it would be impossible to pick out more instructive and more beautiful images. (36)

D-503 claims a poor memory for verses, but his recounting of the poem is alive with detail. And when he paraphrases it, of the imagery he chooses to describe destruction is the most vivid, with metaphors such as "liquid gold" and "black skeletal crosses." When he refers to the entropic harnessing of fire, on the other hand, he actually quotes it, thereby distancing himself from an emotional reaction—revolution is more compelling than entropy. Initially D-503 refers to the meter of the poem, which gives it the structure that he finds comfort in—iambs capture words in unfree movement, entropy. But within the iambs, everything is out of control—swaying, collapsing, shriveling. Although the One State subordinates everything to stasis with the adjective "steel," all it takes is one madman, one poet, and unfree movement will explode into fiery revolution once again. *We* points to Zamyatin's belief that efforts to produce "useful" literature were futile. After all, despite the One State's efforts, D-503, its model citizen, all too easily catches the epilepsy of inspiration.

Despite his own tendency to inspiration, D-503, like the One State, is distraught by others who display it. R-13, D-503's closest friend, is a poet, and his thoughts are always chaotic, uncontrolled, and extremely disturbing to D-503.[34] As a child, R-13 once put spitwads into one of the robot-teacher's speakers, thereby disrupting the flow of One State propaganda. Later, as a One State poet, R-13 should, like his robot-teacher, deliver the law in regulation meter and rhyme, but he instead showers his audience with a baptismal stream of disorderly words: "the words come from him in a stream, they splash from his thick lips" (32).[35] He disrupts the order of the One State, both physically—he rearranges the furniture into nongeometric formations—and verbally—he constantly tells jokes, which disturbs the clarity of thought so prized by D-503.[36] And, with his "inside-out, ridiculous logic" (33) he points out flaws in the One State's mathematical logic—in the eighth entry he draws D's attention to the much-feared concept of infinity. D-503 claims not to be able to understand R-13, because his head is opaque: "I looked at his tightly locked little suitcase and thought: what is he sifting through right now in that little suitcase?" (34). Yet his own writing has the same effect on D-503 as R-13's jokes. As he writes, D-503 makes associations, insights about R-13 that surprise and shock him. Something in R-13's tone reminds him of I-330's questions in the opening march, and he writes: "Dear R. . . . In him there is also (I don't know why 'also,' but let me write down what comes out)—in him there is also something not entirely clear to me" (34). D-503's hand—and by extension his writing—is so out of control that he thinks of it as moving independently; he encloses it in parentheses, but it cannot be contained. R-13 represents that hand, familiar but at the same time alien, "I and not I."

Entry 39 is the last one D-503 writes before undergoing the operation to remove his imagination (*fantaziia*). Everything will finally be clear, and the entropic stasis that D-503 so desires will be his. However, rather than submit to this surgery, D-503 rushes down into a public bathroom so that he can continue writing. There he is comforted by an undisturbed bubble of entropy, its transparency and utility a testament to "the greatest and most rational civilization in all of history" (141). In this static bubble, he meets a fellow citizen who informs him of a great discovery: he has proven that there is no infinity, that the universe has an end. At last D-503 has been given the answer he has sought since the first page of his journal—the unknown "x" has been solved. He can now cast out the question marks and ellipses that make him less of a human being in the eyes of the One State:

> I wanted to put a period already—as the ancients put crosses above the holes where they lowered their dead, but suddenly the pencil began to shake, and it fell from my fingers . . . "Listen," I grabbed my neighbor, "Listen to me, I tell you! You need—you need to answer me: there, where your end of the universe ends? What lies beyond it? He didn't have a chance to answer; from above—on the stairs—pounding . . . (141–42)

D-503 wants to end his journal with the punctuation of certainty, and now that he has received the good news about infinity, he could do so. A decisive punctuation mark would, however, be like a cross above a grave, a marker of intellectual death, and the questioning D-503 cannot accept that finality. He is plagued by question marks that puncture the bubble of entropy in which he seeks refuge. After his long journey of questioning he finds only that there is always another question lying in wait beyond the "final" answer; the only way to rid himself of this infinite questioning is to eliminate that part of his brain that produces questions: the imagination. Entry 39 ends with ellipses, because with his imagination intact D-503 cannot stop interrogating reality.

In a parody of the Proletkult's belief in a literature of answers, Zamyatin adds a decisive ending: a 40th entry written by a lobotomized D-503, which is punctuated almost solely with periods. The only question marks are now aimed not at the One State but at his former "insane" self: "Was it really I, D-503, who wrote these two hundred pages? Did I really at one time feel—or imagine, that I felt this?" (142). These questions might make it seem that something of the questioning revolutionary D-503 remains after surgery, but they are entirely rhetorical: D-503 does not try to answer them. Dispossessed of his creative mind—and of the questioning muse I-330—D-503 is finally able to cast aside his tortured quest for answers. Yet the decisive punctuation of this entry cannot provide emotionally satisfying answers to the questions raised by his journal. Did I-330 love him? Did O–90 survive to have her baby? His final sentence ends with an imperative: "And I hope we win. More than that; I am sure we will win. Because reason must win out" (143). The hope that opens the sentiment belies its final and desperate conclusiveness. Even without an imagination, D-503 manages to leave the door open to chaos.

DYSTOPIAN FEAR

Red Star and *We* both envision the human being as existing on a continuum with uncontrolled beastly desire on one end and dissociative alien intellect on the other. They disagree, however, on where human beings should exist on this continuum and on the role of the writer in placing them there. *Red Star* argues that existence at either pole of the continuum creates a human being at odds with society—a superfluous man—and that writing can achieve an organized harmony of the two extremes, a desired state of being that all people will eventually reach under Communism. In *We,* on the other hand, this equilibrium is presented as unnatural—it denies the tendency of human thought to swing like a pendulum back and forth between the extremes; for Zamyatin the role of literature is to free the pendulum when it becomes stuck in unnatural stasis. *Red Star* and *We* represent the division in the early Soviet period between those like Bogdanov, who believed that literature should support and nurture "ruling ideas" (now the dictatorship of the proletariat) and those like Zamyatin who believed that it should continue to be revolutionary, finding and revealing the flaws in society. A comparison of the first Bolshevik utopia and what is often considered the first dystopia of the twentieth century reveals an instability that would haunt writers throughout the early Soviet period and well into socialist realism. Soviet literature has two roles, one to continually challenge and change reality (Zamyatin) and one to create and maintain equilibrium (Bogdanov). *Red Star* and *We* embody conflicting sides in an ongoing polemic about literature that continued throughout the early Soviet period, a divide over the role of the Soviet writer in transforming society.

Bogdanov's and Zamyatin's views of literature seem incompatible, but together they form the paradox that is socialist realism. Assigned the role of organizing readers' psyches, of attaining the equilibrium necessary to the Communist future, socialist realism defends the status quo and the powers that be; it is entropic. However, socialist realism also has a revolutionary role based on the underlying fear that an equilibrium cannot be permanently achieved—hostile forces must continually be overthrown, kept at abeyance. Later Soviet cultural production is marked by the uncomfortable coexistence of both ruling and revolutionary ideas, of literature as a sedative to maintain the status quo and as a weapon to rouse energies and fight the hostile forces that continually threaten to push the delicately balanced Soviet psyche into either dissociative alienation or uncontrolled aggression. Socialist realism has been said to have a "utopian impulse,"[37] seen in its injunction to overlay the future Communist utopia on the past and present, but it is also infused with dystopian fear, and the greatest fear contained within it is the fear of its own devices. As we will see in the next two chapters, the history of literature in the early Soviet period constitutes a fierce battle to gain control of its villains, to cleanse its texts and its readers of their toxins. In the next two chapters, I show how the strategies of two popular genres in the early Soviet period—satire (chapter 2) and the fantastic (chapter 3)—become distilled in the figure of the villain and thereby become useful tools in the literary hygiene that would come to be called socialist realism, a genre that would always be motivated by dystopian fear.

Chapter Two

He Does Not Love Us When We Are Dirty

> Dear little grandfather Lenin, we want to tell you that we have become very good. We study diligently. We already read and write well. We make lots of pretty things. We wash ourselves carefully every morning and wash our hands every time we eat. We want to make our teacher happy. He does not love us when we are dirty.
>
> —Letter from schoolchildren to V. I. Lenin (1922)

WITH LENIN as the state's father figure, Soviet children needed clean hands to make "pretty things." On propaganda posters, in brochures, and in public lectures Bolsheviks preached the virtue of hot water, soap, and scrub brushes.[1] Physical hygiene became a sign of mental hygiene which could only be accomplished with political hygiene. A 1920 propaganda poster entitled "Comrade Lenin Cleanses the Earth of the Unclean" depicts Lenin perched on a globe with a broom, sweeping the earth free of bloated capitalists, autocrats, and religious figures, the "unclean" (*nechist'*) who would infect Soviet citizens with the ideas of the past. In the battle against intellectual dirt, political rhetoric was filled with terms drawn from the washroom, and removing people tainted by the past would provide a much-needed "cleansing" (*chistka*). At every opportunity the vanguard instructed their pupils on mental and physical cleanliness, using Lenin, the propaganda-poster teacher, as both model and threat: "he does not love us when we are dirty."

More than anything, a clean mind was signaled by clean words. All members of early Soviet society were encouraged to rid their speech of "coarse, rude, and hard expressions" that might signal a dirty mind. Even before the revolution, worker activists often equated swearing with a lack of culture.[2] At least one prerevolutionary trade union prohibited cursing because it was seen as a sign of "the lack of respect for the human personality that exists under the bourgeois system."[3] After the revolution, efforts to clean up workers' speech continued. Leon Trotsky, in his 1923 book *Problems of Life* (*Voprosy byta*), reasoned that "the struggle against 'bad language' is a condition of intellectual culture, just as the fight against filth and vermin is a condition of physical culture."[4] And Trotsky was not alone; Michael Gorham, in his extensive study of language change in the Soviet Union, asserts that there emerged in the 1920s "a dominant discourse of language purism."[5] Campaigns such as the 1923–24 Komsomol (Communist Youth Organization) "struggle for cultured speech"[6] were launched to clean up the speech—and therefore the minds—of Soviet youth. And this language purism extended far beyond merely eradicating swearwords. "Language hygienists" also targeted dialect and nonstandard lexicon and grammar, all of which were connected, like swearing, with political backwardness in the early Soviet period.[7] Dirty, sloppy words communicated dirty, sloppy thoughts. And despite the fact that workers (and avant-garde writers such as Mayakovsky) often saw hygienic speech as bourgeois, there was a concentrated effort throughout the early Soviet period to stop the proletariat from using swearwords, dialecticisms, and poor grammar and compel them to adopt the clean, efficient language espoused by Trotsky, the Proletkult, and the productionists, among others. Throughout the early Soviet period we see satire used as a device to expose and silence the villains who refused to speak the clean language of Communism.[8]

HYGIENIC SATIRE

Propagandists took advantage of increasing literacy in the early Soviet period to make the written word a constant presence in work and leisure-time activities. As citizens moved from factory to gymnasium, they were surrounded by a wallpaper of behavioral instruction generated from every level of society. Hallways, fences, and factories were plastered with propaganda posters, and at every workplace and university "wall newspapers" (*stengazety*) imparted the "culture of everyday life" (*kul'tura byta*) to Soviet citizens. "Culturedness" encompassed an astonishing array of topics from personal hygiene to political awareness to poetry—and all of it in the service of Soviet ideology. One poster might advise citizens to wash their vegetables and the next to read more books. The vanguard of the revolution had an enormous task in imparting this knowledge to a population of newly literates, many of whom did not share their enthusiasm for clean fingernails and Pushkin. Nevertheless, imparting culturedness was given top priority. Reading rooms were quickly set up all over the country, and precious resources were poured into filling them with newspapers, magazines, and books that would promote both physical and mental hygiene.

Many of the best minds of the early Soviet period broke in their pens on this propaganda effort. Posters on hygiene and cultured behavior were designed by major artists and writers of the early Soviet period such as Aleksandr Rodchenko and Vladimir Mayakovsky. Many writers who would go on to create Soviet classics began their careers writing newspaper feuilletons, including Yury Olesha, Mikhail Bulgakov, Valentin Kataev, Mikhail Zoshchenko, and Ilya Ilf and Evgeny Petrov, who all wrote for the railroad workers' journal *The Whistle* (*Gudok*). Humorous pieces based on writing sent in by worker-correspondents used satire as a corrective device, aimed at injecting "culturedness" into the Soviet reader, who would ideally read them while sitting upright in a good chair with freshly washed hands and neatly combed hair, eager to please "dear little grandfather Lenin."[9] Writers who cut their teeth on journalistic sketches and feuilletons made satire a major component of their later poems, short stories, plays, and novels, and the period leading up to socialist realism is therefore considered the golden age of Soviet satire, an age when talented writers aimed their pens at the "uncultured," those who refused the hygiene of the revolution and remained physically, culturally, and ideologically dirty.[10]

In this chapter I examine two satires from the early Soviet period that together provide a case study of the roots of the hygienic impulse behind socialist realism and also the instability it introduces: Mikhail Bulgakov's novella *Heart of a Dog* (*Sobach'e serdtse,* 1925) and Vladimir Mayakovsky's play *Bedbug* (*Klop,* 1929). Both texts use the hygienic strategy of exposure and silencing of an impostor hero. However, whereas *Heart of a Dog* shows the villainy of its impostor to be systemic—everyone in Soviet society is revealed to be like him—*Bedbug* shows him to be the sole exception and safely removes him from a hygienic Communist utopia. Without the contaminating villain, society is kept safe and clean. As we see in following this shift in narrative strategy from *Heart of a Dog* to *Bedbug,* Soviet satire moved in the late 1920s from one that revealed society's flaws to one that removed these flaws. An examination of these two texts reveals, however, the dystopian fear that would travel into socialist realism with this strategy as writers moved from revolutionary diagnosis to engineering the New Person.

"BAD WORDS ARE NOT ALLOWED": MIKHAIL BULGAKOV'S *HEART OF A DOG* (1925)

In Mikhail Bulgakov's *Heart of a Dog*[11] Professor Preobrazhensky transplants human organs into the body of a stray dog, a disposable test subject that is expected to die.[12] Contrary to expectations, the dog is "humanized"—his fur falls out, and he develops opposable thumbs and acquires the power of speech and Soviet documents, all proof of his status as a human being. This newly created human being is soon revealed to be worse than the dog he replaces, a crude, self-interested liar and thief who betrays the men and women who are kind to him. As Professor Preobrazhensky observes the transformation, he gradually realizes that the dog-man's beastly behavior reflects not the heart of a dog but rather that of the organ donor, a petty criminal and tavern layabout. Through the experiment a man who would previously have been forbidden entry to the professor's apartment is allowed in, and chaos and destruction ensue. Professor Preobrazhensky and his Communist nemesis Comrade Shvonder each then begin campaigns to educate and control the dog-man. Their attempts fail, and Preobrazhensky reverses the operation; the human organs are removed. The power of speech gained with "humanization" gradually fades away, and the cursing, rebellious dog-man once again becomes the silent, loyal dog.

In the epilogue of the novel, when the dog-man's human body becomes canine, neighbors are alarmed by his sudden disappearance and summon the police, who enter the professor's apartment and demand that he produce the "human being" (*chelovek*): " 'You mean he spoke?' asked Filipp Filippovich, 'This doesn't yet mean that one is a human being.' "[13] The former dog-man enters, still retaining some eerily familiar human traits, including the ability to utter the line: "Bad words are not allowed!" (91). However, according to the professor's definition of "human," this line no longer qualifies the creature to be a human being, and since most of his physical traits are those of a dog, the police soon leave. We are left with questions. Is the professor right? Does speech qualify one to be human? And if so, what kind of speech? Scholars have viewed Comrade Shvonder as the villain of *Heart of a Dog* and Professor Preobrazhensky as the heroic defender of home, culture, and civilized behavior.[14] However, the imagery used to describe the professor paints a more negative picture—in the operating room he is compared to a murderer, a thief, and a vampire; in these descriptions and others that are outlined below, the professor becomes a villain, not a hero, and his judgment about the nature of humanity falls under suspicion.

Rather than a battle between good (the professor) and evil (Shvonder), *Heart of a Dog* depicts a contest between two Dr. Frankensteins, each of whom attempts to create a human being with "good" words and each of whom holds a different definition of what it means to be human. The professor believes that human beings speak hygienically and that they obey a natural hierarchy. Comrade Shvonder argues that human beings practice an egalitarian speech and a dissolution of individuality in the collective. Neither is successful at changing the dog-man into his particular version of a human being—Sharikov continues to utter bad words until he is physically deprived of the ability to talk. In the failure of these two mad scientists, we see a satirical indictment of the Soviet intelligentsia's campaigns to change people by changing their speech. Professor Preobrazhensky represents the intelligentsia's belief that there is a hierarchy of language and desire, and that climbing this cultural ladder makes one human. Shvonder represents the Communists' fervent belief in Communist propaganda and egalitarian speech as equalizing mechanisms. *Heart of a Dog* is a condemnation of the belief that good words can teach old dogs to be New People. In the end the teachers in *Heart of a Dog* not only fail to change their recalcitrant student, but they themselves are revealed to be beasts clothed in pretty words.

Language Hygiene as Elitism

Heart of a Dog moves full circle by the end: the professor has maintained the walls of his apartment against the revolution and the man who took over the dog's body has been banished (by removing his organs from the dog). In the final scene the professor continues his scientific work in his clean, orderly apartment while the loyal and subservient pet looks on. Nothing has changed. The professor represents an intelligentsia made up of hypocrites, intent on improving the common man, but not at the expense of their own authority and living space. The professor's last name, "Preobrazhensky," is derived from "transformation"[15] and therefore signals his self-proclaimed interest in eugenics, the occupation of many a mad scientist.[16] Yet the professor's only real effort at improving human beings occurs not on the operating table but at the dining-room table. There he works to improve the dog-man with good grammar and fine manners, all of which he sees as lacking in those elevated to power by the revolution. Casting Preobrazhensky, a "hater of the proletariat" (22), as a language hygienist paints the campaigns for "culturedness" as an extreme elitism, where, as the professor proclaims in the epilogue, merely possessing the power of speech does not make one "human"—being human means speaking and behaving like the upper classes.[17]

Maintaining a healthy body and mind requires that the professor maintain linguistic purity within the civilized world of his apartment, that he remain constantly on guard against the intrusion of "bad words" from outside its walls.[18] The professor is a representative of a civilized hierarchical culture that won't let just *anybody* in. Therefore, when the Soviet House Committee demands that the professor give up his dining room to house the common man, he defends it with the ferocity of a guard dog. By doing so, he preserves not only the tangible walls and rooms that separate his civilized work and his civilized life into discrete activities, but also the grammar and lexicon of civilized discourse that separate the people who surround him into discrete groups based on class, gender, and education. He views the House Committee's lowered register as a threat to these divisions and to the clarity of human thought: "Try to express your thoughts more clearly" (18); "I request that you not use such expressions" (21). And he condemns the linguistic egalitarianism of the revolution, rejecting the House Committee's use of "comrade" and insisting instead on the hierarchy and differentiation inherent in prerevolutionary forms of address. He negates their attempts at gender equity by asking who among them is a woman and then instructing her to use the feminine ending for her title. The committee fights back, angrily denouncing the professor's bourgeois forms of address. Nevertheless, they leave defeated and completely silenced: "The four of them silently left the study, silently walked through the receiving room, silently walked through the foyer, and the only thing heard was the heavy, resonant sound of the front door shutting behind them" (22). The door audibly reestablishes the boundary between the professor and the linguistic "ruin" they represent.[19]

After the House Committee departs, the stray dog slavishly admires his master's linguistic power: "What, does he know some kind of word?" (21). Although the dog views the professor as a sorcerer of words, we soon learn that the professor's only real method of controlling others is the power he gains by supplying Soviet officials with rejuvenation treatments. He succeeds in refusing the House Committee not through etiquette and proper grammar but by making a phone call to a very important patient. And his solution to the House Committee's disruptive singing, which has begun to drift into his dining room, is also an appeal to Soviet power: he suggests that they post armed guards next to each revolutionary singer in his apartment building, thereby forcing them to be silent. The professor sustains the integrity of his apartment, his life, and his work solely through the power gained by submission and service to a higher authority. Prior to the operation, the dog suddenly realizes that "a collar is just like a briefcase" (31).[20] His collar subjects him to the command of the professor but also grants him the respect of stray dogs, entry into previously forbidden realms, and food and warmth.[21] In a similar way the professor has been given a "briefcase," his job as a Soviet professor of science, which subordinates him to the state but which also allows him to maintain the boundaries of his apartment.[22] The dog accepts the name "Sharik" in exchange for a place in the professor's world. Preobrazhensky accepts the title "Professor" for a place in the Soviet world. Each lives in an uneasy exchange of submission for power.

The depiction of "Professor Transformation" constitutes an exposure of intellectuals supported by the Soviet state as beasts clothed in civilized discourse, interested only in their own needs and detesting the dirty masses who have invaded their hermetic spaces. Etiquette is merely another language of power, and language hygiene and "culturedness" are elitist campaigns to keep the common man out of bourgeois dining rooms. In his dog-like defense of his apartment and bourgeois lifestyle, the professor is revealed to be, like the dog he takes in, willing to trade obedience for food, warmth, and power but unwilling to share his bounty with lesser dogs and men. The dog-man's rejection of Preobrazhensky's instruction parallels the resentment directed at Bolshevik culturedness campaigns, which were accused of imposing an unnatural language and culture on the Soviet people.

Revolutionary Words

When the dog-man begins to speak, dirty words and bad manners invade the professor's apartment. This carnivalesque challenge to the professor's power does not, however, result in true change. The dog-man's cursing and disdain for hierarchy are put to the same use as the professor's good grammar and etiquette—to gain power over others and fulfill selfish desire. The overthrow of the professor's apartment constitutes an exchange of one linguistic tyranny for another. This revolution begins in the chapter after the operation, which is in the form of a scientific journal of observations kept by the lab assistant Bormenthal under Professor Preobrazhensky's direction. Written, scientific speech is the most inviolable of linguistic media for the professor, and therefore it is the first to fall to the dog-man's revolutionary speech.[23] At first the journal entries are scholarly, filled with scientific information, and clearly punctuated; they fit well with the orderly, grammatical world created by Preobrazhensky. Bormenthal dutifully records the professor's confident observations on the effects of transplanting human organs into the dog, but as the creature develops speech, Bormenthal loses control, a loss signaled by editorial comments in parentheses throughout the notes. The first is found in the middle of the entry for December 29, when human sounds begin to issue from the dog. The next several pages of entries, which chronicle the emergence of speech in the creature, are filled with such annotations, noting changes in handwriting, writing instrument, paper, neatness, and an increasing number of "blots" (*kliaksy*). Along with these disorderly textual insertions, uncontrolled voices, asserting the existence of the supernatural and the irrational, begin to invade Bormenthal's scientific narrative; he notes rumors that Martians have landed in Moscow and that the apocalypse has arrived. Faced with these uncontrolled voices, Bormenthal loses control not only of the text but of his own mind: "I'll go insane" (43).

Significantly, the dog-man's first meaningful statement constitutes a refusal to obey the professor (January 11). This refusal begins a process by which the professor loses control over every carefully structured area of his life. First of all, he must give up his work; when the professor first hears the dog-man curse, he falls, injures himself, and must then turn observation of the experiment over to Bormenthal. Next, he must relinquish his imagined linguistic control; from Bormenthal's account we learn that, faced with the creature's "bad words," the professor's own words lose their supposed efficacy: "For some reason the cursing produces a surprisingly painful effect on Filipp Filippovich. There are moments when he departs from controlled and cold observation of new phenomena, and it seems that he loses his patience. For example, once, when the dog was cursing, he suddenly exclaimed nervously, 'Stop!' This had absolutely no effect" (45). Cursing causes a loss of mental and physical control on the part of the professor; it runs counter to his definition of civilized speech and demonstrates that he has no means other than force to prevent such speech acts in his apartment. Even his ability to use force is lost when Comrade Shvonder assists the dog-man in attaining documents that officially grant him living space in the professor's apartment. With the documents, the capacity for speech, and a little coaching from Comrade Shvonder, the dog-man now lectures the professor in his own dining room:

> "I'm not allowed to swear. I'm not allowed to spit. And from you I hear only, Fool, fool. It's obvious that only professors are allowed to curse in the Resefesar." Filipp Filippovich flushed, and tried to fill a glass but broke it. He drank from another and thought, "If this goes on, he will start to teach me and he will be completely correct in doing so. I cannot control myself." (54)

The professor's frustration with the dog-man's assertiveness causes him to unintentionally echo the destruction wrought by both the dog and the dog-man; he has now become the *source* of ruin, of broken glass and "bad words." Although he claims to control others with kindness, the professor's words are often quite hostile, especially when addressing the dog-man: "Filipp Filippovich irritably exclaimed" (52); "he furiously shouted" (52). And although he celebrates good manners and verbal etiquette, the professor is repeatedly rude to others. He acknowledges in spite of himself that speech does not make one human, and we see that his own speech all too often reveals an animal nature, even before the dog-man enters his life: "he bellowed" (19); "in a serpent voice" (21). The dog-man's vulgarity merely removes the thin veneer of cultured discourse that privileges the professor and his civilized dining room.

After the dog-man acquires speech and asserts control over his own fate and, therefore, over the professor, the dining room is invaded full force by ruin. The sideboard mirror is broken in half, turning the post-operation dining-room scene into a cracked reflection of Professor Preobrazhensky's pre-operation lecture on dining and conversation. Despite his earlier warnings about Soviet newspapers, the professor is now reading a newspaper denunciation written by Comrade Shvonder;[24] and, as the professor predicted in the pre-operation lecture, this activity has a negative physical and emotional effect: "Lightning distorted his face, and through his teeth ragged, mangled, chirping words poured out" (49). Like his reflection, the professor's words are now broken, fragmented. Moreover, the lyrics to one of the dog-man's popular songs repeat themselves in the professor's head, taking the place of his usual operatic offerings[25] and bringing back his earlier dining-room proclamation that "ruin . . . is in the head" (27). The professor loses all control over his emotions as well as his reasoning when the dog-man Sharikov, the embodiment of ruin, enters the dining room in garish clothes. Sharikov's patent shoes with white spats remind the professor of galoshes. But these "galoshes" are a warped reflection of those that protect the professor from the mud of the revolution; they instead disrupt his previous "civilized" behavior and deprive him of self-control. The professor is revealed by the dog-man's revolutionary vulgarity to be himself a beast clothed in eloquence and etiquette, a pretty veneer that peels away when his territory is threatened. And in the end, the dog-man is revealed to be no different, which would make sense if he were truly the professor's illegitimate son, as rumors insist, but the Communist Comrade Shvonder, not Professor Preobrazhensky, is the one responsible for the dog-man's rise to power, and in his creation of a linguistic monster, we see a satire on Soviet beliefs in Communist propaganda and egalitarian language as tools of social change and human transformation.

Comrade Shvonder's Monster

The professor views Bolshevik speech as an assault on civilization and defends his dining room against the words of the revolution: "It is necessary to know not only what to eat but when and how . . . and what to talk about while you eat. Yes sir. If you worry about your digestion, my best advice is—don't talk about Bolshevism at dinner" (24). He warns his colleague Bormenthal not to read Soviet newspapers before dining and outlines a scientific study in which people lose weight and suffer from poor physical reflexes, appetite, and mood after reading the Communist newspaper *Pravda.* In his quest for power, the dog-man therefore not only assaults the professor with vulgarity, but also with Bolshevik speech, which he uses not to establish equality and justice, the goals of the Bolshevik Revolution, but to gain power over the professor. Bolshevik speech is just another form of etiquette and culturedness, ruling words used by the dog-man to wrest power from the professor. Under the guidance of House Committee Chair Comrade Shvonder, the dog-man chooses a new name for himself, "Poligraf Poligrafovich,"[26] from the Soviet equivalent of a saints' calendar—a calendar of technology.[27] In Russian "Poligraf" points to the printing profession (*poligrafiia*).[28] And Poligraf Poligrafovich is indeed a creation of the printing profession, since his new name must be printed in the newspaper in order to gain official recognition. Moreover, once he has an identity and a document that allocates him living space in the professor's apartment, Sharikov then turns to the press to take away the last remnants of the professor's former control over him; just before the operation is reversed, Sharikov is about to use the newspaper to denounce the professor.

Naming the dog-man after the printing profession serves to expose the true nature of the Soviet press, which, like the dog-man, operates throughout the novel as an agent of denunciation and deceit. Moreover, the name, since it fails to change the dog-man into a Soviet New Person, points to the inability of the Soviet press to transform reality with propaganda. The power of the press over reality and over language is as illusory as the professor's or Shvonder's. This is particularly well illustrated by one newspaper article, in which the dog-man's "birth" is announced: according to the newspaper, on January 7, Russian Orthodox Christmas, the professor assisted in the birth of an infant who could play the violin.[29] The press thereby fulfills on the printed page what the professor could not achieve with experiments in eugenics; a musical genius is created and on Christmas no less, thus heralding a new beginning. The article is accompanied by a picture of Dr. Bormenthal, which was stolen by a reporter and which is captioned "Prof. Preobrazhensky." The press has given the professor's powerful name to someone supposedly under his control. As promised, the Soviet press thereby establishes a new identity for the exploited and serves as a weapon to wrench power from the powerful. But the power shift is merely a typo in Bormenthal's case, a miscommunication. As we have seen from Bormenthal's journal, he has no more scientific power than Preobrazhensky. Nor has he any other kind of power—in the end he remains the professor's obedient assistant. Moreover, regardless of the newspaper's account, the dog-man is no musical "prodigy." And when he publishes the name Poligraf Poligrafovich in the Soviet newspaper and thereby gains a Soviet identity, the dog-man remains the same self-interested criminal as the organ donor Klym Chungukin; he steals not only from the professor and Bormenthal, but also from the servants and the House Committee. The dog-man puts on Soviet words as easily and thoughtlessly as he does the Bolshevik leather jacket; both are, however, merely a revolutionary costume that does little to attenuate the selfish impulses of the beast.

The professor, by transplanting human organs into the dog, inadvertently creates a human being. But it is Comrade Shvonder who helps the dog-man attain documents and thereby brings him to life in the Soviet sense: "without documents a person is strictly forbidden to exist" (53). A new Soviet name should signify a Soviet New Person, and through his support of Sharikov, Shvonder seems to fulfill the goals of the revolution—a common man has been officially granted living space in the professor's apartment, and equity has been achieved.[30] Moreover, Shvonder, as a representative of the Communists, seems to have gained power over the professor; he is now able to refuse Preobrazhensky's request for extra living space for Sharikov, and whereas he himself was earlier interrupted and silenced by the professor, he now speaks in longer sentences. Shvonder fulfills his role as revolutionary vanguard by giving Sharikov a voice in the professor's apartment: "Shvonder immediately supported him, 'Excuse me, Professor, but Citizen Sharikov is completely correct. It is his right to take part in discussing his own fate, and especially because the matter concerns documents' " (55–56).

What comes out of Sharikov's mouth is, however, beyond Shvonder's control. When Sharikov openly expresses his refusal to serve in the military, Shvonder turns to him and "courteously" (56) explains his duty as a Soviet citizen. But civility and patient explanation work no better for Shvonder than they do for the professor: "It was Shvonder's turn to be embarrassed" (56). Shvonder's power, and the power of the Communist collective that he represents, is as illusory as the professor's. His role as vanguard is to grant the common man Sharikov free speech, control of his environment, and the enlightenment granted by the ideas of Communism. With these changes, Shvonder believes that the best within Sharikov will come out. However, these changes do nothing but free the beast; Sharikov takes advantage of everyone around him, grabbing every opportunity for power and profit but evading all responsibility. In the end, Sharikov is revealed to be like the Soviet chairman described in the opening scenes of the novel, who uses his newly achieved power only to satisfy his desire for food and sex. The dog is disdainful of such a man, but, under Shvonder's guidance, the dog-man becomes him. Shvonder's Bolshevik words do no more to create a good man than the professor's "civilized" words.

MONSTROUS WORDS

Julie Clarke argues that we fear the Frankenstein monster because he is a "liminal being," at once dead and alive, human and nonhuman.[31] Jeffrey Cohen goes further to identify in the monster a "harbinger of category crisis."[32] The monster straddles borders and incorporates disquietingly incompatible elements into one creature. In *Heart of a Dog* there are two views of the monstrous—two opposing Dr. Frankensteins who come to look on their own creations with horror. Shvonder and the professor each hold a different definition of the human being and of the natural, and when they meet, each believes that the other has crossed the line. The professor is enraged by the House Committee's attempts to pollute the pure space of his apartment, and Shvonder is horrified by the professor's resistance to merging with the outside world. Each sees the monster in the other, and each attempts to change the other through words. When their words fail to have an effect, and the dog-man gains power, they shift their attention to him. Each believes that he should be able to transform the dog-man into a human being. For the professor he represents the unthinkable: power that refuses to speak cultured words. For Shvonder he represents the impossible: selfishness that clothes itself in Bolshevik jargon. However, their creature continues to exist in "category crisis." Although he is silenced in the end, and the professor and Shvonder no longer have to listen to "bad words," Bulgakov's dueling Frankensteins fail to learn the novel's lesson that at the center of the human—and canine—heart is a self-interest and desire for power that cannot be overcome with "nice" words.

When Bulgakov submitted *Heart of a Dog* to the journal *The Depths* (*Nedra*), reviewers were enthusiastic and recommended publication.[33] But in May 1925 Glavlit, the Soviet censorship organization, rejected the novel: "It isn't even worth cleaning up [*chistit'*] *Heart of a Dog*. The piece as a whole is not permissible."[34] What makes *Heart of a Dog* so unhygienic? After all, the novel expresses a common concern of many Communists in the era of the NEP (New Economic Policy) that NEP capitalists, who might appear Soviet but who acted according to bourgeois values, were reversing the achievements of the revolution. One could point to the novel's claim that power was being given to those who continued to behave in a way contrary to Communist belief, exploiting others and fulfilling selfish desire. In the same year, however, Fedor Gladkov's socialist realist prototype *Cement* made similar claims and was readily published. The answer lies not in any specific content but in the novel's overreliance on satirical exposure at the expense of positive example.

As the 1920s progressed, satire increasingly turned from exposure to transformation; *Heart of a Dog*'s failure to follow this trend has been suggested as the reason behind its rejection.[35] The only transformation in the novel is the defeat of the sole active Communist, Comrade Shvonder, who disappears before the end. The final scene is a return to life before the operation; the submissive dog watches as his powerful master plunges his hands into a container of human brains, ready once again to transgress the laws of nature. There is no conclusive triumph of Soviet values in the novel and no solution for controlling the beast other than by force; collars and locked doors are the only way to keep the wolf within human beings (and dogs) under control. *Heart of a Dog* draws on a long tradition in Russian literature of exposing human selfishness and desire for power over others, but it offers no alternative—it focuses only on diagnosis, not cure, and on exposure, not transformation. Because it offers no solution, readers must supply their own, and the text therefore occupies the monstrous liminal space of multiple interpretations. The fact that it has so frequently been read as anti-Soviet would seem to support the censors' decision.

UNMASKING SATIRE: VLADIMIR MAYAKOVSKY'S *BEDBUG* (1929)

In *Bedbug* two beings from 1929—the worker Prisypkin and a bedbug—are unintentionally flash-frozen.[36] Their bodies are discovered and resuscitated in 1979 by the citizens of a futuristic Communist utopia. In the 1929 NEP society depicted in the first four acts of this play, Soviet workers still live a life of sacrifice in rags and bare feet. Prisypkin, on the other hand, has quit his factory job to marry a wealthy businesswoman and has become immersed in a bourgeois world of tuxedos and patent-leather shoes. When he is resuscitated in 1979 (act 5), scientists at first identify him as the laborer he once was, but soon determine that he does not meet the Communist criteria for what constitutes a human being, much less a worker, the highest form of human: "influenced by external mimetic traits—calluses, clothing, and so forth—[the scientists of 1979] mistakenly classified the defrosted mammal as a member not only of 'homo sapiens' but of its highest variant, the working class."[37] When they amend their analysis, the "defrosted mammal" becomes a parasite that more closely resembles the bedbug resurrected with him than the men of the Communist future. The pseudo-human and the bug are placed in a zoo cage as a hygienic, cautionary display, and the Communist future is made safe.

Bedbug is, like *Heart of a Dog*, a satirical exposure of greed in Soviet society, but it is also a condemnation of pseudo-Soviet satire and a manifesto for its reform. Through the time travel enabled by Prisypkin's death and resurrection, we are shown the long-term negative effects of 1920s satire such as *Heart of a Dog* on the Communist future. In the 1929 scenes, the poet Oleg Bayan makes running commentary for the audience on Prisypkin's hypocrisy, but his humorous satirical jabs do nothing to positively alter his target. On the contrary, the satirist only encourages Prisypkin's negative behaviors, creating in him an impostor-hero—the very opposite of what 1929 Soviet satire should do. In the 1979 scenes, the impostor-hero created by Bayan threatens the Communist future, infecting its citizens with bourgeois culture that had long been wiped out before his defrosting. Communist leaders step in to save the day with a new type of satire, a didactic exposure followed by a second crucial step: the containment of society's flaws and hygienic instruction on their cautionary example. This new narration constitutes a literary vaccine that protects the social body from Prisypkin and his negative influence.

1929: A Comedy of (Bad) Manners

Rather than obeying the propaganda mission of Soviet literature, the poet Bayan instead becomes a life coach for the upwardly mobile, giving "lessons to young people—to one poetry writing, to another singing, to another dancing, and to another, well, you know . . . how to borrow money" (64–65). His running commentary in the 1929 scenes of *Bedbug* is a satirical attack on hypocrisy, while at the same time a brilliant lesson in how to live hypocritically—and all delivered for a reasonable price. Whereas Bayan is conscious of the humor in his misapplication of Soviet terms to non-Soviet desires—stage directions show him giggling (54)—Prisypkin takes the poet's rhetoric quite seriously and comes to believe that he, labeled a "proletarian" by his trade union card and by Bayan's eloquent speeches, deserves to thrive at others' expense. Bayan's erudite mockery becomes Prisypkin's ignorant but passionate truth. This is evident when Prisypkin controls his future mother-in-law by threatening to withhold the coveted name that grants him power in Soviet society: "Don't call me comrade, citizen, you still haven't become related to the proletariat" (55). By marrying Prisypkin, his capitalist fiancée and her family will legally acquire the protective cover of the words "comrade" and "proletariat," which in the NEP reality depicted in the play and satirized by Bayan translates into buying power—with his trade union card, the family can acquire more goods. Together the government and the satirist have created an impostor-hero who appears Soviet and sounds Soviet, but who is, like Bulgakov's Sharikov, consumed only with self-interest and consumption.

Bayan's use of Soviet terms is a colorful part of his satirical wordplay, evidenced by his description of Prisypkin's "Red" wedding:

> Not only do I understand, but with the power of imagination that has been, according to Plekhanov, granted to Marxists, I see as through a prism your lofty, elegant, and enchanting class ceremony! . . The bride exits the carriage—a red bride . . . all red,—that is, she's all steamed up; the red stand-in for the father is leading her, the accountant Erlykov, a fat, red, apoplectic man. You are led in by the red groomsmen, and the table is laid with red ham and bottles with red seals. (59)

The "class ceremony" that Bayan envisions with the power of his "Marxist" imagination is in reality a rejection of the working class; the audience has already learned that Prisypkin has given up his job in order to marry a woman with a bourgeois pedigree. Although he retains the trade union card and all the benefits it supplies, Prisypkin has cast off the responsibilities that come with it; he may have a "class ceremony" as Bayan proclaims, but if so, it is of the wrong class. Bayan's repeated use of the word "red" transfers the color of the Bolshevik Revolution to the instruments and products of capitalism: the bookkeeper and the luxury food and drink. Instead of representing justice and equality, red becomes base, physical—the sweaty bride and the corpulent accountant are indeed red, but not the red of revolution. Through it all, Prisypkin remains oblivious to Bayan's satirical jibes and sincerely proclaims at the marketplace: "For my money I demand a red wedding" (58). The only thing he has learned from Bayan's ridicule is that everything can be bought, including the word "red." Bayan showers the wedding preparations with his comical pseudo-Soviet praise, and Prisypkin takes every absurd compliment at face value.

At the wedding reception Bayan demonstrates his chameleonesque ability to accommodate the desire of any audience, delivering a comical couplet and then speaking in an elevated style "like the ancient Greeks" (75).[38] In his impromptu monologue on rhetoric, Bayan subverts the belief of Soviet linguistic engineers in the power of language to change minds. For Bayan, language is all style and little substance; identity is tailored from fashionable words, easily changed by the actor to suit this year's social audience. The impressionable Prisypkin follows his fashion advice, adopting the pretentious "Pierre Skripkin" (*Skripka* is the Russian word for violin) and buying visiting cards imprinted with the new name, thereby proving that a new identity can easily be bought at the local market. "Pierre Skripkin" is all costume and no substance, but his star-appeal is nevertheless a magnet for the starving and barefoot young people. In scene 2, when "Pierre" sweeps into the workers' dormitory with his entourage, he is treated by the young workers like a visiting celebrity. The "Barefoot Youth" wants to dress like him and the "Young Girl" declares "dreamily" that he is carrying out "a cultural revolution in his own home" (64). Prisypkin's "cultural revolution" does not ring in an era of equality, however; it is all Hollywood trompe l'oeil on plywood and papier-mâché. At the marketplace he announces that he will name his future children after American film stars, but his influence at the workers' dormitory signals an even more immediate danger than a future generation of Mary Pickfords and Douglas Fairbanks.

The danger inherent in Bayan's fashionable wordplay becomes physical when the celebration of Prisypkin's marriage breaks out in a fire that kills the wedding party. And it is Bayan's seemingly harmless wordplay that ignites the inferno. In the preceding scene, the comic banter between Bayan and the wedding party becomes increasingly threatening and chaotic, as misunderstandings and malapropisms accrue. When the others adopt Bayan's satirical style, Soviet language breaks down altogether. This is obvious in an exchange between the usher and Bayan, who is playing the piano: "Why is it that you play only on the black keys? The proletariat, I guess, only get half and the bourgeoisie get all of them?" (77). When Bayan protests that he is using both, the usher accuses him of selling out to the Whites (the anti-Bolshevik forces in the Civil War). Bayan's satirical misuse of the color red morphs into the usher's threatening accusation about the color white. The fight for Communism is thereby transformed into an absurd battle over cultural production that smacks of ignorance and paranoia. Too drunk to make sense of Bayan's confusing turns of phrase, the usher transforms each of the poet's expressions into a vulgarity; when Bayan refers to the bride's "petite histoire" the usher repeats "pissoire" (77). As the guests become increasingly intoxicated, such misunderstandings mount, and Bayan, who can no longer control and exploit language to his benefit, becomes the victim of his own linguistic games: the argument turns into a fistfight, a fire starts, and he and the wedding party go up in flames.

In the final scene of 1929, a group of firemen alerts the audience to the danger of reading in bed, an activity that can easily lead to a similar fiery death. Their equation of reading and destruction points to the satirist's potential to destroy progress toward the Communist future. In the final lines of their propaganda ditty, the firemen rhyme "pozharov" (fires) with Zharov, the last name of a Soviet poet criticized by Mayakovsky.[39] Like Bayan, such poets do nothing to extinguish the flame of consumption and selfishness that threatens to destroy the coming of Communism. Firemen, symbolic sentinels of literary style, represent a glimpse of Soviet satire of the future, a collective voice directed at preventing harm to Soviet citizens. Personifications of Mayakovsky's propaganda posters of the 1920s, the firemen urge Soviet citizens to be cautious in dealing with harmful substances such as fire and the poet Bayan. They are unaware, however, that although they have extinguished the fire caused by Bayan's linguistic chaos, his malaprop-spewing pupil lies frozen in the cellar, a potential threat to the Communist future.

The first half of Mayakovsky's play is a satire on satire. Bayan has two audiences, the theater audience who is encouraged to laugh at his clever asides about Prisypkin, and Prisypkin himself, who consistently misses the humorous barbs hidden behind the poet's lavish praise. Although Bayan reveals Prisypkin as a pseudo-Soviet impostor to the theater audience, he does nothing to correct Prisypkin's narcissism; on the contrary, the poet's clever wit only sharpens his target's self-interest. Since Bayan depends on Prisypkin's generosity, he crafts his satire so that its target remains unoffended; and therefore, instead of transforming his pupil into a New Person, his mocking lessons in selling out awaken Prisypkin's self-centered desires. Bayan's character is an attack on Soviet writers who would try to serve capitalism and socialism at the same time. By showing the theater audience how ridiculous and anti-Soviet Prisypkin's pretensions are, Bayan paints the picture of a Soviet Tartuffe, a hypocrite who hides his bourgeois social climbing behind a trade union card, but he negates the impact of his exposé by coaching Prisypkin on how to use Soviet words for selfish ends. He exposes and at the same time helps create a pseudo-Soviet "hero." More important, Bayan does not challenge the theater audience to see Prisypkin in themselves, a challenge that only takes place in 1979, when satirists of the Communist future play a different role in this comedy of bad manners.

1979: Hygienic Narration

If the 1929 scenes of *Bedbug* center on exposing the dangerous pseudo-satirist Bayan and his impostor-hero Prisypkin, the 1979 scenes counter Bayan's negative example with a new vision of the Soviet theater as instructive, sugar-coated spectacle. The resurrected Prisypkin brings with him a series of infectious theatrical devices—dance, music, costume—that create epidemics among the citizens of the future, who have no immunity from these eradicated "diseases." The narrators of the future, set in direct opposition to the self-interested Bayan, set out to vaccinate the remaining uninfected citizens of utopia by warning their audience of the dangers posed by these social viruses, and more importantly, quarantining the infectious Prisypkin to prevent further damage.

The first infectious danger that Prisypkin brings to the future is the anti-Soviet foxtrot, the wild Western dance taught by Bayan at the workers' dormitory as he warns his pupil away from disciplined Soviet movement: "Why are you stomping as though you're at a May Day parade?" (67). He urges Prisypkin to achieve world revolution so that he can show off his mastery of the foxtrot and warns him to ignore the "vulgar dance" of the mechanic, the worker who steadfastly denounces Prisypkin's departure from the working class. Prisypkin learns this lesson well; when the mechanic sings a song warning against abandoning the difficult struggle for socialism, Prisypkin instantly turns away: "Stay away from me with your coarse propaganda" (70). When Prisypkin is resurrected in the Communist future of 1979, the foxtrot has vanished and the only dance available is the type that Bayan has taught Prisypkin to hate: "a dance by ten thousand male and female workers; they will be moving along the square. It will be a merry rehearsal of a new system of field work" (105). Prisypkin, who has brought Bayan's philosophy with him, asserts that hedonistic abandonment to the foxtrot is his due as a former revolutionary: "Why did we try so hard, for what did we spill blood, when I, the hegemony, so to speak, am forbidden, in my own society, from dancing the newest dance to my heart's content?" (104). Under his influence many of the citizens of 1979 abandon their collective Communist dance for the bourgeois dances of the past. We see the result in scene 7, when a young woman who lives next door to Prisypkin is infected with the "ancient disease" (98) of love; she sleepwalks her way through the foxtrot and the Charleston, while reciting poetry and smelling an invisible rose. And she is not alone in her malady—she is followed by thirty chorus girls and a foxtrotting couple.

A reporter serves as narrator of this scene, countering Bayan's comic narration of the 1929 scenes with a hygienic reportage of the dangers of bourgeois dancing. Whereas Bayan teaches Prisypkin the foxtrot, the reporter instructs his audience on its danger. The reporter is the writer of the future, observing and interpreting the vaudeville performance of lovesick women and drunken men as an infectious danger, reporting that Prisypkin's presence has created an "epidemic" (99). In his description of the epidemic, the infected dancers lose their humanity: the chorus line is a "centipede" and the foxtrotting couple "a hermaphrodite quadruped" (99). In 1979, Prisypkin cannot be allowed to dance because his dancing only encourages others to follow him in the base fulfillment of selfish appetites. Under the reporter's narration the audiences onstage and in the theater are encouraged to see the entertaining musical of 1929 as a convulsive effect of disease.

A second epidemic is caused by the resurrection of old, sentimental words. The naive citizens of the future, eager for knowledge, are unwisely given instruction on understanding them—newsboys offer a "complete list of so-called swearwords" and an explanation for the word "alcoholic" (88). Beer-soaked romantic songs and love poetry soon intoxicate and fracture the formerly harmonious speech of the New People. When society finally realizes the danger of Prisypkin's speech, he is placed in a zoo cage with a sign that warns: "Watch your ears—it swears!" (113). The zoo director assures the frightened crowd that special filters, cleaned daily by keepers equipped with gas masks, have been placed on Prisypkin's cage to keep out most of his speech; only the few words that are "worthy" will reach them now. But this silencing is only the first step in containing the beast. Hygienic narration must present Prisypkin's example to the audience as a cautionary tale, removing him from the realm of the human.

Clean Clothes

Prisypkin, in his 1920s tuxedo, is put on display in the final scene like a store-window mannequin advertising what not to wear in the Communist utopia. The zookeeper delivers a lecture on the wardrobe of the "bourgeoisius ordinarius" (112):

> With his monstrous mimicry he lures his prey by pretending at times to be a cricket-rhymester and at times a romance-voiced bird. Back then even their clothing was mimicry; they had a birdlike appearance—a winged and tailed frock coat with a snow-white starched breast. These birds made their nests in theater loges, perched on oak trees at the opera. At ballets, to the beat of the Internationale they scraped one leg against the other, hung upside down from the twigs of their verse, and cut Tolstoy's hair to make him look like Marx. (113)

The description of birdlike mimics applies figuratively and also literally to Prisypkin, who is still dressed in his wedding tuxedo, and who when the cage is unveiled, begins to recite poetry like a "cricket-rhymester," horrifying the onstage crowd. The zoo director's description of mimics also brings us back to the marketplace of the first scene, where Prisypkin buys clothing and culture under the direction of the poet Bayan, another "cricket-rhymester" who has done his best to make everything and everyone "look like Marx" with his red words. Such birdlike mimics seemed harmless in 1929, but in 1979 the threat of the twittering Bayan is revealed in his monstrous creation, the parasite Prisypkin, who now frightens the crowd with his verses and guitar songs. The zoo director's speech also brings the audience watching the play into its metaphor, as they presumably sit in "tailed frock coats" "making their nests in theater loges." His words reduce the audience to animal parasites, an identification reinforced by Prisypkin in his later direct appeal to the audience to join him in his zoo cage. The satirical devices in the 1979 scenes of *Bedbug* are designed therefore not only to expose the obvious pseudo-speakers onstage, but also to reprimand the audience that has paid money to see them.[40]

Prisypkin's birdlike mimicry is countered by the costumes of the Communist future. In Meyerhold's 1929 production of *Bedbug* the sets and costumes of the 1979 future utopia were designed by Aleksandr Rodchenko, who clothed the citizens of the future in production clothing, referred to by the stump-compound *prozodezhda* (*proizvodstvennaia odezhda*), a common costuming device in 1920s constructivist theater productions. Outside the theater, *prozodezhda* was clothing designed specifically for a certain sport, profession, or activity. As Meyerhold's productions often included circus acrobatics and drew on his theory of biomechanics (specific body poses were used to convey emotions), *prozodezhda,* designed with comfort and function in mind, was a perfect fit. Theatrical *prozodezhda* was usually monochromatic and evocative of either work clothing or of military uniforms, which were both designed to remove visual signs of difference and unite individuals into a collective.[41] Rodchenko's citizens of the future are clothed in white *prozodezhda* with white aviator helmets; and the zookeepers are equipped with white gas masks and gloves, covered from head to toe as protection against the infectious Prisypkin.[42] Prisypkin's costume, the black wedding tuxedo in which he was frozen, stands out in jarring contrast to the white background of props and people. Prisypkin is a dark bird, and the New People of the future are clean and pure, differentiated by the fact that they have received the communal identity promised by Communism. The tuxedo, designed not for work but for ostentatious show, is a physical manifestation of his exaggerated laments and drunken romantic wailing; it exposes Prisypkin as a provincial actor, a comic blot on the white landscape of the future, a walking, talking, singing, and guitar-strumming tuxedo.

The exposure of the dark Prisypkin takes place in front of an onstage audience of New People, the citizens of the Communist future. It is a festive public performance, a correction of societal vice that must be communal and public, like the dance of the future. The chairman of the city soviet describes the nature of the performance and its intended goal: "We never turn down a spectacle, which may appear fantastic on the outside but which hides under its rainbow plumage a deep scientific meaning. . . . I cannot but note my gratitude and say a word about our renowned director, who decoded the true meaning of these strange and horrible phenomena and made from them a scientific and merry entertainment" (110–111). The zoo director stands for the Soviet writer, who must not only classify who is human and who is beast but must do it in an entertaining way, a "spectacle" (*zrelishche*) with "scientific meaning" beneath "rainbow plumage." Spectacle is a sugar coating designed to make the bitter pill of truth go down more easily, but importantly, it must be announced as such. Unlike the underhanded and multileveled narration of the sellout satirist Bayan, the chairman's description of Prisypkin is a straightforward and clear condemnation of the impostor-hero.

The chairman's words readily apply to the spectacle at the opening of the zoo exhibit containing Prisypkin and the bedbug. They could also apply to the performance of drunken, lovesick dancers narrated by the reporter. And of course they could also describe the play as a whole. The reporter in the vaudeville scene and the zookeeper—indeed, all the choruses of uniformed speakers of the future throughout the 1979 scenes—fulfill the collective role that the uniformed firemen did at the end of the 1929 scenes, cautioning against the danger of emulating Prisypkin. They are the collective satirist of the future, descendants of the censors of the past, who protect the audience from dirty words and bourgeois tuxedos with humorous ditties and clever metaphors.

Despite Stalin's assertion that it would be a crime not to love Mayakovsky's work, *Bedbug* was not chosen as a prototype for socialist realism in 1934. On the contrary, after its 1929 production, *Bedbug* disappeared from the Soviet stage until after Stalin's death. This can be attributed in part to a 1930s rejection of avant-garde theater in favor of more traditional staging or to a rejection of utopian visions in Soviet literature and theater. Another explanation lies in the compulsion to control audience identification. The play hinges on whom the audience chooses to sympathize with: Prisypkin or the collective. At the end of the play, Prisypkin turns to address the audience: "Citizens! Brothers! My own people! Dear ones! Where did you come from? So many of you?! When did they unfreeze all of you? Why am I alone in the cage? Dear ones, brothers, come join me! Why am I suffering?" (115). Do audience members recoil in horror? Or do they join him in his cage to sing his romantic songs and share his laments? Do they choose the foxtrot or the communal dance? Will they shed their dark tuxedos for the bright clothes of the Communist future? The problem in *Bedbug* is that the audience is invited to choose.[43]

THE DEATH OF SATIRE?

Satire seems directly opposed to "organizing the human psyche," the role assigned to writers by proletarian groups in the early Soviet period (see chapter 1). After all, satire reveals flaws and inconsistencies in society and in people that disturb the equilibrium envisioned by Aleksandr Bogdanov. It is a revolutionary device, a diagnostic tool. Socialist realism, on the other hand, is founded on the idea of cure, and therefore the dystopian fear introduced with this diagnostic mechanism must be dispelled by the end, the disease eradicated. Bulgakov's novel uses the strategy of exposure and silencing to provide a pseudo-cure—the dog-man is silenced and his final words are an act of obedience to Professor Preobrazhensky, the language hygienist: "Bad words are not allowed!" The fact that the professor is himself guided by self-interest and a desire for power means that the dog-man's victory merely substitutes one impostor for another—the beast in the tuxedo gives way to the beast in the leather jacket who gives way once again to the beast in the tuxedo. Mayakovsky's play, on the other hand, gives some hope of change in the translation of beastly desire into collective desire by the multiple speakers and choruses of 1979. The beast's final appeal to join him in his cage leaves his audience with a choice, however, and socialist realism must ensure that only one choice remains in the end.

These readings are partial explanations for why Richard Chapple, in his study of Soviet satire, argues that satirical "unmasking" faded as a literary strategy after the adoption of socialist realism: "The party's attempt to remove the unmasking aspect of satire eliminated not only one of the classical criteria for satire but also the flowering of its own satire."[44] Chapple sees this elimination as the inevitable conclusion of a long campaign against Soviet satire. This campaign was, however, against only a certain type of satire; Soviet critics such as Vladimir Blium argued that the problem was not the unmasking strategy of satire per se but rather its target:

> The target of satire must be an *individual* phenomenon, not a *social* one. Now the satirist must become a "moralist," depicting ugly phenomena as exceptions, as distortions of a reality which has every tendency towards health, towards growth, towards vigour, towards normality; and these tendencies must occupy the foreground, . . . otherwise the work will be either unconscious lies and slander against the new life or a deliberately counter-revolutionary act.[45]

Blium's call for the remaking of Soviet satire is emblematic of more general proletarian demands in 1925 for the party to manage non-proletarian writers and grant hegemony over literary production to the proletarians. The party responded to these demands by issuing a proclamation on June 18, 1925, entitled "On the Policy of the Party in the Field of Literature," which refused their request for exclusive control of literature. Despite this refusal, the document expresses the desire to eventually rid Soviet literature of those writers who failed to actively support the party: "Thus, as the class war in general has not ended, neither has it ended on the literary front. In a class society there is not, nor can there be, a neutral art."[46] While the beginning of the First Five-Year Plan is often seen as the source of attacks on "fellow travelers" (Trotsky's term for those writers who were not Communists but who more or less supported the revolution), the 1925 proclamation sets the stage for these attacks. In this climate it is hardly surprising that *Heart of a Dog* was rejected by Soviet censors. As Blium argues, implying that problems were not "individual" but "social" could produce only "unconscious lies and slander against the new life or a deliberately counter-revolutionary act." And Prisypkin's appeal to the audience to search for their own inner beast similarly suggests that his defects are widespread. Sharikov and Prisypkin are meant to challenge readers to look within themselves and their society. Socialist realism on the contrary encourages readers to see the villain as an outside threat.

The debate over satire died down in the opening years of the First Five-Year Plan, but it sprang up again during the summer of 1929, with Blium once again leading the attack. And by 1930 the staging of satirical plays was becoming increasingly difficult, despite earlier popular and critical successes; both Bulgakov and Mayakovsky fell under attack by Soviet critics along with other satirists.[47] A number of satirical journals were closed down in 1932,[48] and with the coming of socialist realism in 1934, Soviet satire seems to fall silent. However, the hygienic impulse behind it does not. What does change is a distancing of the villainous beast from the societal psyche. As socialist realism progresses, the dirty beast becomes increasingly negative, morphing from the self-interested wheelers-and-dealers of the NEP era into the saboteurs and Nazis of the socialist realist era. The positive hero's success and socialist realism's transformative function rest on exposing the misdirected selfish desire that is embodied in the beast and then silencing it, but no longer would the beast ask readers to look within themselves to find his reflection.

In socialist realism the beast transforms from an extreme of the human psyche—Bogdanov's view—into a virus, an unnatural presence in the purified psyche that must be eradicated. And the constant seeking out and destroying of this toxic invader naturally results in the mounting paranoia and purge mentality of the 1930s. The socialist realist hero must not only learn to control selfish desire—it must vanish entirely, replaced by collective desire, and therefore the beast must disappear before the final scene—his clothes, his songs and his wild dances are too seductive, too dangerous to appear in the happy endings of socialist realism. They must be translated into the white-clothed parade of the Communist future. Does this require a "fantasectomy," as Evgeny Zamyatin's *We* suggests (see chapter 1), or is there room for fantasy in socialist realism? I turn to this question in the following chapter.

Chapter Three

Things That Should Not Be Found

> The proletarian state must educate thousands of first-rate "masters of culture," and "engineers of souls." This is needed so as to return to the whole mass of working people that right to develop their minds, talents, and abilities that they have been deprived of throughout the world. This practically attainable goal imposes on us, writers, a strict responsibility for our work and social behaviour. That not only places us in the position, traditional for realistic literature, of "judges of the world and of people," and "critics of life," but also entitles us to a direct participation in the construction of a new life and the process of "changing that world."
>
> Possession of that right should inculcate in each writer a consciousness of his duty and responsibility for the whole of literature and for the things that should not be found in it.
>
> —Maksim Gorky, "Soviet Literature": Address Delivered to the First All-Union Congress of Soviet Writers, August 17, 1934

BY THE TIME GORKY gave his address to the First Congress, it was a well-worn truism that Soviet writers were to enlighten the proletariat and help build the Communist future. During the First Five-Year Plan, many of them had left their solitary writing lives for "direct participation in the construction of a new life," getting down and dirty in their newly assigned roles as propagandists and correspondents at construction sites and factories. They had worked hard to acquire the physical dirt that came with honest labor and to shed the intellectual dirt that supposedly came with their class backgrounds and education. One might think that Gorky's audience—members of the newly formed Soviet Writers' Union—

would therefore be above suspicion. However, Gorky's ominous warning about their "duty and responsibility" indicates that even they might still harbor and transmit "things that should not be found." In their life and work Soviet writers were to be, like the heroes they created, models of "work and social behaviour"—but could they be trusted?

According to the *Communist Manifesto,* the "ruling ideas of each age have ever been the ideas of the ruling class."[1] "Engineers of the soul," unless they came from the proletariat (the majority of them still did not), could not help but be tainted by these ruling ideas—toxic thoughts that could poison the very people they sought to enlighten. According to early Soviet scientific studies, university education created spiritual, intellectual, and physical degeneration if not combined with physical labor. A buildup of toxins was generated by intense mental effort, and if allowed to accumulate, these toxins would induce a decline in consciousness and an upsurge in individualism—they could even lead to insanity.[2] Thinking was dangerous work. Non-proletarians who joined the Communist Party worked hard to prove that they had been cleansed of these bourgeois toxins, but fellow travelers, although valued for their talent and experience, had done nothing to prove themselves. They and their often difficult and ambiguous writing were viewed with suspicion by Communists eager to safeguard the unsullied minds of the proletariat, especially those who were newly literate and would have little resistance to the toxic fantasies of the past.

According to *The ABC of Communism* (1919), the proletariat had been crippled by the separation of mental and physical labor under capitalism and would with enlightenment gain great cultural power: "You may or may not become a professor; but in any case you must produce values."[3] The task given to Gorky's audience was to heal the divide created by the proletariat's lack of education, to enable them to "produce values." As is apparent in Gorky's speech, writers had a "duty" and "responsibility" to keep it clean. Since their own literary imaginations were suspected of harboring dangerous toxins, what hygienic strategies could Soviet writers use to ensure cleanliness, to make fantasy safe and therefore prevent the proletariat from becoming toxin-filled clones of the bourgeoisie they had fought to replace?

When socialist realism was officially adopted in 1934 Soviet writers were told to depict "reality in its revolutionary development," that is, to show the present and past as moving toward Communism. Accepting this as a "utopian impulse," scholars have viewed socialist realism as relentlessly positive and uncritical—which does not account for the portrayal in these texts of toxic villains.[4] By approaching the socialist realist text through its villains rather than through its positive heroes we see that "reality in its revolutionary development" is not just a "utopian impulse" but also a hygienic impulse. Socialist realism demands a continual cleansing of the Soviet psyche, a maintenance regime composed of dirty characters and purifying plots intended to keep the Soviet reader "clean," a cleansing task that involves an introduction and subsequent eradication of fantastic hesitation.

HYGIENIC NARRATION

Tzvetan Todorov's highly influential but narrow definition of the fantastic text posits that such narratives maintain a state of doubt about the nature of reality until their very end.[5] Scholars after Todorov broadened his definition, however, to make the fantastic a mode[6] or impulse[7] running through many literary texts, with subgenres of "speculative fiction" categorized by a reader response that is built into the text through narrative strategies or character reactions (fantasy, horror, science fiction, utopia, dystopia, alternate history, magical realism, and many others). The label given to this response varies: "hesitation" (Todorov), "estrangement" (Darko Suvin), "astonishment" (Eric Rabkin), "fear, awe, and confusion" (Farah Mendelsohn), among others."[8] But in all cases, the key to these theories is the importance of reader response—projecting and predetermining it. For this reason, socialist realism falls squarely into the category of speculative fiction, as it intends a similar reader response caused by the villain's presence. It differs from Todorov's vision of the fantastic only in that the threat of fantastic hesitation to the Communist future must be fully expelled from the narrative at the end. While this difference is important, focusing on it alone masks the narrative's essential mechanism: doubt. Doubt about the Communist future must be introduced so that it can be vanquished, its spectacular erasure assuring that "reality in its revolutionary development" becomes the sole reality available to readers at the end. The subversive nature of the fantastic is thereby erased and the text cleansed of villainous doubt.[9]

Socialist realism resembles those forms of speculative fiction that present an alternate reality as completely logical and possible. Science fiction, for example, annuls fantastic hesitation by presenting a set of rules that govern the textual world, usually extrapolations of theories drawn from some branch of the natural or social sciences.[10] When defining science fiction, which he views as marked by "cognitive estrangement," Suvin therefore incorporates an intellectual component in his definition of its fantastic mechanism.[11] The reader is estranged from the reality in which he or she exists but then provided with an explanation that makes this estrangement acceptable—the unnatural world is made natural. Joanna Russ therefore claims that science fiction can be understood only by using the filter of the science utilized by the text—not through conventional tropes.[12] In socialist realism the science behind the fiction involves much more than an understanding of Marxist history. Socialist realism rests on a concept of the human psyche as one that perceives reality only via the words used to describe it and that can therefore be changed by these words. This enthusiasm for the transformative power of language, which permeated early Soviet culture, coalesces in the socialist realist idea that writers can "engineer souls" through the written word.

This engineering feat utilizes a hygienic narrative strategy wherein fantastic hesitation is introduced into the text via the villain and then expelled. The reader depends on a "clean" narrator for this expulsion, one who translates the individualism, selfishness, and alienation of the villain into collective desire. The effect intended by socialist realism is possible only when fantastic hesitation is decisively silenced within the text, and the hero—and reader—rejects the villain's example. Engineering the appropriate reader response—packaging the beast and the alien to be repulsive to everyone at all times—would always remain a central concern of Soviet writers. In this chapter an unlikely pairing of novels serves as a case study of the mounting anxiety over reader response in the early Soviet period and of the strategy developed to deal with it: one novel written before the First Five-Year Plan, when the role of the writer and narrator were radically redefined, and one published at its conclusion. Together they give us a glimpse into the evolution of socialist realism's hygienic impulse. Yury Olesha's *Envy* (*Zavist'*, 1927) illustrates a problematic use of the fantastic that fell under attack in the latter half of the 1920s. And Lev Kassil's *Shvambraniia* (*Shvambraniia*, 1932) provides an unexpectedly strong example of the socialist realist solution to this problem. Both novels begin with storytellers who are disconnected from the physical world and from the collective, first-person narrators who nostalgically describe prerevolutionary culture, but they part ways in their treatment of the potentially toxic fantasy generated by these narrators. In *Envy*, although doubt is ultimately cast out and society within the novel is thereby protected from its toxins, the alien imagination is the perspective of the narrator for much of the story, forming a potential threat to the Soviet reader, who might identify with him. In *Shvambraniia* the first-person narrator has already been transformed—a mature Soviet writer overlays a Marxist interpretation of the past onto the perceptions of his younger self. His retelling of earlier imaginative escapes from reality constitutes a perfect example of "reality in its revolutionary development"—the young boy's journey to a virtual world is cleansed of bourgeois ideas and doubt and transformed from a static, escapist fantasy into a dynamic journey to consciousness, an awareness of Marxist history and the ability to filter all events through this awareness. The villainous unreliable narrator within the childish writer is exposed and translated into a socialist realist narrator, a voice that transforms his former self into a Soviet writer.

By the end of *Shvambraniia*, the immature narrator's encounters with a series of villains have eradicated all doubt, and he has matured into a Soviet writer. The childish storyteller grows up, a maturation process that requires an erasure of escapist fantasy and a translation of fantastic hesitation into socialist realist surety. To accomplish this translation, the writer must submit to the collective imagination by channeling an artistic vision that is handed down from above: "reality in its revolutionary development." It is a willing liquidation of self, an erasure of the prerevolutionary vision of the writer as genius and prophet, one who attempts to convey a unique vision of reality via a narrator who spins the story in a new way. In socialist realism innovation becomes increasingly unimportant; what remains crucial is that the narrator controls reader response, with precision first evoking and then dispelling fantastic hesitation. In anticipation of Gorky's speech at the 1934 Writers' Congress, *Envy* and *Shvambraniia* show that one of the most important "things that should not be found" in Soviet literature is the unreliable narrator, the ultimate villain of socialist realism.

UNRELIABLE NARRATORS: YURY OLESHA'S *ENVY* (1927)

Nothing seems farther from the construction novels of socialist realism than Yury Olesha's *Envy*.[13] There is nothing overtly anti-Soviet about the novel, but the transformation expected of later socialist realism never quite comes about. In fact, nothing at all seems to happen in the seemingly aimless narrative. In part 1 the indigent Nikolay Kavalerov describes the daily life of the Soviet engineer Andrey Babichev, who has taken him in off the street and given him a job and a place to live. When Andrey's protégé, the famous soccer player Volodya Makarov, suddenly returns to take his place, Kavalerov writes a letter of protest to Andrey and leaves his apartment. Kavalerov then wanders the streets, where he accidentally meets Andrey's brother Ivan. Although he knows next to nothing about him, Kavalerov vows to follow Ivan, which he does throughout part 2. Ivan turns out to be as aimless as Kavalerov; he does little but talk, telling stories and encouraging rebellion against the Soviet New Person. Ivan invites Kavalerov to take part in a "conspiracy of sentiments,"[14] a plan to stage a final parade of people representing the old emotions. Yet again his plan is all talk; nothing comes of it, because Ivan can find only one representative, the envious Kavalerov. Kavalerov also hatches a plan—to kill his former benefactor Andrey Babichev and thereby gain revenge and fame. But nothing comes of his conspiracy either. Instead Kavalerov listens to Ivan's fantastic stories, watches Volodya's soccer game, and gazes at the lovely Valya, the embodiment of the Soviet future, but he never acts. At the end of the novel, Ivan and Kavalerov give up their former quest for fame and glory and in the final scene agree instead to share the widow Prokopovich in her enormous bed. In the concluding lines of the novel, Ivan proclaims allegiance to the only emotion left to them—"indifference" (*ravnodushie,* 94).

Envy is a novel where the central characters wander without purpose, making plans that are always unfulfilled. Between fanciful stories and aimless ramblings the reader catches glimpses of the New People—Andrey Babichev, Volodya Makarov, and Valya, but the novel does not center on them. On the contrary, *Envy* centers on its unreliable narrators, who, rather than lead readers to "reality in its revolutionary development," instead lead them to *question* what is real—they produce a text that is fantastic, not socialist realist. *Envy* is a "conspiracy of narrators," a final parade of the villainous alien imagination, which suspends the reader in the liminal realm of the fantastic, cast into a limbo of never-ending hesitation over the nature of reality. Although this conspiracy is exposed and rejected in the end, nothing is offered to take its place.

Distortions of the Alien Imagination

Kavalerov, the first-person narrator of part 1 of *Envy*, prefers to observe the world from odd angles, heights, and distances, peering into convex street mirrors or looking through the wrong end of the binoculars:

> I find that a landscape looked at through the wrong end of a pair of binoculars becomes brilliant, bright, and three-dimensional. The colors and the contours are somehow more defined. A thing stops being a known thing, and suddenly becomes ridiculously small, unusual. This evokes in the observer the ideas of a child. Exactly as if you were dreaming. (47–48)

Because of such assertions by Kavalerov, his narration is often seen as an example of what his contemporary Viktor Shklovsky called "estrangement" (*ostranenie*) (the defining factor of the fantastic according to Darko Suvin). According to this idea, literary language is differentiated by a disruption of the reader's familiar, comfortable perception of the world, epitomized in the childlike freshness of a dream that Kavalerov claims as his own. The resulting "strangeness," acceptable in a Soviet novel of the 1920s, becomes villainized in later socialist realism. The convex street mirror that Kavalerov loves requires that he face away from the world (he describes it as seeing from the back of his head), and the wrong end of the binoculars artificially distances him from what he observes. Socialist realism, on the other hand, is intended to bring the reader closer to the world—albeit a redefined world—and the people around him or her. Kavalerov asserts that his vision is revolutionary—it tears down "the laws of the world" (48). It offers, however, nothing to replace what it has torn down. The world becomes smaller and "stranger," but it does not become the harmonious whole promised by socialist realism. On the contrary, the narrator becomes increasingly isolated from other people and from the physical world.

Even without the aid of convex mirrors or backward binoculars, Kavalerov's observations are distorted by the envy of the novel's title. This is evident in the following observation he makes about Andrey Babichev:

> But everything in his behavior says: you—are a philistine, Kavalerov. Of course, he doesn't announce this. Probably he hasn't even thought anything like that. But it's obvious without words. Some third person announces it to me. Some third person forces me into a rage while I watch him. (17)

Kavalerov considers himself to be an omniscient narrator, able to discern and report the thoughts of everyone he observes, but in the above passage he relies on a "third person" to "announce" it to him. This seemingly objective and authoritative "third person" exists, however, only in Kavalerov's head, created by the envy of the title. Because of his envy, Kavalerov thinks that everyone occupies a place in the world that rightfully belongs to him. The people he observes are undeserving doppelgangers, to whom Kavalerov attributes the feelings and motivations that he would have were he in their places. Kavalerov accuses Babichev of a lack of imagination, but Kavalerov himself can only imagine the people he observes as being like *him*—full of spite and envy and seeking personal glory.

Moreover, he filters the world through other people's imaginations. Kavalerov sees himself and those around him as characters from formulaic adventure stories, reenacting hackneyed plots. When he spies Volodya's photograph, he imagines a fellow "Tom Virlirli" (43) seeking glory and fame, but blocked in his pursuit by the villainous Andrey Babichev. When he sees Valya on her balcony, he imagines her to be a damsel in distress, awaiting his own beautiful words to free her from the bondage imposed by Babichev. And when he observes Babichev himself, he imagines him as the evil villain, set on subjugating the hero to his will and "utilizing" (39) the heroine. The unique vision attributed to the bourgeois writer is revealed through Kavalerov's narration to be instead highly derivative.

Through inserted letters, memos, and phone conversations, Kavalerov's vision of the New People is exposed for what it is, an envious distortion of the world around him, filtered through the hackneyed plots of other people's narratives. In his letter to Babichev Volodya proclaims his love for him and his desire to vanquish the remaining bourgeoisie and become a machine, thereby painting a picture of himself not as a Tom Virlirli but as the New Soviet Person. An overheard phone conversation reveals that the damsel-in-distress Valya does not fear the "villain" Babichev, from whom she seeks comfort, but rather the "hero" Kavalerov, who has frightened her by speaking in his "figurative language" (*obraznyi iazyk,* 40). Finally, in his interoffice memos the "villain" Babichev is revealed to be concerned not with Kavalerov's destruction but with the composition of candy wrappers: "best of all would be something from science (poetic—geography? astronomy?), with a serious name, and with a tempting sound: 'Eskimos'? 'Telescope'?" (16). The man with "no imagination" (16) channels his creativity to the good of Soviet society—his imagination is industrial, Soviet: "the color should be dull blue—chemical, not romantic" (17). The literary vision that Kavalerov imposes on the world is one that cannot accommodate Babichev's imagination as anything but villainous. It blinds Kavalerov to Soviet "reality in its revolutionary development."[15]

These snatches of narrative reveal that it is Kavalerov, not Babichev, who "utilizes" people around him—to fill the roles necessary to his preconceived plot, which is borrowed from the well-worn pages of the books he has read. Through his eyes, the world around him is made not "strange" but all too familiar, filled with villains and heroes from the hackneyed melodramas of the past. At the end of part 1, when Kavalerov meets his mentor Ivan Babichev and asks where he came from, Ivan answers: "I myself thought myself up" (49). Similarly, Kavalerov "thinks himself up." He imagines himself to be the Western chivalric hero signaled by his name, which is derived from "cavalier," a hero who will rescue Valya from her balcony, join forces with Volodya, and defeat the evil Babichev. However, he is incapable of acting as such a hero. Other than the one phrase said to Valya as she passes him in the street, Kavalerov makes no attempt to woo her. Similarly, his vow to kill Babichev comes to nothing. Kavalerov is a "cavalier" incapable of completing a quest. In the end, he realizes that such a vision as his has no place in the Soviet imagination. But in part 1, he still believes that he can be a Soviet child on Babichev's sofa: "Now I sleep on an excellent sofa. On purpose I move so as to call forth a ringing from its new, tight, virginal springs. . . . I fall asleep like a child. On the sofa I make a flight into childhood" (24). Kavalerov asserts throughout part 1 that he can be reborn into a new kind of hero, a "Soviet" hero, and thereby participate in the Soviet world and attain Soviet glory, but he fails time and again to do so.

Kavalerov ends the novel not on Babichev's couch but on Anechka's enormous bed, where he escapes from the responsibilities that come with sleeping on Babichev's couch. Earlier in the novel, Kavalerov envisions a life beneath the bed's mirrored headboards:

> Kavalerov thought, "If I were a child, Anechka's little son, how many poetical, magical constructions my child's mind would have made, gripped by the power of the spectacle of such an extraordinary thing! Now I'm an adult, and

> now I can only detect the general contours and a few details, but as a child . . . As a child, not governed by the laws of distance, scale, time, weight, gravity, I would have crawled in the corridors formed in between the boxsprings and the sides of the bed. I would have hidden myself behind the columns that now seem to me no bigger than test tubes; I would have put up imaginary catapults on barriers and would have shot them at enemies losing strength as they fled across the soft spongy ground of the blanket. I would have received foreign ambassadors under the arc of the mirror, like a king in the novel I'd just read. I would have gone on fantastic journeys along the carvings, climbing ever higher and higher along the legs and backsides of cupids, as one climbs on a statue of Buddha, not quite able to take the whole thing in at once, and from the top arch, from a head-spinning height, I would have thrown myself into the horrible abyss, into the icy abyss of the pillows. (71)

Kavalerov's vision of life in Anechka's bed epitomizes his own narratorial point of view. Although it seems a celebration of the freedom gained by returning to a childlike vision, at the beginning of this reverie, Kavalerov admits to the limits of his imagination—as an adult he is incapable of the "poetical, magical constructions" of a child. He can only deliver "general contours" of the world. A child, according to Kavalerov, is free of the laws of physics, "distance, scale, time, weight, and gravity," but Kavalerov can only achieve this freedom in artificial lenses and the mirrors in Anechka's headboard. His freedom is really a derivative, self-destructive escapism—in Anechka's bed he would be isolated from Soviet time and would wander through a static, shapeless realm, gazing at a reflection of himself, of his own psyche, which is formed from scraps and bits of other people's novels and myths, "the backsides of cupids." Kavalerov is capable of seeing only isolated parts of the greater whole, the Buddha that is too large to take in at once. Even before his retreat into Anechka's bed at the end of the novel, it is clear that he can only focus on isolated fragments of the world around him. Andrey Babichev, whom he observes through much of part 1, is always reduced by Kavalerov's observation to a birthmark or a pince-nez, rarely if ever seen in his entirety. Anechka's bed with its convolutions, carvings, and fragments of mirror is a microcosm of Kavalerov's brain, comfortable, fanciful, and isolated from the outside world, where nothing can be seen in its entirety. As Anechka's child, he would be forever crawling and hiding among the folds of his own psyche.

Time and the Toxic Hero

Socialist realism requires that every narrative, no matter when it is set, be filtered through the prism of the Communist future. What happens now or in the past can be shown only "in its revolutionary development," moving toward that future. The imaginative journeys that would take place in Anechka's bed are, however, removed from time, stretched out, made epic, or frozen—they are never joined to the forward arrow of the Soviet timeline. Kavalerov's fate in retiring to Anechka's bed at the end of the novel is symbolic of his narrative exile from the Soviet space-time continuum to the timeless, eternal space of his own imagination, which stands in direct opposition to that discussed by Volodya in part 2:

> The revolution was . . . well, what? Of course, very cruel. But why? It was magnanimous, right? It was kind for the whole clockface . . . Right? You have to be offended not just for the space of two seconds, but for the whole clockface . . . Then there is no difference between cruelty and magnanimity. Then there is one thing: time. The iron logic of history as they say. And history and time are one and the same thing, doubles. (69)

Volodya argues that in order to understand individual events, they must be weighed against all of time. When all emotions, desires, instincts (the extraconscious) are harnessed to the idea of the "whole clockface," an understanding of Marxist history and one's place in it (consciousness), then they change. When Volodya expresses envy for the machine in his letter to Andrey, this emotion comes from a desire to help build the Communist future, not a desire to take center stage in the Soviet construction pageant. Envy, Kavalerov's main narrative filter, is changed by the whole clockface to become a productive emotion. With his teammates he expresses no envy, instead "searching in each of them for remarkable traits and abilities" (69). He diminishes his own achievements in order to magnify theirs. And when Andrey Babichev claims to love Volodya "both as a son and as a new person" (68), he demonstrates that the whole clockface does not destroy the emotions of the past, as Ivan claims, but instead alters them. Loving Volodya solely as a son would mean focusing on the moment, but loving him as a "new person" requires that love be weighed against Marxist history, and since the new person represents the final conclusion of that history, loving Volodya as "new person" acknowledges the whole clockface.

Kavalerov's narration of part 1 is difficult to follow because there is no "whole clockface" to guide the reader; the only thing uniting his rambling narrative is the emotion of the title: envy. Kavalerov envies the New Person's moment in the spotlight, and wants only to stand in his place. His symbol for this coveted moment of fame is a waxwork figure that Kavalerov saw in a museum when he was a child. As he gazed at the dying French president Carnot, frozen in a "greenish cube," the young boy could hear the "rumble of time" (26). Kavalerov wants to be immortalized in such a museum exhibit, his name in capital letters below a wax figure:

> And everyone seeing it will say: "Ah!" and will remember some kind of stories, maybe legends: "Ah, that's the one who lived in a remarkable time, hated everyone and envied everyone, who bragged, got carried away, was tormented by great plans, wanted to accomplish a lot and did nothing—and it ended with him committing some repulsive, vile crime." (26)

Kavalerov's vision of fame is not only removed from the space-time continuum, isolated in a greenish glass cube, but it is also removed from direction and purpose. Visitors to Kavalerov's exhibit will judge him to be a man incapable of conscious action, one who "did nothing." His wax figure will be placed there not because of an act that won him fame but rather because he is the subject of "some kind of stories, maybe legends," vaguely envisioned tales of failed potential and unfulfilled intention—like his own narration—that will end in a "repulsive, vile crime" (hence his vow to kill Andrey Babichev). Not surprisingly, the self that Kavalerov envisions in the glass cube is the superfluous man, the nonconformist antihero of Russian nineteenth-century literature who dreams of great deeds but accomplishes nothing, placed by "stories, maybe legends" in a "greenish cube" where time is suspended forever.

Several times in the novel Kavalerov encounters echoes of the frozen "greenish cube" of fame that he saw as a child, and in each of them, because of his own failure to act, he remains unseen and unheard. The first is at the airfield, where a crowd of people gathers on a green field to celebrate the invention of a new type of airplane. Prevented from joining them, Kavalerov calls out, and they turn, frozen in expectation, but he cannot speak and so his opportunity is lost. In the conclusion of this scene, Babichev turns to him: "He had no eyes. There were just the two dull, shining discs of his pince-nez, like mercury" (35). Kavalerov's primary goal is to be seen, to be recognized by the powerful Soviet New Person, but here, as throughout part 1, Babichev is made blind to him by Kavalerov's inaction and emotional distance from Soviet reality. Another chance at the "greenish cube" comes at the soccer game, when the ball unexpectedly lands at Kavalerov's feet in the stands. Players and spectators are frozen (against a green background), and all attention is directed at Kavalerov, who is once again incapacitated by his focus on the importance of this moment. Babichev, who sees the whole clockface, finds the moment to be insignificant and easily throws the ball to Volodya on the field, much to the delight of the spectators. By the time of the scene at the soccer match (in part 2), Kavalerov's inability to view reality through the whole clockface has caused him not only to lose his place as first-person narrator (part 1) and hero, but even as a character in the Soviet plotline; at the soccer match, he has become invisible to Babichev and to Valya, who "looked at Kavalerov not seeing him" (88). He calls to her, but "she did not hear" (88).

Volodya's teammates, as they leave the field, acquire the admiring gaze of an audience that Kavalerov so desperately wants: "They were gaping with the news—the details of height or build, severity of abrasions, heaviness of breathing, complete disarray of clothing, From a distance everything had a lighter, holiday impression" (87). In this moment, each player is recognized for the individual effort he has put into the apparently effortless teamwork displayed on the field. The Soviet spectators' vision of the players is detailed and realistic, in direct opposition to Kavalerov's own vision. In the crowd's observation we see a re-creation of the task of the Soviet writer, to show team achievement and to deliver a "holiday impression" of movement forward, in other words to show "reality in its revolutionary development." It is clear that Kavalerov can be neither appreciative, realistic observer (narrator/writer), nor team-playing, selfless object of observation (hero). When he describes his childhood encounter with fame at the museum in part 1, he fails to acknowledge that the exhibit he so vividly remembers, the "greenish cube," was a record not of the French president's great or vile deeds, but of his own death. *Envy* itself serves as such a "greenish cube," testifying to the death of the alien imagination, represented by Kavalerov's distorted narration in part 1 and his failure as hero in part 2.

Conspiracy of Toxic Sentiments

Part 1 of *Envy* is an exposure of the poisonous imagination, the unreliable narrator as toxin, awakening doubt and never quelling it. Some scholars claim that the third-person narrator of part 2 provides an objective contrast to Kavalerov's unreliable first-person narration.[16] However, the narrator frequently undercuts his supposed omniscience by repeated expressions of doubt over his own narratorial assertions. For example, he ends chapter 1 by telling us that Ivan worked as an engineer before the war, but begins chapter 2 with an expression of doubt about his own assertion:

> But was he ever really an engineer? But didn't he lie? How the idea of an engineer's soul, closeness to machines, to metal, to blueprints didn't suit him! It would be easier to take him for an actor or a defrocked priest. He himself understood that his listeners didn't believe him. He himself spoke with some kind of playfulness in the corner of his eye. (57)

The narrator's version of reality in part 2 comes to him through the stories and legends of Ivan, whom he considers to be completely untrustworthy. A blaspheming liar who eternally struts across an imaginary stage, Ivan revels in his dishonesty and in his audience's disbelief. The narrator of Part 2 seems to agree with Ivan: "But if this is fantasy [*vydumka*]—so what? Fantasy is the sweetheart of reason" (54).[17] Part 2 begins, however, with a flashback to Ivan's childhood, where it is clearly revealed that fantasy is *not* reason's sweetheart. Ivan's childhood is a never-ending battle between father, the rational man, and son, the fanciful child, over who gets to narrate reality. The father wants to impose a fact-based narration, drawing on his background as a historian and classicist. And the son wants to narrate a world of fantasy and imaginative fun.

When the boy claims to have invented a dream machine, the father demands empirical evidence, and when the machine fails to induce a dream about a famous Roman battle, the father claims victory. However, one of the servants has a dream remarkably similar to the one requested, and the father is plunged into doubt. Then the father himself has the dream, which contains details about the battle that are not given in the accounts of historians. It would seem that fantasy—and therefore Ivan—has finally won a decisive victory over the father's rational belief in history and science. In support of this victory, we then learn that the father has seen a giant, orange bubble outside his window, supposedly caused by another of Ivan's inventions—further proof that Ivan's fancy trumps his father's reason. However, faced with his father's shame and fear young Ivan admits that he was lying: a balloonist was demonstrating his new technology that day over the city. We are once again back on the firm ground of the father's reason-based world. However, just when the truth appears to be established, the narrator questions this most rational assertion—the incident could not have occurred, because the date that Ivan claims for the flight is far too early in the history of aviation. We are left with the question of who to believe—Ivan, his father, or the doubting narrator. Adding to this confusion is the fact that the adult Ivan starts his story with the words "And it seems to me" (54). From the narrator's presentation of Ivan's stories we are left with no decisive winner in the battle between father and son and fantasy and reason. Ivan's inventions are all viewed through several layers of "it seems": the narrator's parenthetical comments, the father's doubt, and Ivan's own storytelling, in which he seems to relish fiction more than fact.[18]

If truth is not important to Ivan's stories, then what is? Part 2 reveals that Ivan's narratives exist only to infect others with the envy, shame, and fear that he himself feels. The dream machine and the bubble maker evoke discord in his family and anger and shame in his father. And the potion he invents to cure warts instead causes a flower to grow from them, and instead of relief, the invention elicits only negative emotions in the woman who uses it and finds herself with a flower growing out of her face: "Moral torments tortured her. She hid her face in a scarf, the flower lovingly tickled her lips, and this tickling sounded like the whisper of a depressingly spent youth, like the spirit of some single kiss chased out by the stamping of feet" (55). Ivan's childhood inventions all shake the foundations of belief systems and turn confident, self-assured adults into angry, shameful doubters. Ivan is at heart a nihilist, tearing down dreams of happiness rather than building them, which is evident in his story of an event from childhood, when he attacked a little girl at her birthday party: "I grabbed her by the back of the head and knocked her forehead against a column several times. At that moment I loved this girl more than life itself, I bowed down to her—and hated her with all my might" (66). Ivan claims to celebrate the noble emotions of the past, but none of them are pure for him—love can only be experienced with hate or envy. His "conspiracy of sentiments" seems to be a celebration of beauty and whimsy, of dreams, bubbles, and flowers. But it is really a celebration of negative feelings, a parade of spite and ill will. Through his stories Ivan externalizes his own feelings of envy and fear—he infects the world around him with toxic fantasy.

This is also true of "Ophelia," his machine designed to "do everything" but intentionally denied utility. He ruins this tribute to the new world by giving it the negative, haunting emotions that lie at the heart of all his inventions—anger, envy, hatred, shame, and fear: "Able to do everything, she sings our romances, foolish romances of an age gone by, she collects the flowers of an age gone by. She falls in love, is jealous, cries, dreams . . . I did this" (73). Kavalerov is drawn by Ivan's stories of Ophelia into the world of the fantastic, where he is stranded between reality and fantasy, no longer sure what is real and what is unreal, and in this liminal realm, he is able to experience only the negative emotions that Ivan himself is capable of feeling. The New People, who view reality through the whole clockface, are impervious to Ivan's inventions, but Ivan's disciple, the only "hero" he can find, is not. Only Kavalerov can see Ophelia, because he views all of reality through the lens of envy and she is only visible in this spectrum.

At the end of *Envy*, Ivan and Kavalerov exist in a sort of quarantine in Anechka's bed, free to indulge their alien dreams and toxic emotions, but unable to infect others with them. Although Kavalerov wants to be a Soviet child, he realizes at the end of the novel that he has no place in the Soviet future, that he is, rather than an innocent child, "lazy, dirty, and lewd" (93). This realization signals the sterility of the old world and the old imagination. Anechka sees Kavalerov as a "grandfather," and she herself is described as the polar opposite of the young, lithe Valya: "The Widow Prokopovich is old, fat and loose. You could squeeze her out like liverwurst. . . . The widow Prokopovich is the symbol of my masculine humiliation" (25). By going to the "old, fat and loose" widow, whose face is like a "hanging lock" (37), Kavalerov loses the power to procreate—Volodya will now marry young fertile Valya and sire the Communist future.[19] But more important, both Kavalerov and Ivan will be deprived of procreation in a literary sense; their words and stories are now destined to stay within the muffled confines of Anechka's bed and their own heads, unable to infect others. Ivan once claimed that his words were eternal: "I don't talk, I engrave my words on marble" (66). But in the new age they vanish as though scratched in sand. The final words of the novel are a parody of the collective language of the new world: "And today, by the way . . . listen: I . . . I'll tell you something pleasant . . . today, Kavalerov, it's your turn to sleep with Anechka. Hooray!" (94). The New People, however, have evolved so far that they are unable to hear these words of surrender to a sterile future. The "hero" Nikolay Kavalerov and the storyteller Ivan Babichev retire into the eternal disconnected present of the alien imagination, deprived of an audience and a place in the Soviet future. Their envy and spite are no longer heard by the New People around them. Yet despite their silencing and expulsion from Soviet society in the book, they are allowed the last word, and as critical response to the novel reveals, the lingering poison of their toxic fantasies makes *Envy* too hazardous for Soviet literature under socialist realism.

THE NONTOXIC WRITER

When it was first published, Yury Olesha's *Envy* won the praise of important Soviet cultural figures such as the writer Maksim Gorky and Commissar of Education Anatoly Lunacharsky, who deemed Olesha "a new name inspiring the highest hopes."[20] Moreover, *Envy* received a positive review in the Communist newspaper *Pravda:* "The novel exposes the envy of little people, of the petty bourgeois flushed out of their lairs by the Revolution, of those who are . . . against the majestic reorganization of our economy and our everyday life."[21] However, the *Pravda* critic expresses one significant concern: "[Olesha's] vacillations regarding his heroes, the ambivalence in their very delineation—is beyond all doubt. And, of course, this ambivalence is the greatest defect of Olesha's interesting novella."[22] Despite this "defect," *Envy* could still be considered a *Soviet* novel in 1927, deserving of praise even in *Pravda.* However, after the redefinition of literature that occurred during the First Five-Year Plan, *Envy* could no longer be seen as "interesting"—concerns about its "vacillations" were transformed into accusations that it suffered from a "lack of socialist perspective."[23] Satirical exposure of non-Soviet elements of society, which won the novel praise, was no longer enough to warrant its inclusion in the Soviet canon. The condemnation of *Envy* constitutes a decisive moment in the decade-long battle between Marxist critics and fellow travelers, whose literature—like Olesha's *Envy*—was often accused of ambiguity bordering on the counterrevolutionary. Mistrust of these writers lay deeper than their refusal to shape their texts to the necessities of Soviet propaganda. Few of them came from the proletariat, and a common stereotype of the intellectual in the early Soviet period, especially among proletarian groups, was of a cold, unfeeling elitist. The noun *intelligent* (a word that includes not only what we would call "intellectuals," but any white-collar worker) was often used in proletarian journals as a derogatory term.[24]

This attitude is strange, given that many of the writers contributing to these journals were themselves *intelligenty,* but as Lynn Mally points out, most members of the Proletkult believed that *intelligenty* could purge themselves of the toxic past through selfless work for the proletariat.[25] *Intelligenty* petitioning to join the party were therefore advised not only to read Marx and Lenin, but also to merge with workers on factory floors and construction sites, thereby gaining something that could not be found in the pages of books and pamphlets, something long suppressed within them: a diminished or dormant "heart." This "heart" could, however, be awakened by working side by side with the proletariat. Students and white-collar workers took part in voluntary labor at factories and in fields, intended to free them of toxins and awaken long-suppressed natural instincts—according to the *ABC of Communism,* "Labour should be a need, like the desire for food and drink."[26] Many a non-proletarian applicant to the Communist Party was told that he "should go into production, prove himself, and apply to the Party there."[27] The purifying balance of body and mind acquired both on the factory floor and in the classroom would create a New Person who could both design and build the Communist future.

The First Five-Year Plan (1928–32) marks a turning point in the development of the Soviet hero and of the Soviet writer. It was a time centered on a vision of metamorphosis—of a war-torn country into an economic superpower and of a fragmented people into a single class. Massive resources were pumped into educating the proletariat, and at the sites at which the Five-Year Plan was to be fulfilled—factories, hydroelectric dams, collective farms, and construction sites—"human material" was to be reengineered through physical labor. Writers were encouraged to travel to these sites not only to document these changes but so that they too could look back at their poisonous former selves in the third person and at their former work as alien. The writer who once led others into literary escapes of adventure and fantasy had now to become a follower—of the party's and by extension the people's instructions on the containment of the alien imagination.

The Five-Year Plan was to forge alien toxin-filled writers into *Soviet* writers. But what did that actually mean in terms of narration? After the Five-Year Plan it became vitally important that the writer provide a narrator who was not only reliable but also an infallible defender of the Soviet vision of life and of history. In order to "remold" the reader, a steady voice was needed to sort hero from villain, to distinguish "reality in its revolutionary development" from that which would prevent the coming of Communism. In *Envy,* narration is suspended in the eternal present generated by fantastic hesitation, wherein the narrator and by extension the reader finds it impossible to choose between potential futures—they therefore remain eternally stranded outside "reality in its revolutionary development." In *Shvambraniia,* on the other hand, a novel published at the end of the Five-Year Plan, we see a narrator who has transformed so that he can translate the alien dreams of his former self into "reality in its revolutionary development." Written on the eve of the adoption of socialist realism, *Shvambraniia* lays out a vision of the Soviet writer and narrator that illustrates how toxin-filled intellects can be changed into Soviet heroes and more important into Soviet writers. This Soviet coming-of age story reads as an instruction manual for the transformation of literary imagination.

REMAPPING THE ALIEN IMAGINATION: LEV KASSIL'S *SHVAMBRANIIA* (1932)

Lev Kassil's autobiographical *Shvambraniia* was published in 1932 at the end of the First Five-Year Plan; it is a coming-of-age novel, in which a mature narrator looks back on a childhood spent playing "Shvambraniia," an elaborate game of pretend in a make-believe land. Both *Envy* and *Shvambraniia* have first-person narrators, but unlike *Envy,* the narrator of *Shvambraniia* undergoes transformation into a Soviet writer. Looking back on his childhood, this narrator chronicles his childhood games and his gradual acquisition of consciousness, inserting Marxist explanations for the gut reactions of his younger self to the world around him. But the young Lyolya, as yet unaware of Marxism, rejects the real world and turns to the imaginary continent of Shvambraniia, a land of happy endings, for the justice that he cannot find in the real world. Lyolya invents Shvambraniia while sitting on the punishment bench with his brother Oska, stewing over the injustice of adults, and the imaginary land is expanded and modified as the boy becomes increasingly aware of the injustices meted out on a larger scale by the class system in which he lives. He has no Marxist labels such as "class struggle" or "opiate of the masses" with which to describe the world around him, but a sort of revolutionary instinct prompts him to demand justice, even if it takes place only on the butcher paper of Shvambraniian documents or in the schoolboy notebooks that constitute Shvambraniian chronicles. Through the course of the novel the reader learns that such dreaming, even if motivated by noble intentions, is in the Soviet world a seductive and potentially dangerous occupation.

Unlike the unreliable narrators of *Envy*, the narrator of *Shvambraniia* has transformed into a New Person, who can filter the alien, disconnected, and toxic dreaming of his younger self through the future-oriented consciousness of his mature self. In his narration of the events of his childhood, the mature narrator shows how, through contact with villains who represent his own worst impulses, the alien imagination that crippled the narrator as a child was abandoned. As a result of the villains' example, he is moved to translate individual desire for a Westernized literary fantasy into the collective desire of socialist realism. Through a palimpsest of narrators, we are allowed to see both the seductive attraction of fantasy and its potential danger if undirected. We are then shown its potential benefit if used to build Communism. *Shvambraniia* is labeled a "novel" in the lengthy subtitle, and on its pages the little boy's naively scribbled chronicles are reshaped by the mature narrator to fit the mold of a socialist realist novel, a novel centered on transformation. Written in the year in which the Soviet Writers' Union was formed and on the eve of the adoption of socialist realism, *Shvambraniia* can be read as a blueprint for rewriting the literary imagination, for transforming the writer from empty dreamer to "engineer of the human soul" by exposing and translating the villain both within himself and within society. In the process the escapist fantasy of Shvambraniia is transformed into "reality in its revolutionary development."

Immature Fantasy

In the early Soviet period, applicants to the Communist Party were required to submit an autobiography, in which they described their journey to consciousness. Igal Halfin has shown the important part that the First World War played in these autobiographies, which usually included an explanation for the petitioner's attitude toward and participation in the "imperialist" war. Halfin views this (re)writing of the past as comparable to socialist realism's recasting of past actions in light of the coming Communist future, its use of "reality in its revolutionary development."[28] Similarly, in the prerevolutionary portion of *Shvambraniia*, the mature narrator describes his gradual disillusionment with the war, as his younger self becomes increasingly aware of a sharp contrast between the noble battles of Shvambraniia and the increasingly harsh reality of the real war. This part of the novel is a writer's apology for his childish prerevolutionary imagination, in need of the Bolshevik Revolution to change it into that of a mature Soviet writer.

The narrator presents his childish attraction both to the war and to Shvambraniia as an understandable if misguided escape into fantasy by an immature writer who has been exposed only to bourgeois culture. Prerevolutionary Shvambraniian battles, fought in the boys' parlor, are informed by the noble but deceptive descriptions of World War I that filter into their imagination from the press: "The daily bulletins from the front are decorated with beautiful and vague words that cover up all kinds of war unpleasantness: losses, defeats, the retreat of armies. And all this goes under a name that is sonorous and festive: the theater of war."[29] The newspapers turn war into a theatrical spectacle, embellishing and ennobling the mounting failures of the Russian empire. Adding to the allure of journalistic accounts, postcards, calendars, and boxes of candy are covered with beautiful pictures of brave and gallant soldiers in victorious battle. Lyolya and his brother Oska are seduced by this advertising, and, as Lyolya is exposed constantly to the beautiful "theater of war," his invented Shvambraniia imitates this candy box world filled with brave soldiers and beautiful battles, where the combatants line up neatly like chess pieces into straight rows of good guys and bad guys. The little boy's creation of Shvambraniia echoes the beautiful bourgeois propaganda with which his life is decorated.

Lyolya's childish fantasy of Shvambraniia has its equivalent for adults, as we learn when he eavesdrops on their conversations about the theater: "Arguing and getting carried away, they debated the deeds of various heroes at yesterday's show. They accused made-up people, defended them, loved them and hated them just as Oska and I did, when we played Shvambraniia. And we came to the conclusion that this kind of art was Shvambraniia for adults" (275). Children raised on adventure tales and advertisements become adults lost in a fantasy world, where the justice and nobility lacking in the real world is performed nightly. Moreover, they are not content to keep the spectacle within the walls of the theater: the whole world must become a stage. A group of wounded soldiers comes to Lyolya's hometown to recuperate, and their arrival is transformed into a public performance. The townspeople hold an amateur night for them, complete with poetry, piano recitals, gymnastics performed by schoolchildren, and a song from the local pharmacist. But the soldiers must also perform; the wounded are driven into town in the coaches of the nobility, accompanied by fashionable ladies from a local charity who are dressed as nurses. The soldiers are "washed, freshly shaven, and perfumed" (103), with ribbons decorating their crutches. And when they arrive at the theater, the ladies of the town direct their attention not to the stage but to the soldiers in the audience: "'No, this is simply scandalous,' the ladies whispered, disenchanted, 'Only trifling scratches . . . If only there were one serious case!'" (103). At the end of this dual spectacle, the townspeople enthusiastically request a speech from a soldier who has risen. But the soldier's soliloquy is disappointing. He rises not to thank the townspeople for their celebration, but to request an end to the performance: the wounded have spent three nights without sleep on their journey.

And, upon arrival, they have been presented only with the townspeople's fantasy of a homecoming; instead of rest and medical attention, they are given ersatz nurses, beribboned crutches, and singing pharmacists.

Part of the boy's journey to becoming a Soviet writer involves learning to see past the stage decorations of the "theater of war." And, as the war progresses, the spectacle does become less enchanting to Lyolya; at a later parade staged to celebrate a Russian victory, in place of perfumed ladies the boy now sees hooligans, reeking of alcohol: "They infected the air with their howling" (105). Lyolya, like these rabble-rousers, is drunk with war. And it takes the voice of one of the real soldiers, the son of the neighbor's cook, to sober him up. Asked to read a letter addressed to the soldier's mother, the boy recites "in a joyful voice" (93), but in the letter he finds a reality at odds with that painted on candy boxes: the cook's son has lost an arm in battle. Although Lyolya tries to comfort the grieving mother with the suggestion that her son will win a medal, the chapter concludes with his realization that such words are "foolishness" (93). In reading to the illiterate cook, the boy becomes a medium between reality and audience. This is his first official role as storyteller, interpreting reality for an adult audience, rather than relating his fantasies of Shvambraniia to his little brother. He is responsible for the emotional coloring of that reality just as he will be when he matures into the writer represented by the adult narrator. Lyolya has been trained to interpret war as beautiful, but in the letter and his reading of it he finds a reality at odds with the storybooks he has read; both the hero in his tale and the audience who listens have been crippled by the system for which they sacrifice—the son is unable to write (because of his lost arm the letter has been dictated to someone else) and the mother is unable to read. In trying to gild reality for her, as the newspapers and the advertisements have done for him, the boy realizes that what he has said is "foolishness." And in this description of his own youthful foolishness, the mature narrator moves his immature self one step closer to becoming a Soviet writer, who must listen not only to his own voice but to that of the people.

One of the final performances of the "theater of war" occurs when Lyolya and the other schoolboys are allowed to witness a mock battle performed before the ladies of the Charity Club. The ladies enjoy the event, shrieking and covering their ears. Lyolya, however, cannot help but see a difference between the "theater of war" and the reality of even a mock battle: "The battle, by the way, was very ugly and not at all as it was depicted in *Niva*" (111). And the black-and-white division of the world into "us" and "them" vanishes when one "Russian" soldier is singled out as being German (much to the embarrassment of his son, a classmate of Lyolya's), a nod to the fact that the common people are not enemies, but are moved around the battleground in false divisions of ally and enemy. Moreover, the soldiers are not the idealized, noble warriors of candy-box illustrations, but rather unruly hooligans, more interested in flirting with the older female students than charging into battle. Finally, to the boy's surprise, there is no decisive victory; when asked who won the mock battle, the colonel has to think a moment before deciding. When Lyolya gets home to his eagerly awaiting little brother, he sadly relates: "the war, it turns out, isn't at all beautiful" (113).

The first part of *Shvambraniia* therefore paints a picture of the prerevolutionary writer as naive child, beginning to peek beneath the glitter and tromp l'oeil that hides unpleasant bourgeois reality from his stagestruck imagination. By the time of the revolution, the suffering of the common soldiers has begun to seep through that beautiful wrapping, and the boy begins to suspect that the world constructed by bourgeois propaganda "isn't at all beautiful." The concepts of hero and villain that drive the little boy's fantasies about World War I and Shvambraniia begin to be muddled, when in the mock battle he is no longer able to distinguish which is which. Disenchanted at last with the "theater of war," Lyolya and his brother turn even more enthusiastically to their own fantasy escape, Shvambraniia, where the illusory divisions between hero and villain can more easily be maintained.

Lyolya and the Muses

In order to write Soviet fiction, the immature writer in *Shvambraniia* needs to relearn how to distinguish hero from villain in the redefined postrevolutionary world in which he lives, and his immature fantasies of Shvambraniia continually get in the way. Before the revolution, the lessons of his private school, like bourgeois propaganda, only helped to isolate the young writer from reality: "The old books and teachers who enthusiastically narrated tales of heroes with crowns told us nothing about people who made things. They raised us to be shirkers, helpless ones, good-for-nothings, or members of a haughty cast of pure-spitters [*chistopliuev*]—people of 'pure intellectual labor'" (50). And instead of the noble values of his beloved Shvambraniia, Lyolya finds only prejudice and injustice in his lessons. History classes justify the killing of innocent people by Ivan the Terrible and literature classes provoke anti-Semitic laughter. As a result, Lyolya soon realizes that school cannot answer his "spiritual questions" (79). He increasingly turns for satisfaction to Shvambraniia, but in the mature narrator's retelling of the revolution and Civil War, we soon learn that no fantasy world can truly answer his spiritual questions; only the transformation of the real world can do so. The narrator's recounting of his childhood disillusionment with Shvambraniia constitutes a maturation of fantasy and at the same time of morality. By writing about his experiences, the Soviet writer remaps reality in its revolutionary development onto childish escapism.

After the revolution, Lyolya's private upper-class boys' school becomes a coed public school. Just as he had fantasized, the upstairs and the downstairs people become equal, and "unsuitable acquaintances" are given an education. Significantly, therefore, when he first sees the initials for the new "One Socialist School," Lyolya confuses them with those that he and his brother always imprinted on their top-secret documents—he thinks that the world has learned the "One Secret of Shvambraniia" (151). In a way they have, since the Socialist School embodies the justice and equality of their invented land. However, Lyolya is horrified when the values of Shvambraniia leave their paper world and sit down at the desk next to him; he reacts to the public schoolboys as though they are still "undesirable acquaintances," stealing what is rightfully his. Little Lyolya has no tools with which to connect imaginary, abstract concepts of justice with the physical world. His happy endings are designed to remain virtual. However, after he enters the Socialist School, he encounters several mentors who help him to discern Soviet heroes from Soviet villains. Shvambraniia anticipates the teacher/disciple relationship that informs later socialist realism in two unlikely muses who enter the little boy's life after the revolution and help him to mature into a Soviet writer. The first is an older schoolboy who helps him to see that his favorite teacher and the class hero are both really villains, intent only on nurturing the beast within the immature dreamer.

The first mentor that Lyolya encounters is the older schoolboy Stepka Gavrya, who like Lyolya had spent his childhood dreaming of a mythical land. With the revolution, however, Stepka has left behind this alien dreaming: "'I don't dream of Atlantis any more,' said Stepka firmly, 'Why in the world would I need Atlantis now? Nowadays I don't have any time even without it. Revolution. . . . and instead of the private school we have the O.S.S—it means the One Socialist School!'" (153). He berates Lyolya for being an "intellectual" (*intelligent,* 155) and for his escapist attraction to Shvambraniia. But he does not reject the intellect. Instead, under his guidance, the boys begin studying again, but no longer the esoteric and useless subjects that so frustrated Lyolya before the revolution. Now he is caught up by the romance of real-world situations found in mathematical story problems. He and the other boys begin to direct their intellect at the physical world. Stepka guards the boys, however, from becoming too entrenched in the physical world by battling and exposing another student leader as villain: the overly physical Bindyug, an example of the extra-conscious gone amok.

Bindyug, the school's star wrestler, leads the boys in throwing off the harsh restrictions that had existed in their school before 1917. He embodies the violent, primal nature of the revolution grown out of control and destructive, resolving all conflicts with physical force and using the disorder of the times to declare an end to studying. With the entrance of female students, he soon turns school into a perpetual party, with drinking, dancing, and fistfights in the cloakroom. Having looted the local liquor store, Bindyug ensures that a steady stream of alcohol enters the classroom, and the schoolboys quickly become drunk on wine and freedom. Like a devil on Lyolya's shoulder, the beast Bindyug prods him to indulge every selfish whim, even if it proves to be at the expense of his schoolmates. Stepka steps in to expose the imbalance in Bindyug by directing his own brand of schoolyard satire at the bully: "'Your fist is cool, but your head is a fool,' said Stepka" (187).

Known for his physical strength and wrestling ability, Bindyug has previously been undefeatable, but Stepka reveals that the collective is even stronger. And, under Stepka's influence, Lyolya begins to be drawn away from Bindyug and toward the collective. A key moment in this shift arrives when Lyolya is entrusted with the school's sugar supply, and Bindyug suggests that they skim a few cubes from the top. Lyolya, who has been piling up a treasure of Shvambraniian sugar in a box at home, is tempted. However, he rejects the offer; cheating the former unjust school officials was one thing, but now his own "comrades," including Stepka, are on the school's soviet (organizational committee): "I couldn't cheat them, even for Shvambraniia" (172). Of course, Bindyug reacts to Lyolya's egalitarian impulses with violence, and Shvambraniian sugar is stained for the first time with real blood. Through this confrontation with the bully, Lyolya begins to reject the selfish individualism of the beast. The other boys soon follow suit. The change in the boys becomes apparent when Stepka arranges a math competition between the former private schoolboys and the former public schoolboys. He encourages them not to use notes or to copy from one another: "We wouldn't cheat our own, would we?" (217). Lyolya and the other boys enthusiastically agree. But when they win the competition, it turns out that Bindyug has ignored this vow. As he is lifted on high in celebration, a crib sheet falls from his pocket; and the former private schoolboys, infused with the collective spirit, immediately admit the deception and share first prize with the competing class. Hero is exposed as villain and his selfish desire to win is translated into a collective desire for justice.

Stepka also helps expose one of the teachers, Semion Alekseevich Kirikov, whose involuntary insertion of nonsense sounds "e-e-m-mue-t" into his speech causes the boys to nickname him after the French silent "e": "But sometimes it seemed to me that there was something elusive, malicious and strange in this good-natured old man. It came out at the end of some of his jokes—visible but silent like the 'mute e' in written French" (191). Kirikov's speech defect symbolizes the defect in his thinking and in his influence over the boys. But the defect is concealed beneath his masterful storytelling, and he quickly becomes their favorite teacher, entrancing them with tales of adventure. Among his accounts of battles and big-game hunting, Lyolya detects subtle jabs against the Soviet regime. And in a final class, Kirikov's criticism becomes explicit, as he lectures against Bolshevik enlightenment: "The Bolsheviks have turned Russia back . . . e—m-mue-et . . . to primitive communism . . . to the initial darkness . . . chaos . . . ruin" (192). Then he reverses Stepka's efforts to join the public-school boys and the private-school boys into a single collective; he divides them into "troglodytes" and "anthropods" and mockingly urges them to embrace Bolshevik primitivism and return to all fours. The hypnotic storyteller turns his audience against the progress of socialism and encourages them to regress to the selfishness of the beast.

As his classmates grunt and bound around the classroom like apes, Lyolya feels drawn to join in. However, he is kept from doing so by Stepka, who points out that Bolshevik electrification has put an end to all darkness; Stepka then runs to fetch the president of the school soviet, to put an end to what he considers anti-Soviet speech. When they return, Stepka accuses Kirikov of being a "bourgeois" and a "saboteur" (194). Through Stepka's exposure, Lyolya's eyes are opened, and he suddenly recognizes his teacher as a speculator who had earlier been arrested by authorities. "E muet" is unmasked and removed from his teaching post. Bindyug, in protest over Kirikov's removal, leads a general protest to reinstitute uniforms and school prayer and to reject the public-school children; under his influence, the private-school "troglodytes" throw all the public-school "anthropods" out the windows. Once again, Stepka counters Bindyug's influence, dramatically making a hero's entrance on the commissar's horse to denounce the villains Kirikov and Bindyug. Stepka enchants the schoolchildren by suggesting that they write to the children of France and propose that the "e muet" in French be abolished like the hard sign in Russian. He exposes the insidious speech of the storytelling teacher, thereby exposing the bourgeous imagination which helps bring out primitive selfishness in its audience.

Toward the end of part 2 Stepka seems to regress to his prerevolutionary life of dreaming about imaginary places when he and Lyolya get caught up in the town's enthusiasm for the theater. It is opening night, and they both have roles in a play filled with Shvambraniian names: "And on the island of Rhodos, where there lived a Fork de Forkos . . . in short, there were many other lines that ended in 'os'" (278). But before the curtain can rise, Stepka selflessly answers the call for volunteers to help fight the Whites in the Civil War. He abandons useless fantasy for revolutionary reality and gives his life for the Soviet Union: "He died as a hero, Stepan Gavrya, seeker of Atlantis, and about him they said many different things" (325). Of course, the mature narrator's own recounting of Stepka's positive influence on his younger self is one of these things. And through writing about Stepka he identifies the immortality that can be gained through sacrifice for the collective. But the Lyolya of part 2 is still too immature to grant eternal life with his pen. Lyolya must take one more step in relocating his imaginary Shvambraniia into the real world, a step that occurs under the guidance of a new mentor, who draws the young writer into building a Soviet children's library, where his imagination can be redirected from alien dreaming to Soviet "reality in its revolutionary development."

Stepka serves as a revolutionary muse, jolting the young boy's imagination away from the selfishness embodied by the villain Bindyug. Stepka dies with the revolution, and another teacher, Lyolya's cousin Dina, comes to open a Soviet children's reading room and to guide little Lyolya to his final step to maturation in part 3. Because of Stepka's efforts to draw Lyolya away from Shvambraniia, the young writer's psyche is now split between the collective utility of the Soviet imagination and the self-centered uselessness of Shvambraniia. In keeping with this split, he divides his time between the reading room, a symbol of the Soviet imagination, and an abandoned mansion, the new setting for the brothers' games of Shvambraniia: "Ugor's house all at once looked like an ancient boyar's tower, a fair booth, and the hanging gardens of Semiramide" (293). It is evocative of legends, myths, and fairy tales but also of the class system that existed before the revolution, when wealth allowed one to follow whimsy instead of the laws of practicality and symmetry. Windows are of different sizes and shapes, many of them stained glass, and artists have painted mythological creatures and exotic animals on the exterior walls. The mansion is a product of the alien imagination, beautiful and fanciful, but out of sync with the necessities of real people. The many noisy weathervanes and metal ventilators prevent inhabitants from working or sleeping. And the structure, poorly designed, has deteriorated after the owner's death—the cracked window frames let in the cold, it shakes in the wind, and the sagging floors are a safety hazard. Therefore, the rooms of the mansion prove an exciting and dangerous place for Lyolya and his brother Oska to act out the intrigues and battles of Shvambraniia.

There is more than physical danger in their games. One day the boys fall through the rotting floor to the basement, where they meet their old teacher "E muet," who proves as much of a danger to their development as he was in the Socialist School. Kirikov has set up an illegal still in the basement of the mansion, but he convinces the boys that he is an alchemist, the "Don Quixote of Science" and that he has discovered the "elixir of worldwide joy" (302). Lyolya and Oska help Kirikov gather firewood for his elixir, and he helps them embellish the stories of Shvambraniia. Kirikov is a master storyteller, both in school and in the basement of Shvambraniia. In school, Kirikov encouraged the boys to follow the beast. And in the mansion, he spins drunken stories of Shvambraniia that further immerse the boys in the useless dreaming of the alien—their time spent with Kirikov in "Shvambraniia" is time spent away from the children's reading room and the propaganda efforts that will build the Communist future.

Kirikov's villainous influence is countered by the boys' cousin Dina, a young Communist who tries to draw them away from Shvambraniia: "She was just a little surprised that in such an interesting time there was still a need for the supernatural. She said that it was simply a shame and that it was time to work" (305–6). Dina redirects Lyolya's creative energy away from the mansion and into the reading room, channeling his love of stories and words into collective activities and propaganda work. Lyolya soon becomes the editor of the children's magazine *The Fearless Thinker,* a title illustrative of the courage it will take the boy to turn his intellect away from the comforting, escapist fantasies of Shvambraniia and toward the propaganda work necessary to the Soviet writer. Dina also redirects his love of theater when the children of the reading room put on a talent night. Unlike the theater experiences Lyolya has had previously, the children's performance does not provide an escape from reality but rather creates a new reality: onstage and in the audience, members of the former elite are now mixed with "unsuitable acquaintances." And Lyolya suddenly realizes that in the reading room, the "landless" children, one of the items on his prerevolutionary "list of the world's injustices" (313), now have a place of their own. Lyolya is transformed by this experience and selflessly offers to share his secret store of "Shvambraniian sugar" for use at the talent night. As the other children and their parents have tea with sugar, Lyolya imagines Stepka Atlantis giving his approval for this magnanimous act. By rejecting the villains who embody his own inner alien and beast—the drunken storyteller Kirikov and the selfish bully Bindyug, Lyolya is transformed into a hero worthy of the transformed dreamer Stepka, whom Lyolya is finally able to both emulate and (re-)create on the printed page.

In this evening of egalitarian theater, Lyolya conclusively rejects the beast and the alien and thereby acquires the clean and sober vision of a Soviet writer and becomes a storyteller worthy of Dina's reading room. This transformation is symbolized not only by the unifying performance of the children and Lyolya's donation of Shvambraniian sugar, but also by the final event of this transformative evening. At the conclusion of the talent night Lyolya is told that he will be the first to view Dina's new work of art, a painting entitled *View onto a Moonlit Night in Winter* (319). As he looks at the beautiful painting in a gilded frame, Lyolya suddenly realizes that Dina has merely placed a frame around a window looking out onto his hometown. Dina explains:

> "So you need a gold frame! Then Pokrovsk turns into Shvambraniia, eh? Oh—you! . . . Let me explain, kids," said Donna Dina. "It's all the fault of an old proverb: 'All is good where you are not.' But the well-known Communist writer Franz Mehring wrote this: 'The proletariat does not need to build a world in the clouds, because they can establish their kingdom here on earth. And so we have the proletarian revolution so that it's good right where we are!" (320–21)

Unlike the gilding provided by the theater of war, Dina's gold frame does not disguise reality but rather draws the viewer's attention to it. And when he sees the "painting" Lyolya suddenly loses all interest in Shvambraniia, which now can only be viewed as "unreality" (320). The real, sparkling, nighttime scene within the gilded frame is far superior to the gilded reality that he has concocted in his imagination.

After viewing Dina's "painting," Lyolya's attention is drawn to the real world, as though a gilt frame has been placed around each person and each object that he sees. Because of this, he can now easily and conclusively defeat the villains who earlier drew him away from Soviet reality. Lyolya has a final confrontation with the beast Bindyug, who has battled against the children's reading room and who now takes his anger out on Lyolya. But things have changed; as Lyolya is attacked by Bindyug, the other children of the reading room band together to defeat the bully. As a collective, they expel the beast, an act that is later echoed by society as a whole—the mature narrator informs us that years later the adult Bindyug was banished as a kulak. This dual expulsion of the beast—by Lyolya and by society, is echoed by the dual expulsion of the alien Kirikov. After viewing Dina's "painting," when Lyolya returns once again to the mansion, the veil of fantasy is removed and he can see only the seaminess of the place and of Kirikov, whom he finds drunk and semi-conscious. Lyolya suddenly realizes that the "elixir of world-wide joy" is in reality home brew; and he is stunned when the "alchemist" equates his moonshine with Shvambraniia: "Your Shvambriia is also . . . e-muet . . . a type of home brew . . . a homemade fantasy, a dream of your own brewing" (327). Both Kirikov and Lyolya are revealed to be intoxicated and incapacitated, one by alcohol and one by Shvambraniia. Shvambraniia and Kirikov lose their charm for Lyolya, and the alien is expelled. And when Lyolya tells a commissar about the still, this expulsion is echoed by society as a whole: Kirikov is arrested and his influence over Soviet youth comes to an end. The beast and the alien are both defeated, and Lyolya throws himself full force into the propaganda efforts of the children's reading room.

With the newly acquired vision of a Soviet writer, when Lyolya then goes to a Bolshevik armored train car to deliver propaganda posters, he sees the revolution itself in a new way: "For the first time I saw the Revolution in its own workaday, businesslike manner. Point-blank, up close I looked at it not from Shvambraniian heights or from the gap in my garden gate. And the business of these newly seen people seemed to me difficult, dangerous, but the only real business" (333). Useful work has now become more attractive than fantasy for the boy. Significantly, as the train leaves, Lyolya sees an important symbol of Shvambraniia transformed from fantasy to utility. Before the revolution, the boys placed the queen of Shvambraniia (a chess queen), who holds the "One Secret of Shvambraniia" (a note written by Lyolya), in a "grotto" made of seashells that sits on their mother's dresser. The mother has traded this luxury item for kerosene, and as the train pulls away Lyolya sees a hand extended to empty the strange ashtray that he earlier saw being used by the revolutionaries in the darkened train car—now, however, it is clear that the ashtray is the former "grotto of the Black queen" (334). This magical symbol of Shvambraniia is thereby transformed into an everyday object, useful, as one of the revolutionaries earlier remarked, for "military hygiene" (332). As the train pulls away, Lyolya's Shvambraniian fantasy is reduced to the ashes falling from the Shvambraniian grotto onto the ground: "Ashes and stubs poured from it, ashes and stubs" (334).

Useful Fantasy

In *Shvambraniia,* we see that the writer's role is defined as one of seeking out the unbalanced extremes of the Soviet psyche—the alien and the beast, exposing them and then establishing an equilibrium that will allow him to build the Communist future. By his example the reader thereby achieves a balanced psyche, the goal of socialist realism. To achieve this goal, one final step is needed: translating the desires of the villain into the collective voice, and in the narrator's final heavy symbolism about the purposes of Soviet literature, Shvambraniia provides instruction on the transformation of useless Shvambraniian fantasy into useful Soviet fantasy.

While dismantling the abandoned mansion to provide fuel for the reading room fireplace, one last event signals the potent danger of Shvambraniian fantasy for the children. The ledge that supports little Oska, who has climbed to the third floor to admire the view, begins to collapse, and he is saved at the last minute by the commissar, a simple uneducated man, who has earlier routed Kirikov from both the school and the mansion. He and Dina are in love, and their union symbolizes the joining together of the newly enlightened proletariat and the newly grounded intelligentsia. Together they ensure the safety of the children in their charge. Oska, through the destruction of Shvambraniia, is saved both physically and mentally—according to the mature narrator, his little brother had begun to doubt the reality of the world around him, preferring the hazardous view from Shvambraniia. Lyolya's storytelling, like Kirikov's, was harmful. Only by dismantling Shvambraniia can the brothers embrace Soviet reality and merge with the collective:

> I stood in a chain, passing to the left the planks I received from the right. They transformed in my hands. From the right I received them as pieces of Shvambraniia. To the left I gave them over as firewood for the library. . . . It was pleasant to feel that the left comrade was just as connected to you as the right one, and the right one to the next one, and on and on . . . I stood as a living rung of a ladder along which the ghostly Shvambraniia went to useful combustion. (335–36).

Oska is saved. Lyolya becomes one with the collective. And Ugor's house, a symbol of useless fantasy, is transformed into firewood, used to heat the reading room, where the psyches of Soviet children will be shaped. As the schoolchildren stand on the ruins of Shvambraniia, little Lyolya recites the "last Shvambraniian poem," in which he bids farewell to Shvambraniia and declares that "it's time to get to work": "Fairy tale to ashes, Fairy tale to dust / Better than a fairy tale reality will be!" (338). This final Shvambraniian proclamation is in effect a statement of purpose for the Soviet writer, who is instructed to depict reality "in its revolutionary development." With the revolution, fantasy has acquired a direction and a purpose, and as a Soviet writer Lyolya will prove reality superior to fantasy, just as he has done on the pages of *Shvambraniia*.

And to prove little Lyolya's point, the mature narrator brings us back to the reality of the present day; in an epilogue, he recounts his trip home to celebrate the birth of Oska's first child and the completion of *Shvambraniia.* He reads *Shvambraniia* to his family, and the grown-up Oska heartily approves of his brother's condemnation of the imaginary land: "The author was successful in exposing the futility of such dreams" (342). But he finds one thing lacking: "You want to take away from us the right to dream" (342). Oska pulls out *The Communist's Guide* and reads a passage to prove that dreaming is still sanctioned in the Soviet Union:

> "To maintain our enthusiasm we don't need any kind of illusion or deception . . . This is our great happiness. But it doesn't mean that we don't need any 'dream' (Lenin's terminology) . . . The class that holds the power in its hands, changing the world through work, is always inclined toward realism, but it is also inclined toward romanticism, that is what Lenin meant by our 'dream.' It's no longer an unattainable fantastic star, it's not a comforting chimera. It's simply our plan itself, our five-year plan and further five-year plans. . . . That's what you should have talked about," finished the scholarly Oska. (343)

Oska's critique of *Shvambraniia* not only imprints the requisite stamp of Leninist approval on the book, but also points to a new direction for the Soviet imagination, one that can only be taken by a writer who has made the transformation from Shvambraniian fantasist to socialist realist. The epilogue serves as a quick fix to assure the reader of Oska's point. Shvambraniia has not vanished with its destruction. Instead, it has been transformed into something tangible—the book that is being held in the reader's hands. Dreaming is still allowed.

In an early chapter of *Shvambraniia* entitled "Brain Work and Manual Labor" (51) the narrator recalls relations between his family and the people who lived downstairs. Unable to understand the technology on which their everyday life depends, Lyolya's mother and father must send down for someone to repair their broken light switches and toilets. Yet despite their reliance on the downstairs people, they view them as "unsuitable acquaintances" (52), beastly sources of lice, germs, and bad habits: "And Mama would say 'golden hands' and then count the silver spoons" (51). Nevertheless, Lyolya wants to acquire the golden hands of his unsuitable acquaintances; they can make tangible, useful objects, whereas he and his brother can build only "lifeless models of things, cardboard ships, paper factories" (53). But *Shvambraniia* is not merely a condemnation of the upstairs people and a celebration of the downstairs people. The upstairs people also have something to offer; as the mature narrator notes, his downstairs neighbors were unable to read and write, and were forced to appeal upstairs to have letters or documents read to them or written for them. The narrator likens the relationship of the downstairs and the upstairs people to that of a blind man and a lame man traveling together, dependent on one another for survival. They are crippled by the system in which they live but gifted with something necessary for the journey to Communism. The beastly downstairs people have the golden hands. But the alien upstairs people have the golden ideas, the fairy tales and adventure stories that contain the happy endings Lyolya so loves. The golden ideas are simply disconnected from the physical world, and therefore never realized.

Lyolya has been formed into an alien dreamer by his existence in the upstairs world. He proclaims that in Shvambraniia every citizen is able not only to read the contents of books but also to bind them—hands and brains are equally developed in every citizen. But like everything upstairs, Shvambraniia is composed only of thought and paper; it exists solely in the boy's imagination and on the maps, proclamations, letters, and ransom notes written by Lyolya to document the geography and history of Shvambraniia. It is just another cardboard construction, a "toy model of a remarkable world" (53). The mature narrator's recounting of *Shvambraniia,* on the other hand, is the story of how a toy model is made real by the Bolshevik Revolution, of how the childish dreamer matures into the Soviet writer, who still constructs paper worlds, but who can also bind them. In the golden hands of the mature Soviet writer, the golden ideas of Shvambraniian fantasy are transformed into Soviet reality.

The land of Shvambraniia is an invention of the upstairs paper world, created by a childish dreamer who is fondly mocked by his older self, the mature and firmly grounded Soviet writer-narrator who is given the task of "ideologically remolding" the reader by retelling his own encounters with the villains Bindyug and Kirikov as he travels the path to psychic equilibrium. The reader is encouraged to follow Lyolya on his journey by the fact that the people who guide him are so sympathetic, relentlessly brave, and cheerfully industrious. The heroine Dina is beautiful and admired by all. The hero Stepka Atlantis gives his life for the cause. Under their guidance, Lyolya has learned that Shvambraniia pales in comparison with Dina's Soviet reading room and that Shvambraniian heroes pale in comparison with the real-life revolutionary sacrifice of Stepka Atlantis. And all this is done by his mentors' exposure of the villains and instruction on harnessing their negative power for the collective good. By empathizing with Lyolya's journey, the reader has, according to the guidelines of socialist realism, come to a similar revelation.

The triumphant collective destruction of the mansion and Lyolya's hymn to reality are not enough to assure that Shvambraniia achieves the socialist realist task of "ideologically remolding" the reader. The novel is given an epilogue, where we move into the present, where life is indeed better for all the characters as a result of their abandonment of Shvambraniia. Lyolya is now a Soviet writer, able to dream in a new way, and Oska is a Soviet scientist-propagandist, able to influence real people about real events (he has just come from delivering a speech to the Water Transport Active Worker's Group on the Spanish revolution). Most important, Pokrovsk is now the Soviet town of Engels, a shining symbol of Communist enlightenment and progress. This trip to the present demonstrates that the narrator has earlier depicted "reality in its revolutionary development"—the events of Lyolya's childhood have led his family and his town closer to Communism. The adult Lyolya and his activist brother Oska give an epilogic "roll call" of the people in their childhood and their subsequent fate. Those who displayed Soviet values are rewarded with important positions or glory and those like the kulak Bindyug with exposure and expulsion. This sorting out—seen also in Mayakovsky's *Bedbug* (1929), when the zookeeper separates the human from the nonhuman (see chapter 2)—becomes the job of the Soviet fantasist, who must identify the villains—the beastly kulaks (Bindyug) and drunken alien dreamers (Kirikov)—and silence them, subsequently translating individual desire and useless fantasy into collective desire and useful, socialist realist dreaming. Bindyug and Kirikov are not allowed to speak at the end of Shvambraniia, as Prisypkin does in *Bedbug.* And every trace of the immature narrator has vanished; the nostalgic recounting of the past has ended and with it selfish desire and doubt about the future. We are left only with an adult narration of collective desire and socialist realist surety.

AN IMAGE CAN KILL

Socialist realism centers on the obliteration of doubt, and by doing so it constitutes a unique and ideologically charged use of the fantastic. Through the introduction of a villain, socialist realism incorporates hesitation as an essential component of its transformative mission—it is introduced so that it can be exposed and eliminated. Fantastic hesitation is silenced and the reader supposedly begins to see reality in the Soviet way, "in its revolutionary development" toward the inexorable arrival of the Communist utopia. The epilogue of *Shvambraniia* serves as a warning to the Soviet reader—and writer—about the seductiveness of fantasy. The adult pragmatist Oska finds his brother's retelling of their childhood game to be too fond, too nostalgic; and he angrily rejects Lyolya's playful suggestion that his newborn daughter be named after the heroines of Shvambraniia: "We've bred enough unreal mongrels" (340). Oska's coldness provides a sharp contrast to the narrator's nostalgic remembrance, thereby reminding the reader that there is a danger in Shvambraniian dreaming. Escaping to other realms produces fantastic hesitation, a liminal suspension between two worlds, and socialist realism is haunted by the fear that a reader might choose the wrong one. On the final page of the epilogue, the narrator hangs the Shvambraniian coat of arms over his door as a "warning" to be vigilant about "secret Shvambraniians" (347). Such escapist dreaming, even when dutifully silenced and translated into "reality in its revolutionary development," always carries with it the danger of misidentification.

In *Shvambraniia* we see the socialist realist strategy fully formed, two years before the official adoption. Fantastic hesitation is externalized in villains such as the alien "E muet" and the beast Bindyug, who try to poison the narrator with their toxic doubt. Through their expulsion from society and the mature writer's rewriting of his former self, hesitation is conquered and the narrator's psyche is balanced, preparing him to become a Soviet writer and balance other psyches. In *Envy,* although fantastic hesitation is expelled from the society within the text—the New People no longer see or hear Ivan and Kavalerov—it is never conclusively silenced for the reader. After all, the alien Ivan is allowed to speak its final lines and therefore remains a toxic threat to the reader until the very end. One can imagine Oska's—and the

Bolsheviks'—consternation at the fate of *Envy* in the late twentieth century, when Western scholars would celebrate it as "an all-inclusive weapon aimed against a 'universal' system, Soviet Marxism, most particularly as prostituted by the régime."[30] Introducing fantastic hesitation via the villain carries the risk that readers might absorb his toxic thought.

Olesha spoke about the dangers of negative characters at the first Congress of Soviet Writers in 1934, where socialist realism was officially adopted:

> When you depict a negative hero, you yourself become negative. From the depths of your soul you raise up something bad, dirty—that is, you convince yourself that something bad and dirty is in you, and because of this, your conscience takes on the heaviest psychological load. Goethe once said, "I wanted to read *Macbeth* one more time, but I couldn't risk it. I was afraid that in the shape I was in, reading it would kill me." An image can kill the artist.[31]

According to Olesha's account, by 1934 the antihero, the mainstay of Soviet literature in the 1920s, had become toxic waste from the literary garbage pit, a hazardous agent best kept crated and labeled with a stern warning for the Soviet writer: "an image can kill." Olesha's speech reads as an extended apology for creating such toxins in the past and a fervent vow to do better in the future. He focuses on his own most notorious hero, Nikolay Kavalerov, a Soviet-era Macbeth who fails in his quest to kill the sausage king Andrey Babichev. Olesha confesses to loving Kavalerov and investing much of himself in what critics subsequently called "a vulgar and worthless individual":

> I said to myself, "This means all this ability, all that is your own, all that you consider to be your strength, is instead insignificant and vulgar." Could this be true? I wanted to believe that the comrades criticizing me (these were communist critics) were right, and I believed them. I began to think that what I considered treasure was in fact poverty.[32]

In the conclusion of his speech, Olesha suggests: "It is necessary to choose what is best within oneself in order to create a complex person who can serve as a model. The writer must be an educator and a teacher."[33] Speaker after speaker at the first congress made similar declarations. Under socialist realism, officially adopted at this conference, the writer would become a teacher and guide for Soviet readers, engineering their souls by means of model heroes who were, unlike the antiheroes of the early Soviet period, worthy of imitation.

However, the inclusion of potentially attractive villainous characters and the fantastic hesitation that they evoke begins an inevitable and continual retooling of Soviet literature and of the Soviet villain, revealed most markedly in censorship of new works and in substantial changes made to new editions of previously published texts throughout the Soviet period.[34] It is commonplace to assert that the entire Soviet period was infused with paranoia about the influence of anti-Soviet forces on its citizens. I would go further to argue that the evolution of Soviet literature can be understood *only* if one takes this fear into account. To protect the reader from their seductive charms, 1920s antiheroes were transformed into more clearly defined socialist realist villains, who then became more and more cartoonish as socialist realism evolved. This exaggeration of the negative qualities of the villain continued in the hopes of removing any sympathetic response in the reader. And in some texts the villain was removed entirely, which led to a charge of "conflictlessness" (*bezkonfliktnost'*) in the 1950s, when Andrey Sinyavsky would assert that "there are books in which *all* the heroes are positive."[35] Yet Soviet writers never entirely let go of their villainous toxic fantasies. They could not. For, without them, socialist realism could not exist.

Chapter Four

Lost in Translation

> Her son spoke less and less; and at the same time she noticed that occasionally and with increasing frequency he used new words unintelligible to her, and that the coarse, rude, and hard expressions dropped from his speech.
> —Maksim Gorky, *Mother* (1907)

THE HISTORY of prerevolutionary Russian literature is one of secret societies, censorship, arrest, and exile, as writers attempted social change through the printed word. Maksim Gorky's *Mother* (1907), one of the earliest prototypes for socialist realism, ends with the title character beaten by tsarist police as she hands out propaganda pamphlets written by her imprisoned son. As the police close in, she assures the crowd of the mighty and mystical power of the words they are being given: "The word of my son is the honest word of a workingman, of an unsold soul. . . . It goes to you, working people, incorruptible, wise, fearless. Receive it with an open heart, feed on it; it will give you the power to understand everything, to fight against everything for the truth, for the freedom of mankind."[1] The fearless words of both the flyers and the woman who "feeds" them to the crowd are transformative, remaking the scattered people into a collective, nourished into a healthy organism by a newfound understanding of injustice. This scene communicates one of the foundational beliefs of the revolution as represented in socialist realism, that one "unsold soul" can engineer other souls and collectivize the world with healthy words cleansed of "coarse, rude, and hard expressions."

Soviet focus on this linguistic power is in one sense predicated on its dark side. In the wrong hands words can poison the organism by creating the exploitation and ignorance that the mother battles. Marx envisioned human history as a long story of class struggle, and by extension, the history of ideas as the struggle between "ruling ideas" of the "ruling class" and the ideas that will rise up to overthrow them.[2] In this struggle words are either exploitative or revolutionary, but they are never innocent. *The ABC of Com-*

munism describes prerevolutionary bourgeois education as using this power to subdue the proletariat:

> If any of the children of the workers, happening to be exceptionally gifted, should find their way into the higher schools, in the great majority of instances the bourgeois scholastic apparatus will serve as a means of detaching them from their own class kin, and will inoculate them with bourgeois ideology, so that in the long run the genius of these scions of the working class will be turned to account for the oppression of the workers.[3]

Prior to the revolution, the best of the proletariat was thereby "inoculated" against Marxist truth with bourgeois words, which entered their bloodstream and in vampiric fashion transformed them into something alien. The Bolsheviks expected to turn this power to their own benefit by inoculating Soviet citizens against the words of the past. This educational effort extended far beyond the classroom, as linguistic vaccines were disseminated through theatrical performances and instructional lectures, and reading rooms served as clinics to immunize Soviet citizens with written propaganda filled with the curative words of the new ruling class, the proletariat. Eventually all poisonous words would be eradicated by the vaccine of Soviet literature and the world would be spoken and written about only in the pure words of the New Person, who would be immune to infection by the unhygienic words of the past.

The Russian language had already been altered dramatically after the revolution, inundated with a torrent of new acronyms, stump compounds, industrial terms, and political jargon.[4] Many "linguistic engineers" of the 1920s then endeavored to speed up the process of change by introducing egalitarian vocabulary and grammar and abolishing exploitative and hierarchical terms. Many fought to eradicate bourgeois titles and forms of address and replace them with "comrade" or "citizen." Members of the Proletkult even campaigned to rid Russian of capital letters, considered to promote inequality.[5] Russian orthography was compared to the starched collars of the bourgeois intelligentsia and reformers argued for simplified spelling that would make literacy more accessible to the masses.[6] Through these changes, linguistic engineers sought to transfigure the vocabulary and grammar of Russian into one of equality, a change that would transform speakers' minds and create healthy social bonds. If no one could give voice to the language of selfishness, inequality, and exploitation, then these diseases of the Communist social order would cease to exist.

Linguistic engineers of the early Soviet period believed that changing language would change minds, and utopian dreamers imagined a language that would not only describe but actually help build their sanitized utopia.

Velimir Khlebnikov, inventor of the futurist "transense language" (*zaumnyi iazyk*), expressed the impatience and brashness of the revolutionary period when he declared in 1917: "An overview of the fundamentals of language has already been accomplished, . . . This knowledge is essential in order to transport man to his next stage—a single common language—and that we will do next year."[7] Esperantists operating in Russia were perhaps the most pragmatic of the single-language proponents, but they were only one of the many groups and individuals to jump on the one-language bandwagon. Followers of Nikolay Fedorov believed that a pre-Babel universal language would one day be recovered by a congress of scientific linguists.[8] And a worldwide language, either artificial or organic, became a common motif in Soviet science fiction.[9] Perhaps most important, in the early Soviet period the linguist Nikolay Marr formulated his theory of language evolution that ended in a worldwide unified language. It was the only approved linguistic theory in the Soviet Union of the 1930s and 1940s: one language, one theory, one mind. As 1934 approached, Soviet literati developed a strategy that would produce such a linguistic purity and unity, a hygienic impulse that edged consistently toward socialist realism. This chapter will examine two production novels that show a drastic but predictable evolution of the collective voice and the hygienic impulse during the First Five-Year Plan, when the writer was urged to eradicate the self and channel the collective voice in increasingly exuberant literary celebrations of collective effort.

CONSTRUCTING A NEW VOICE

The collective voice is designed to harmonize the discordant desire of the villain—the dirty, self-centered words of the beast and the seductive, escapist storytelling of the alien—all the while drawing on its energy. In the previous three chapters, each of the texts I have examined ends with the exposure and silencing of villainous voices, accomplished by excluding the beast and the alien from society (Prisypkin of *Bedbug* and Kavalerov and Ivan of *Envy*), by removing their ability to speak in an independent voice (D-503 of *We* and Sharikov of *Heart of a Dog*), or by depicting their acquisition of the collective voice (Leonid of *Red Star* and Lyolya of *Shvambraniia*). Yet in each of these texts an echo of the villain can still be heard at the end. Bogdanov's Leonid may be cured, but we are left not with his voice, but with that of the Earthling psychologist, who assures us that Leonid is insane. Zamyatin's D-503 is obediently happy in the final entry that he writes, but the One State's blissful writer still fails in his quest to inhabit the pronoun "we." Bulgakov's dog-man can no longer speak, but his self-centered master continues to do so, his voice and his power over others stronger than ever.

Mayakovsky's Prisypkin is ensconced in a cage and his infectious words filtered, but he still manages to leap out of his protective enclosure to invite the theatrical audience to join him. Olesha's Ivan Babichev is safely quarantined in the widow's enormous bed, but he is still allowed to speak the novel's final lines. And Kassil's Shvambraniian storyteller, the closest to a socialist realist hero of all these characters, is chastised in the epilogue by his brother, a Soviet pragmatist who finds his fanciful account just a tad too dreamy and nostalgic for the Soviet era. Whatever the political stance of the writer, early Soviet texts were consumed with the difficulty of eradicating individualism and embracing the collective voice.

The production novel sets itself apart from this general trend in that it focuses on physical labor, the Soviet holy of holies, and by doing so, it brings forth one of the strongest expressions of the collective voice in the early Soviet period. As I discussed in chapter 3, physical labor was seen to transform non-proletarians, not just by burning off toxins generated by intellectual labor, but also by connecting isolated thinkers to other people, making them physically and mentally part of a collective, ready to abandon selfish, escapist dreaming in order to manufacture the Communist future. The plot of the production novel is like an assembly line, putting together characters and events that transform the hero into the personification of Soviet society—a whole greater than its parts. This is a major reformulating of literary character, in which the goal is not to create a vivid hero and villain but rather to strip these literary conventions of individuality. Characters who remain verbal at the end of the production novel can exist only as literary loudspeakers for the collective.

The absorption and translation of desire achieved by the hero of the production novel echoes the changing role of writers in Soviet society during the First Five-Year Plan (1928–32), when they were urged to travel to factories and construction sites to chronicle the transformation of society. Encouraged to write in groups or at least to channel the collective voice emanating from the ambitious projects of the plan, they worked at eradicating the writerly self. In Fedor Gladkov's *Cement* (*Tsement*, 1925)[10] and Valentin Kataev's *Time Forward!* (*Vremia, vpered!* 1932)[11] the heroes experience an emptying of self, a willing absorption of villainous desire and the translation of this desire into a collective voice. By completing this process, the Soviet hero becomes not only a personification of society as a whole, but also an avatar for the writer, who must undergo a similar transformation as Soviet literature moves toward socialist realism. The writer must become, as Lenin so famously argued, a "cog" in the greater machine of society.[12]

This chapter takes up the simultaneous translation of the hero and writer in the production novel to show that there is a dramatic change in the nature of this translation between the 1925 *Cement* and the 1932 *Time*

Forward!, a change that reflects increasingly frantic attempts to contain the villainous voice. Despite its status as a prototype for socialist realism, in *Cement* the individualistic voices of its attractive villains, a beautiful female revolutionary and a decisive man of action, haunt the collective ending. *Time Forward!*, on the other hand, makes its villains unattractive both physically and spiritually and makes the silencing of the villains' voices loud and strident, thereby reflecting the transformation of the literary text that takes place in the First Five-Year Plan. In *Cement* the heroes completely give up individuality as they absorb and translate the villainous voice, but whereas *Cement* depicts this process as being extraordinarily difficult, *Time Forward!* demonstrates the hero's increasing ease in accomplishing this strategy. Moreover, by having many of these characters be writers at a Five-Year Plan construction site, *Time Forward!* demonstrates the Soviet writer's need to embrace the example of the hero, to shed nostalgia for the self and thereby transform from prophet on the hill to cog in the machine and from revolutionary to engineer of the human soul.

TRANSLATING THE VILLAINOUS VOICE: FEDOR GLADKOV'S *CEMENT* (1925)

Cement begins with Red Army soldier Gleb Chumalov returning from revolution and the Civil War to find his home and his beloved cement factory in ruins and his fellow citizens fighting over the scraps that remain.[13] Throughout the novel, Gleb and his wife Dasha fight to rebuild the factory and to free their minds of the hierarchy, inequality, and exploitation of the past. They achieve this by reacting against strong figures who lead society at the beginning of the novel but are revealed to be villainous influences by the end: Comrade Badin, the chairman of the Executive Committee of the Soviet, and Polya Mekhova, the leader of the Women's Section. Throughout this book I have shown how the antiheroes of early Soviet literature are increasingly vilified, a fact made especially interesting in *Cement*, because the villains at first seem stereotypically heroic—a bold, charismatic man of action and a beautiful, brave female activist, both heroes of the revolution. In villainizing these characters, we see a renunciation of revolution in favor of collectivism and obedience to the Communist Party.

The energy of Badin and Polya produces dramatic results in the revolution and Civil War, but when constructive work is required, they reveal other aspects of their personalities: his aggression and her cries for justice produce no movement forward—they only feed the fires of never-ending revolution. Before Dasha and Gleb transform, they are sexually attracted to these leaders who represent the energy and blindness of revolution—Dasha has an affair with Badin and Gleb with Polya, but as they acquire consciousness, they are able to overcome desire for revolution—depicted as sexual desire—and move toward an asexual parenting of the collective, emptied of any desire other than service to others. By the end of the novel, Polya and Badin have failed in their transformation into hero and have become villains: Polya the alien dreamer and Badin the selfish beast, their speech toxic to the Communist future.[14] Dasha puts an end to her affair with the aggressive and uncontrolled Badin, and Gleb is no longer attracted to the weak and easily controlled Polya. As part of their own transformation into heroes, Gleb and Dasha learn not only to reject these villainous examples but also to acquire a new collective language that can translate nostalgia into forward-looking optimism, self-centered desire into collective desire, and fantastic hesitation into socialist realist surety. After a long struggle, the novel concludes with a solemn party purging and a joyous celebration in which the collective voice speaks through these transformed heroes.[15]

Silencing the "Woman in Curls"

Polya Mekhova, the beautiful and courageous leader of the Women's Section, seems an unlikely villain, but her expulsion from the Communist Party in the final chapter of *Cement* signals that she has become a dangerous influence to those she leads. Even from the beginning of the novel she is a curious combination of conflicting impulses, invigorated by any opportunity to overthrow those in power and at the same time drawn to submissive relationships, declaring herself to be a "weak woman" in need of a man's "strength" (*sila*).[16] Ironically, both desires—to be overpowered in private life and to overpower in public life—constitute a return to the power dynamics of the past and are unacceptable in the postrevolutionary period of reconstruction depicted in the novel. Gladkov's choice of a female character to epitomize reactionary desire reflects what Anne Gorsuch, in her study of gender in the 1920s, describes as an overriding anxiety about women and their potential incompatibility with Soviet culture: "By virtue of their association with the private, women were thought to embody the dangers of a reactionary past."[17] Polya's desire to return to the gender politics of the past is condemned throughout the novel and contrasted with Dasha's physical and mental struggle to achieve equality with the men around her. At the beginning of *Cement* Dasha has acquired the physical symbols of the Bolshevik woman—every scene emphasizes her "masculine" short hair and red kerchief, while Polya is introduced in a chapter subsection entitled "Woman in Curls" (56).[18] These curls constantly escape the control of her red kerchief, the symbol of her status as a new Soviet woman, and by the time of the party purges, she has stopped wearing the kerchief altogether, a loss that symbolizes her rapidly deteriorating mental state.[19]

Polya's descent into madness is caused by her inability to accept the suffering of the children and displaced people who starve in the streets. Yet despite her compassion, she is unable to take action to help them, as Dasha the collective mother does.[20] Desire for the past enfeebles her, making her able to recognize but unable to fight the aggression, self-interest, and exploitation that have reemerged with the capitalist devices of the New Economic Policy (NEP). When Dasha acquires the inner strength to lock her door in the aggressive Badin's face, he enters Polya's unlocked door and rapes her: "She did not fight, crushed by the darkness. She could not fight. Why, when it was unavoidable and inevitable?" (254). Polya equates the rape with the changes in Soviet policy and gives up hope: "It's impossible to save myself from him . . . the revolution has turned into commerce . . . And this . . . It's all one" (256). The novel presents her rape and madness as a gendered deficiency, a failure to adjust to the changing needs of society.[21] Because of this failure, Polya eventually becomes unable to distinguish her dreams and hallucinations from the reality that surrounds her and becomes the embodiment of fantastic hesitation, trapped in a liminal world in which every revolutionary success is tainted by failure.

By the end of *Cement,* Polya has completely stopped working and has become mired in a long-lost fantasy: "Comrade Lenin on Red Square . . . How long ago! It was like a dream, like images from early childhood" (253). Caught in nostalgia for a time of excitement and dramatic change, she is wearied and bored by the current work, constantly doubting and challenging party policy. Her voice, continually pointing out the injustices of society, was effective in the "childish" days of October, yet she never matures to acquire the ability to see and convey "reality in its revolutionary development," picking out and displaying those details of the present that reflect rather than contradict the Communist future. Her revolutionary words are programmed to fight those in power, so that now she rails against the Communist Party itself. At the party purge her words have a dangerous effect on the crowd: "And the whole crowd immediately cried out; they began to make a discordant racket, and shook their fists at the committee and at each other . . . 'Comrades! . . It's true . . . The little woman speaks well' " (281). The purge committee berates her for demonstrating destructive "left childishness" (*levoe rebiachestvo,* 280) in her speech[22] and urges her to be silent: "You are the head of the Women's Section. You lead an organization of women. Yet you say unsuitable things before workers and these same women. This just won't do, comrade" (280). Polya's condemnation at the party purge is followed by unanimous praise for Dasha, who has by this time acquired the ability to see "reality in its revolutionary development": "This is a real worker and party member" (281). After the party purges Polya descends into madness, and Dasha not only takes Polya's place as leader of the Women's Section but also vows to "fix" her "broken" comrade. Until she has done so, Polya will remain silent, and in the concluding triumphant factory opening, Polya is neither seen nor heard.

As Dasha matures toward full consciousness and gradually attains the ability to filter all desire through the collective, Polya serves as a cautionary tale of childish regression to the past. At the beginning of the novel, when Gleb returns home from revolution and the Civil War, Dasha becomes like the weak, childish Polya for a brief moment, but her unwillingness to give in to her inner child distinguishes her from Polya and sets the stage for her eventual transformation into a Soviet New Person:

> She could not tear herself away from him and childishly [*po-rebiach'i*] babbled in a singsong voice: "Oh, Gleb!" . . . But that only burst from her heart for one moment, and in that moment Dasha felt Gleb's old power over her. . . . Gleb could no longer grab her with all his might, pick her up like a child [*rebenka*] and carry her off into the room as he used to do in the first years of their marriage. (8–9)

She resists the impulse to submit to Gleb, since a return to this comfort would mean a return to inequality and loss of her new collective identity. Instead, Dasha asserts her equality by calling him "comrade" and refusing to consider reconciliation until he has accepted her as an equal. This rejection of Gleb is difficult for Dasha, and throughout the novel she is drawn to the hierarchical relationship that Gleb demands—when she is with him she must "battle with her feminine [*bab'ei*] weakness" (8). It is telling that this "feminine weakness" arises during several instances of sexual violence, for example, when Badin assaults her: "through her veins flowed a wave of feminine [*bab'ei*] weakness, of troubled pleasure" (129). Dasha's disturbing excitement at the prospect of rape is a symbol of a more general desire on the part of all the characters of *Cement* to return to the destructive power dynamics that order society into a hierarchy, revealed not only in sexual relationships but also in the pull of NEP capitalism on the newly conscious proletariat. However, there is no space in Soviet society for the hierarchy of the past, and Dasha successfully fights the nostalgic pull of desire that comes when confronted with Gleb's dominance and Badin's violent attack.

Although this resistance paints Dasha as the most evolved of the characters in *Cement*, when she sacrifices herself to save Badin, her action comes not from conscious thought but from an unconscious compassion for the collective, which she later describes: "Comrade Bad'in is a remarkable party worker [*rabotnik*] . . . and she, Dasha, is a blade of grass" (133). Dasha's sacrifice could be justified were it not for the fact that Badin has just tried to rape her and has earlier shown a disregard for the collective, issuing harsh commands that cause the peasants to revolt and the factory reopening to be delayed. Dasha, who is not yet fully conscious, cannot recognize the growing danger that Badin's personal charisma represents as the country moves from war to peace. After witnessing his decisiveness with the peasants and his seeming respect for her after her act of heroism, Dasha's instinct leads her to trust him. Showing that unconscious instinct can be easily misguided, she then has sex with him, establishing a bond between them that she cannot break until she has acquired full consciousness, thereby overcoming her own desire for the past.[23]

Dasha's use of "comrade" when she first sees her husband at the beginning of the novel shows that she has begun her acquisition of the new Soviet language, which is intended to transform individuals into a collective. She still must become fluent, however, a fluency that she attains, like Gleb, only in the final chapter. The first step in her acquisition of the new language occurs while Gleb is still at war; after Dasha's last-minute reprieve from the firing squad, her speech changes: "She no longer said anything to anyone, and she learned to speak words only when they were necessary and to the point" (175). She silences the old Dasha when she speaks to other people, but an internal voice still asserts her longing to submit to her husband and child. To learn the words necessary to translate individual desires into collective desire, the newly literate Dasha struggles to read Lenin and August Bebel's *Women and Socialism* and leads others to knowledge by teaching them to read.[24] But only after her daughter Nyurka's death, which symbolizes the death of her own childlike former self, is she able to overcome her own personal desire. The sign that she "grows up" is that she then submits to the power of the new language: "And the words revolution, battle, work, party . . . the main thing in these words was that they were immense, inevitable, that she carried them within herself,—where there was no death, where she herself was only an invisible speck of dust" (249). Now Dasha carries "within herself" not a physical child, but words that will give birth to a new world for all children. Her submission to the new language inevitably requires that she bend to changing definitions, passed down from above. Thus, when the newly formed society is under attack, Dasha views Badin as a "remarkable party worker." As the outside danger dies down, Badin's aggression becomes a threat to reconstruction, and her relationship with him must end. Again, after her daughter's death, Dasha is finally able to silence him: "Comrade Bad'in, go away at once and don't sputter here in vain!" (251). Badin has been redefined, just as Dasha's notions of "mother," "wife," and "home" are redefined.

By the time of the party purge, Dasha has gained the ability to speak for the collective and to screen out all words that are not pertinent to that collective. While Polya and Sergey discuss the coming purge (both will be expelled from the party), Dasha sits, writing a report: "She did not see Sergey. She did not see Comrade Mekhova. What did their talking and worrying matter to her?" (270). The new Soviet words Dasha is writing in the report completely absorb her. Polya complains to Sergey that Dasha no longer "understands" her. But it is not a matter of understanding; Polya's words fall completely outside Dasha's field of perception: "Dasha was silent. She did not hear what Polya said" (270). In the concluding scenes of the novel, Dasha is on hand to translate Polya's inappropriate nostalgia into a forward-looking steadfastness: "The past has died without return . . . We will build a new life . . . Love is still love, Gleb, but it demands new ties . . . Everything will burn out, get shaken up, and we will figure out how to tie new knots" (314). At this point Dasha seems to have no desire at all, except to serve the masses by supplying the children's homes and maternity homes and repairing the childlike Polya. By rejecting the charismatic aggression of Badin and the comforting, childlike submission of Polya, she empties herself of individual desire and absorbs and translates their villainous revolutionary desire into constructive action for the collective and their hierarchical sexual desire into a new kind of love with "new ties," translated by a collective voice, which can express only enthusiasm and joy, absent of sacrifice.

Silencing the "Drunken Beast"

Just as Polya represents Dasha's inner child, Badin represents Gleb's inner beast: "when [Badin] was close to Dasha, a drunken beast [*zver'*] raged in his eyes" (127); and "[Gleb's] eyes were filled with beastly [*zhivotnoi*] malice" (33). After Gleb's initial violent encounter with Dasha, he rejects Badin's tactics—"to break her with one blow" (101)—and begins to see in her a "riddle" (37) that must be solved in a different way. Nevertheless, throughout the novel Gleb struggles with his desire to overpower Dasha and force her into submission. This struggle is paralleled by his efforts at the factory to abandon revolutionary force and learn to work within the system, again a struggle in which Badin serves as a foil for Gleb's transformation. At the beginning of the novel, when Gleb is denied entrance to Badin's office, he reacts with violence, ignoring the protests of Badin's secretary, pushing aside the guard, and breaking down the door to find Badin threatening a subordinate with the firing squad. Gleb echoes Badin's threat by loudly and angrily demanding that the Economic Council be shot for their neglect of the factory (he proposes the same solution at the Children's Home). We find out later in the novel that Badin's orders regarding forced grain requisition in this scene produce chaos and unrest among the peasants and that Gleb's initial aggressive behavior in the factory offices accomplishes nothing at all. Revolutionary violence has no place in the postrevolutionary world being built in the novel.

Throughout *Cement,* Gleb's and Badin's relationships with women echo their effectiveness as leaders in society. At the beginning of the novel, Gleb wants to force every situation, both in his home and at the factory, and when he fails to overpower Dasha, he has an affair with the submissive Polya, which temporarily fulfills his desire for power: "He had only to embrace her, pick her up, and press her to him like a child [*rebenkom*]" (218).[25] While he has this unequal relationship with Polya, however, Gleb cannot manage to reopen the factory. By the end of the novel, when he has learned to move through the proper administrative channels and to work peaceably with other leaders at the factory, his attraction for the submissive Polya predictably fades: "Gleb . . . no longer felt for her the former tenderness or sympathy: she was too pitiful and helpless" (312). Emptied of the desire to dominate others, he is no longer attracted to the object of that desire.

Badin, on the other hand, never overcomes his beastly nature, and when Dasha turns him away, he rapes Polya repeatedly in the final chapters. At the end of the novel, when Gleb looks at Badin, he sees "something heavy, inhuman [*necheloviech'e*], living in his blood" (303). It has often bothered critics that Gleb moves from uncontrolled anger at Badin in this meeting to calmly accepting a place beside him on the dais at the factory opening.[26] But it is important that the meeting is closed; when Gleb openly expresses his rage against Badin only party members are present. At the factory opening in the presence of the unconscious crowd, Gleb suppresses his anger as Badin speaks to the crowd. Badin says "everything necessary" (315), but he does not *feel* the crowd, as Gleb does. Never having acquired an empathy for the collective, Badin "stands alone" (311). High above the crowd, he revels in his role as leader, driven only by self-interest. Glaring at the aloof, unfeeling man, Gleb vows to remove the "careerist." It is in this moment that he emerges into consciousness. This vow is aimed at Badin the "careerist," not Badin the romantic rival; Badin must be removed not because he threatens Gleb's own relationship with Dasha—a personal concern—but rather because he threatens equality and the country's economic resources. And, due to his acquisition of political consciousness, Gleb now knows that he can no longer break down doors but must instead act through appropriate channels. Proof of his enlightenment comes in this final scene, when he shares the dais with Badin and restrains himself from destructive and inefficient action against him. Gleb is thereby able to refocus on the factory opening and his role as spokesman for the masses.

In the opening chapters, Gleb's speech evokes his inner, uncontrolled beast. His words are like Badin's—revolutionary, aggressive, and military—and therefore inappropriate for reconstruction: "He yelled it out in a voice too big for that box—at the top of his voice, as he had in the army" (28). Confronted with the puzzling bureaucracy, Gleb fights them with "cobblestone words" (99). In the revolution and Civil War, Gleb's revolutionary speech was effective; character after character proclaims that it was Gleb who led him to join the party. And, at the beginning of the novel, revolutionary words are still needed. When Gleb first returns to the factory in the opening chapter of *Cement,* his former workmates are all complaining about the lack of work, but their complaints do not form a collective voice: "to each man it seemed as though only he alone complained" (26). Although his words are loud and "military," Gleb unites the workers by speaking the common internal desire of each man: to reopen the factory. He speaks the instinctual desire of the collective, and with his revolutionary words Gleb battles the prerevolutionary language of bureaucracy, which still exists. Due to "jabbering" (*gorlopanstvo,* 21) at the offices, workers have abandoned the factory; Gleb's speech draws them back and inspires an interest in the future: "Because of his words tomorrow will be completely different" (68). Yet his revolutionary words only induce short-term bursts of energy and work; at this stage, despite frequent inspiring speeches, Gleb cannot reopen the factory. His speech is fragmentary, lacking in the control and direction a conscious speaker would have; he frequently pauses, utters sentence fragments, and often seems at a loss for effective words when confronted by authority figures.

Dasha serves as a mentor to Gleb in acquiring the new language. When violence will not overcome Dasha's resistance, Gleb becomes a silent observer of her interactions with others, and at the Children's Home he immediately notices her new way of speaking: "And Dasha answered the manager's complaints by hitting her in the face with words (Gleb had never before heard such a voice)" (43). Katerina Clark writes that *Cement* is a "scrambled version" of the socialist realist "master plot," partly because there is no clearly defined mentor/disciple pattern,[27] but if we approach the journey to consciousness as an acquisition of language, we find that Dasha is clearly Gleb's mentor.[28] She teaches him to listen to and to speak the new language, serving as a model for him and reminding him of other sources as well: "What kind of *ABC of Communism* have you studied, Comrade Gleb?" (34). When Gleb finds the newly literate Dasha struggling over Communist texts, she offers him books by Lenin: "We communists must pump ourselves full of learning" (74).

When Gleb first returns, she uses the word "comrade" in greeting him, an effort to remind him of the transformation that has occurred. Gleb's reaction shows, however, that he has not learned the new language: "This is not an insult but a blow. You go up to a person, and you hit your head against a wall. It's shameful and painful" (9). Gleb feels that he is approaching a "person" (*chelovek*) and instead is met with a "comrade" (*tovarishch*). He cannot understand that, for a conscious citizen, these two words are synonyms. Until he can accept Dasha as "comrade," she will not tell him about her experiences during his absence: "I still have no words [*iazyk*] for you" (36). She continually judges him on his ability to handle words, and, when Gleb has developed sufficiently, Dasha finally tells him the story of her own transformation: "Now it is possible to lash you with words too" (163). By the end of the novel, he has learned the lesson Dasha has sought to teach him: "He no longer had the power for such words, because she, Dasha, had taken away this power from him and turned it into dust. And it wasn't simply a woman before him now but a person, equal to him in strength" (296). In acquiring an understanding of the words "comrade" and "equal person," Gleb moves a step up the ladder toward full consciousness.

Dasha aids in Gleb's language acquisition, but the true mentor in *Cement* is played not by an individual but by the Soviet governing apparatus; it serves as the consciousness driving societal instinct and developing consciousness in those receptive to it. Gleb struggles to comprehend documents and books at the factory offices, and specialists at the factory smile at his "foolish questions" (212). Yet, despite his hard work, he fails to gain an understanding of the bureaucratic complexity on his own; he must go to the Central Bureau of Industry for help. When he returns, Gleb faces Badin, armed with the proper documents and with a new language: "Sullenly, sternly detached . . . it was as though he was not speaking but reading from a paper" (265). Whereas Gleb's speech at the beginning of the novel consists mostly of unfinished phrases punctuated by elliptical dots, his speech now shows no such fragmentation and hesitation, and each sentence is firmly punctuated. One paragraph contains eleven sentences ending in periods and eight sentences ending in exclamation marks; there are now no ellipses at all (266). The halting, emotional speech of the former Gleb has become "hard" and useful, like the cement of the title. When Gleb returns, armed both with the proper instincts and with the new "conscious" language, he can reopen the factory.

Michael Gorham describes the "charismatic Bolshevik" of the 1920s: "He becomes one with the crowd, or *becomes* the crowd, articulating its concerns purely and immediately . . . abandoning his preordained, written words and articulating spontaneously the crowd's immediate, inner concerns."[29] Gorham argues that Gleb's final speech reflects this spontaneity, noting that his "unpolished speech" is contrasted with Badin's "ringing rhetoric."[30] But I would modify this interpretation. Gleb does "become the crowd" at the factory opening: "We are all one spirit" (316). And his words seem to come from the crowd: "What was his life, when it was a speck in this ocean of human lives? . . . He had no words, no life separate from this roaring mass" (316). He is able to articulate the crowd's desires; they resoundingly agree and approve of everything he says. This would seem a return to his earlier speech, even in style: short phrases, ellipses, lack of firm punctuation. But it is not "spontaneous" speech; we have seen the dangers of such speech in leaders like Polya Mekhova, who can only articulate the complaints and worries of the unconscious crowd. At the factory opening, on the other hand, Gleb must not only express the crowd's instinctual desire, he must also direct that desire. Gleb notes the volatility of the masses, "always ready for outbursts" (308). But he can now guide that volatile instinct in the appropriate direction: "Our brains and hands shake . . . not from effort, but because they need new work. We are building socialism, comrades, and our own proletarian culture . . . Toward victory, comrades!" (317). In his speech, Gleb can be seen as an avatar for the Soviet writer, who is expected to eradicate self in order to absorb the desire of his audience and then translate it into a collective voice that bows to the higher authority of the Communist Party.

PARTY-MINDEDNESS AND THE SOCIALIST REALIST TEXT

Between the appearance of *Cement* in 1925 and the author's death in 1958, thirty-six editions of the novel appeared, and Gladkov reworked every one, making changes in plot, style, and characterization.[31] Major revisions in the text were made in 1932, 1947, and 1950 (corresponding to the formation of the Writers' Union in 1932 and Zhdanov's attacks on writers following World War II). The translation that is commonly read in the West is from the 1920s. Therefore, a reader of the novel in English would have a radically different impression than someone reading a more recent Soviet edition. Robert Busch writes that the changes "transformed a novel with organic ties to the experimental context of the 1920s into one reflective of Socialist Realism."[32] Together these rewrites should constitute an extraordinary record of the evolution (and cementing) of Soviet ideology. Remarkably, that is not the case. The original novel can easily be read, as the previous pages demonstrate, to fit within the definition of socialist realism. At the end of *Cement*, with the exception of Badin, all the pseudo-speakers and revolutionary speakers have been removed from the party and their destructive voices silenced—they do not speak or even appear at the factory opening. As in any socialist realist novel, Gleb's vow to remove Badin shows that there is work yet to be done; the factory opening and the party purge are only the first steps toward the bright future. The only changes that can be seen to turn the novel into "one reflective of Socialist Realism" are stylistic—modernist experimentation is replaced with a simpler, more accessible style.[33] Why then, were so many other changes made to *Cement*?

Gladkov's continual revisions provide a vivid illustration of "party-mindedness" (*partiinost'*) at work, the state of mind that supposedly led the Soviet writer to shape plot and characters to fit current party concerns and priorities. This is seen most clearly in the changes made to Dasha, who becomes unrecognizable in later editions. Gladkov's editorial changes to Dasha reflect a societal backlash against the emancipated woman—in 1936 early Soviet policies on women and the family were reversed and support for the individual family unit reinstated.[34] By 1958 (the final edition before Gladkov's death) Dasha is transformed into a devoted Soviet housewife. Her party work becomes less important—instead of being elected chair of the presidium, she is elected only a member and no longer makes an important proposal. And her home becomes more important to her and much cleaner—references to mice, mold, and insects disappear. Conditions in the Children's Home are also better, so her decision to put her daughter there appears more positive. And now, instead of ignoring Gleb and criticizing him as a "bad communist" (78), she cooks meals and makes up a bed for him. The 1958 Dasha is less defiant, hostile, and physically threatening with her husband, replacing "comrade" with "dear" (*rodnoi, milyi*) when she addresses him. She no longer has sex with others, nor does she push Gleb into a relationship with Polya.[35] These dramatic changes in Dasha transform her into a more typical Stalinist-era heroine.[36]

L. N. Smirnova notes the effect of similar changes on Gleb's character: "He appears to be more patient, more attentive to the people around him. His responsibility for his acts and words is strengthened."[37] Indeed, in the reworked versions of *Cement*, Gleb becomes less violent and more politically aware. At first reading, these changes seem mild—Dasha appears to be much more radically changed than Gleb. However, the transformations to Dasha's character also change Gleb's. As Dasha begins to cater to him, Gleb is no longer so confused by her, reduced to begging and pleading, and he is less jealous and violent. They still part, but only so that Dasha can care for Polya. Gleb must master his jealousy, which is now totally unfounded and somewhat difficult to understand. His fate is therefore no longer in Dasha's hands. Moreover, because Dasha does not reject him so strongly, Gleb no longer has an affair with Polya; her "childishness" is less attractive to him, even at the beginning of the novel. Gleb is reworked into a character with much more control, one who easily subdues his instincts, emotions, and desires to consciousness. Gladkov felt it necessary to defend depicting his characters as all good or all bad.[38] Gleb, however, was never good enough.[39]

Gladkov's rewriting of *Cement* epitomizes the socialist realist image of the writer and the malleability of the literary text. Under socialist realism, the writer could no longer sit in an ivory tower, indulging a privileged and independent observation of the world from afar, his inviolable words etched in gold and genius. In his many reworkings of *Cement,* Gladkov willingly submits his novel to the demands of society, displaying a monk-like obedience to the goals of the party. This transformation of the Soviet writer, often attributed to post-1934 socialist realist culture, had already taken place during the years of the First Five-Year Plan. By the end of the 1920s writers from Russian Association of Proletarian Writers (RAPP) and *Literaturnaia gazeta* were being organized into brigades and sent to construction sites, factories, and collective farms to write about the Five-Year Plan. Literature, like everything in Soviet society, was to become industrialized, and writers therefore set personal five-year plans for literary production and joined with other professional and amateur writers to compose collective pieces about the projects of the plan. Thousands of correspondents were recruited from the ranks of factory, construction, and agricultural workers and with minimal training sent to work with and write about their fellow workers in a style and structure accessible to them. Writing no longer required special training or talent or a call from the gods, and writers lost their previous status as prophets dispensing wisdom. At construction sites and in factories, they were to take on active roles as journalists, agitprop workers, librarians, and teachers. And they were expected to become experts in the field they were writing about, transforming themselves from elite observers of life into useful participants at the work site—part consultant, part teacher, and part reporter, and ever-obedient to the demands of the party.[40]

REWRITING THE WRITER: VALENTIN KATAEV'S *TIME FORWARD!* (1932)

Time Forward! has been identified as a "turning point" in the development of the Soviet novel and of Valentin Kataev's career.[41] In May 1930 his satirical fiction, like that of so many fellow travelers, fell under attack—the charge was that his heroes lived "selfishly."[42] Kataev dutifully responded to this criticism by setting off to witness firsthand how real-life Soviets behaved at the massive construction projects of the First Five-Year Plan.[43] The result of this journey is *Time Forward!,* which chronicles an attempt to break a cement-pouring record at a construction site in Siberia. The novel begins and ends with the ringing of an alarm clock, and in the twenty-four hours in between, safety guidelines of cement-pouring are ardently debated, cement is poured at a frantic but efficient rate (despite injuries, the intervention of human wreckers, and nature's fury), and personal lives are put on hold so that this collective of workers can move time forward. In the course of completing their production feat, some workers gain both an understanding of and an emotional connection to collective work and to the Communist idea of time. Others that fail to embrace the group effort become outcasts. *Time Forward!* uses the transformational process as a commentary on the changes in Soviet literary culture during the Five-Year Plan—by making many of the characters into writers who participate in and write about the production feat. The novel reads like a manifesto for the Soviet writer during the plan, a call for submission of the literary imagination to the needs of the collective. More important, in its depiction of Soviet time as that eternally repeating moment of transformation and the Soviet writer as successful only when integrated into that moment, it presents a fully formed vision of socialist realism two years before its official adoption.

Internal Clocks

The engineer Margulies has no need for the alarm clock that opens and closes *Time Forward!:* he is inextricably connected to each worker and every piece of equipment at the construction site, and time for Margulies can only be measured by their movement: "Time was not an abstract concept for him. Time was the number of turns of the drum and the pulley, the raising of the scoop, the end or beginning of a shift."[44] His connection to the site, a sprawling, interconnected mechanism of muscle and machinery, is so compelling that he tunes out his own biological rhythm, suppressing hunger so that he can follow the cement-pouring, even though he is not on duty.[45] Margulies watches the workers, timing them with an inner clock set to their movement, thought and feeling. As the workers move to the mechanized rhythm of the scoops and pullies, other people are also drawn in to watch, mesmerized by the hybrid of human tissue and machine gears that makes up the pulsing, beating timepiece of the work brigade; the entranced spectators begin to count off in unison the loads of cement poured, their chanting like the ticking of a great human clock.

The conservative engineer Nalbandov, a villainous foil to Margulies's character, is cut off from this human timepiece by a disconnect between heart and head that prevents him from feeling the Communist ideas he so fluently spouts. Without this feeling, he must rely on the cold, inhuman mechanisms of his fine gold watch as he guides an American businessman around the construction site, the fevered pulse of human-machine hybrid dulled by distance as the two pause to observe the construction site from afar. The American criticizes the new Soviet city that adjoins the site—it lacks the "noise of time" (342); Nalbandov mechanically counters his arguments, but repeatedly thinks to himself: "He is right" (343, 344, 377). Both see time only in the sense of tradition, of the past, and by fighting the attempt to beat the cement-pouring record, Nalbandov tries to keep time to its traditional pace; disconnected from the flesh-and-metal clock of the construction site, he can hear only the rhythms of the past. Margulies's time cycles to the scientific beat of "reality in its revolutionary development":

> At that time Nalbandov thought that this was technologically unfeasible. It went against academic traditions of laying concrete. Margulies had the audacity to disregard these traditions. Nalbandov cited science. Margulies insisted that one had to look at science dialectically. What was a scientific hypothesis yesterday would become an academic fact today; what was an academic fact today would become an anachronism and a bypassed stage tomorrow. (368–69)

Nalbandov is cut off from other people, able to hear only his own heartbeat, his own self-interest. Therefore, he does not celebrate the victory of the collective when the cement-pouring record is broken but instead worries that he has missed a chance at fame. His subsequent reckless attempt to break the new record is halted by Margulies, who constantly guards the integrity of the Communist future—he refuses to allow another try until the quality of the poured cement can be checked. Nalbandov's future is set to the rhythms of the past and he leaves the construction site old and sick at the end of the novel, defeated by time. Margulies, on the other hand, ends the day vital and youthful, proposing marriage to the young Shura—after the shift has ended, of course. In this way the two engineers at the construction site neatly divide into hero and villain, the villain alienated from the collective, timing life by his own heartbeat, and the hero ignoring his own biological rhythms until the human clock signals time for dinner and romance. The hero silences the villain's pleas to set the collective clock to the beat of the past and translates the villain's vision of time into Soviet time.

The temporal movement in *Time Forward!* is not as linear as one might expect in a work of Soviet literature focused on constructing the future. On the contrary, time is circular. The novel begins with the ringing of an alarm clock and the news that a new cement-pouring record has been set. The novel ends with the ringing of the same alarm clock and the news that another new record has been set. What is important in this accomplishment is not the cement-pouring itself or the structure built with this cement, which is hardly mentioned, but rather the pouring of new people into the flesh-and-blood collective timepiece. The production feat is simply a test to divide people into heroes and villains, integrated members of the timepiece and those who are expelled from time. Time in the novel is like the stationary train car that houses the newspaper editorial staff at the construction site: "The train car stopped in space but continued to move in time. Time rushed along, every minute altering the space around the car" (345). Time seems to move forward while in reality staying in one place, an endlessly repeating 24-hour period in which production feats are accomplished and through them people are assimilated into or expelled from the eternally repeating cycle of Soviet time.

This train car epitomizes socialist realism, which is designed to give the appearance of forward movement while repeating the same transformative process in each text. Like a derailed train car, the reality depicted by socialist realism is frozen in a moment of eternal uniform repetition. When the day is done, the same twenty-four hours must be restarted to test a new batch of potential members of the collective. Those who fail the test posed by the production novel are expelled from time as defined by socialist realism—they no longer have a place in the repetitive movement of "reality in its revolutionary development" and are condemned instead to a temporal limbo where nothing changes and where they are eternally disconnected from the pulse of the collective, just like Ivan Babichev and Nikolay Kavalerov of *Envy.* Unlike Ivan and Kavalerov, however, these villainous characters play a crucial part in the transformative function of socialist realism—they serve as a foil that repulses the hero. The hero encounters in the villain's monstrous stoppage of time an externalized version of his inner selfish desire and begins to doubt the reality, that is, the humanity, of his inner self. Fantastic hesitation vanishes, however, as he transforms his psyche to fall into sync with the rhythm of the collective, thereby translating individual desire into collective desire, and by rejecting the villain and that part of himself that the villain represents, he vanquishes fantastic hesitation. According to the precepts of socialist realism, the reader would follow his example.

The Villainous Foil

A good example of such a villainous foil is the worker-poet Sayenko. Even before he physically enters the text, Sayenko has been satirically exposed by one of the most inexperienced writers at the site, who constructs a propaganda poster, a cardboard cross inscribed: "Here rests Nikolay Sayenko, from the brigade of Ishchenko. Rest in peace, dear laborer in truancy and drunkenness!" (210). His status as one of the undead is reinforced by the setting in which we first encounter him, wandering aimlessly across "the graveyard of ruined machinery" (247) where he has gone to gamble with his fellow worker Zagirov. The chapters centered on Sayenko are not so much concerned with his exposure and expulsion, since he is depicted as dead to Soviet time from the very beginning, but rather with the rescue of Zagirov from Sayenko's clutches and from the static, dead time of capitalism into which Sayenko has lured him with the promise of easy money. Every setting that Sayenko chooses for his daylong drinking and gambling binge is infused like this "graveyard" with death and stalled time. Sayenko and Zagirov end the day in a quiet village, relaxing in front of a store covered in painted timepieces, all eternally stalled at two o'clock—time has stopped for Sayenko and through his influence for Zagirov.

Introducing the villainous Sayenko to the text also introduces the danger of reader misidentification. After all, Zagirov has been misled by Sayenko's seductive promise of effortless reward. Could the reader be as easily swayed? Zagirov's loss of every possession, including his shoes, makes such a fate unattractive. Added to this, Sayenko is made so repulsive, so bestial, that Zagirov eventually must flee his seductive undead voice for the collective voice, and abandon "dead" time for Soviet time in order to retain his own humanity. At the "graveyard of ruined machinery," far removed from the construction site and therefore from Soviet time, Sayenko interrupts Zagirov's pleas for mercy to fall into a monstrous fit of inspiration: "He panted, guffawed, threw himself on all fours, struck his elbows against the ground. Zagirov looked at him in horror. He fell, pulled himself up, lilac saliva on his lips as in an epileptic fit. 'Stop! Wait!' he shouted, gasping for breath, 'I'll lose the verses. Go away! Don't get in my way or I'll kill you!'" (248). This act of writing is depicted as a frightening loss of physical control and an aggressive attack on the poet's audience. Zagirov is frightened and reacts to Sayenko's attack of inspiration as to something monstrous, inhuman. Under Sayenko's influence, Zagirov enters that liminal space of the fantastic, where he is confronted with an externalized version of his own greed and self-interest, and the image he finds in this physical realization of his inner self has little resemblance to a human being. Sayenko is animalistic and exploitative like the desire that led Zagirov to abandon the cement-pouring feat for the easy wealth promised by his game of chance. Sayenko's straddling of the boundary between animal and human causes Zagirov to doubt his own humanity and eventually to reclaim it by returning to the construction site.

In their journey from "graveyard" to "graveyard"—the marketplace, the peaceful village, and finally a coffin-maker's shop—Sayenko, and through his influence Zagirov, becomes less human, more animal-like. And, although Zagirov begs Sayenko, "Be human" (249), he himself is transformed into a beast by their association: "The light went out in Zagirov's eyes. He bared his white, rat teeth and like a trapped animal turned his head in all directions" (249) and "[Zagirov] looked directly at him with dry shining dog eyes. 'Now you will be my lackey,' said Sayenko" (399). Later, growling "like a dog," Zagirov attacks Sayenko and calls him a "kulak dog" (435). Through exploitation both master and slave are dehumanized. As they sit among coffins in the coffin-maker's shop, a storm threatens, and Zagirov expresses concern for their comrades at the construction site; the "deceased" Sayenko, on the other hand, curses the site: "sweep everything clean!" (434). When the storm breaks out, Zagirov, horrified by Sayenko's lack of humanity, flees, losing in his escape all sense of place and time. Suddenly the sun comes out, and with it Zagirov's consciousness: "He came to. He came to his senses" (454). He miraculously finds himself at the work site, reestablished in Soviet time and space, just as an injured comrade is led off—Zagirov takes his place and helps beat the record.

Sayenko has served his purpose—the conversion of Zagirov, who rejoins the human timepiece freed of self-interest and dreams of easy fortune. Beyond that inspiration, Sayenko has no further use in the novel and is expelled, along with his selfish desire. In his final scene he is depicted as a wild animal, afraid and alone in the dark: "He steals from shadow to shadow like a wolf, carefully avoiding the streetlamps and floodlights" (487). He circles the railroad car that holds the printing presses of *Komsomolskaia Pravda,* an image of Lenin prominent on its side. Sayenko, who earlier wrote poetry in the "graveyard," now spies a single poet working inside the well-lit car, laying out type, an echo of the book's opening, where another poet sits in the sleeping car of a moving train, reading an article about economic issues while his brightly lit train compartment speeds through the dark night toward the construction site. These poets are linked to the collective, connected to Soviet time, occupying brightly lit train cars caught in a moment of never-ending change. They are in the light, but the poet Sayenko, by embracing the stasis of his self-centered dreams, is a creature of the night. When he races after a well-lit moving train at the end of the novel, Sayenko misses it and remains alone in the dark: "Finally, he falls behind" (489).

Time Forward vs. the Frozen Moment

In *Time Forward!* capitalist art is depicted as a paper dream, a lie that prevents the viewer/reader from linking with the collective clock and is contrasted with the "reality in its revolutionary development" of the production feat, which seems future-oriented but which is in reality focused on the present, on the struggle to transform all human beings, to link them to the beat of the collective clock. This is seen most clearly in the character of the American Foma Yegorovich. During an unexpected stoppage of work, as others rush frantically to restart the cement-pouring process, Foma instead sits down to read a magazine, relaxing, gazing at the advertisements, and dreaming of the goods he can one day buy. Foma has denied himself every comfort while he earns enough money to return home and open his own business. In the meantime he lives a lonely life, wandering from country to country and construction site to construction site, disconnected from the human clock and taking solace in the frozen moments of time pictured in his magazines. His favorite advertisement contains a photo of a well-stocked refrigerator being opened by a beautiful young woman, whom he has named "Maggie." Foma rarely thinks of his real-life wife in America, preferring to dream of this lovely "Maggie" and the bounty she points to. Like the food in the advertisement Maggie is perfect, fresh, imperishable—she will be forever young and beautiful. Foma removes himself from Soviet time—never-ending change—to enter the suspended, static moment of this advertisement, where nothing ever moves; it is a seductive vision of an inviting future cleansed of the dirt and deprivation of the construction site. When work starts up again, Foma cheerfully joins the effort to set a new cement-pouring record but never feels the beat of the collective clock. His body works to an ordinary, mechanical clock, starting and stopping when the whistle blows, and his mind moves to the silent siren call of the beautiful Maggie, a static dream disconnected from time.

When the cement-pouring record is broken, Foma learns that his beautiful dream has been shattered by the crash of the U.S. stock market. As other workers celebrate the cement-pouring record, Foma rips up the advertisement and drinks himself into a stupor, surrounded by torn fragments of the beautiful Maggie and her promise of the perfect life. Later in the night he awakens: "A silence washed over the deserted earth for thousands of kilometers. It became clear to Foma Yegorovich that on the entire planet he was alone; there existed not one living creature—neither beast, nor bird, nor fish, nor human, nor bacteria" (506). Foma, by embracing the static capitalist dream, has failed to transform into a New Person; now he is eternally disconnected not only from the Soviet timepiece, but from all of nature—the natural world is silent, nonexistent for him. He has failed the test posed by the production novel and has been expelled from time. In the end he watches out a window, separated by a pane of glass from the other workers who join forces—after quitting time—to put out a fire (set by Sayenko); his fellow workers are now as distant from him as the objects in the beautiful advertisements. Because of his dreaming, Foma will always have a pane of glass or a photographic lens separating him from Soviet time and from other people. The frozen moment of time adored by Foma is remarkably similar to the greenish glass cube of frozen fame desired by Nikolay Kavalerov in Yury Olesha's *Envy* (see chapter 3). However, unlike *Envy*, *Time Forward!* enters the Soviet canon, partly because Foma, unlike Kavalerov, is silenced long before the end of the novel and his frozen moment replaced by the dynamic linking of several key characters into Soviet time. Moreover, his alien, self-centered dreaming and Sayenko's beastly self-centered desire are translated into "reality in its revolutionary development" and collective desire. This translation is done by Georgy Vasilevich, a Soviet writer who is saved from Foma's fate by entering Soviet time and subordinating his mind and his writing to the transformative beat of the collective timepiece.

The Disconnected Writer

The many writers in *Time Forward!* fall into two groups, those keyed into the human timepiece, locked into the moment of eternal change, and those like Sayenko who are disconnected from it. To be *Soviet* writers, they must connect themselves to the repeating 24-hour cycle of Soviet time; only then can they serve their role of connecting others. Two writers from *Time Forward!* separate themselves from the collective—Georgy Vasilevich, the "famous novelist," and Semechkin, the "special correspondent," and their detachment is in each case symbolized by the use of artificial lenses. Georgy Vasilevich looks at the construction site through binoculars and Semechkin through darkened goggles. The poet Sayenko, who wanders the graveyards and coffin shops outside the construction site, is easily exposed as a beast, dead to Soviet time. Georgy Vasilevich and Semechkin, however, give the appearance of Soviet writers but like Sayenko occupy a dead time zone, unable to perceive Soviet time, even when they are immersed in the hustle and bustle of the site.

Semechkin, through his darkened goggles, views the world around him only in relation to his own needs and desires. His writing serves this self-interest; for example, when a worker swears at him, he decides that it is an insult to his profession and plans a series of articles to battle swearing. His writing revolves not around party goals or the people's needs, but his own desires, and since the world around him operates according to a different clock, he is perpetually confused:

> Around him stood the enormous, complicated, shining difficult world of the construction site. And Semechkin could in no way assimilate this world, enter it, love it. This world and Semechkin were incompatible. Between them stood an invisible but insurmountable barrier . . . Smart, poisonous, ill-willed Semechkin was hostile to this world. (300)

Semechkin's disconnect, symbolized by his goggles, prevents him from seeing anything positive at the construction site. Like the American Foma Yegorovich, Semechkin is separated from Soviet time by a glass barrier, able to see what is happening but only through the distortion of self-interest.

Semechkin never takes off his goggles, and through them the world is darkened, its colors inaccurate, and everyone that he looks at seems to be a villain, not because they threaten the future of Communism, but because they fail to bow to his sense of personal dignity and his ambitions for success. Without a clear vision of temporal movement, he cannot fulfill his role as a Soviet writer, sorting hero from villain, bringing the former into Soviet time and expelling the latter. Therefore his speech and his writing can only confuse, distract, and isolate the listener/reader: "And Semechkin in a muffled bass voice continued to pile up phrase after phrase. He let loose such a fog that soon even he stopped understanding himself" (303). Later, during the cement-pouring, the water supply suddenly dries up—Semechkin has arranged to install a water meter to improve cost-accounting, an act that will take an hour and a half away from the cement-pouring effort. Semechkin readily stops the flow of Soviet time, interested more in the future promise of wealth than in the transformative moment that comprises socialist realism.

The chief engineer then orders that Semechkin be locked in a barn for the duration of the shift. Like the other characters who are expelled from time—Sayenko and Foma Yegorovich—Semechkin ends up alone and in the dark. Still wearing his dark lenses, he nevertheless writes a dispatch exposing the brigade's "scandalous" (486) treatment of him. Oblivious to the brigade's achievement of the cement-pouring record, Semechkin reads his expose aloud to Communist Party secretary Filonov: "Filonov wrinkled his forehead in agony. He was trying to understand, to clarify Semechkin's main thought. In a dull, offended little bass voice, Semechkin continued to pile up phrase after phrase. The phrases were hazy, long, full of poisonous suggestions" (493). They are interrupted by the brigade leader Ishchenko, who places on the table his petition to join the party. Ishchenko has only recently learned to read and write; nevertheless, his petition is completely clear: "Filonov immediately grasped every detail of it by the light of the burning lamp" (494). The well-educated journalist's darkened view of the world is countered by the simple worker's illuminated text.

Georgy Vasilevich, the famous novelist, has committed to writing a newspaper sketch about the construction site, but when he first appears in the novel, he has a serious case of writer's block—he is separated from the collective much like Sayenko and Semechkin, distanced by space and mindset from the people he plans to write about. Concerned only by his own discomfort, he prepares to write in his hot, drafty room, placing improvised paperweights on sheets of blank paper and lamenting that he must use a pencil instead of his customary pen. Roughing it in an uncomfortable room, which might have given the writer insight into the difficult lives of the working people, offers little guidance, as is evidenced by his first written lines:

> The world opens up in my window like a rebus. I see a multitude of figures. People, horses, wicker baskets, wires, cars, steam, letters, clouds, mountains, train cars, water . . . But I don't understand their common bond. And there is a common bond. There is some kind of mighty interdependence. I have absolutely no doubt about this. I know it, I believe in it, but I can't see it. And this is agonizing. To believe and not to see! I'm beating my head against the wall, but I can't solve the rebus. (278)

Georgy Vasilevich cannot discern the relationships among people, and therefore the entire construction site is for him an unsolvable puzzle. After he writes these lines expressing his frustration, he underlines the words "believe" and "see"—there is a disconnect between his ability to "believe" in the Communist future and his ability to "see" this future superimposed onto the present. He has yet to acquire the vision of a Soviet writer, who must be able to perceive and describe the relationships existing among all people and the purpose intertwining all events. Instead, he can only make lists of things observed, connected by commas and ellipses rather than by the repetition that moves reality through its revolutionary development. As he writes, he must continually ask himself: "But what kind of connection could there be among all these details?" (280). In his hotel room, high above the construction site, he can find no answer. His narration of what he observes is indeed repetitive, but all that he can repeat at this point are unanswered questions—he lacks the transformative answers of the Soviet writer.

Frustrated by the unbearable heat in his room, Georgy Vasilevich walks around the hotel, peering out the windows through binoculars. One by one he sees characters who have been described in earlier chapters of *Time Forward!*, but unlike the narrator of these chapters, he has no idea who these people are or what their function is at the site. As he moves from window to window the famous writer observes each person and concludes his observation of each with a question. These questions reveal his own alien imagination, which is intent on solving the riddle of the individual, not the group: "Who are they, these people, each of them separately?" (287). His mind is still the mind of a prerevolutionary writer, observing people from a distant height and trying to depict "each of them separately." Through the artificial lenses of his binoculars, each scene he observes undergoes a visual distortion, whereby people become separate and distinct, stripped of the connections that would be visible were he to view "reality in its revolutionary development." Therefore, although he asks question after question, he receives no answer, instead following each question with a hopeless "Who knew?" Sometimes he touches on the truth as presented earlier by the narrator of *Time Forward!*, as when he describes Sayenko: "in his gait there was something sinuous, doglike" (289). But he ignores this insight, and, instead of judging this "canine" worker as a wrecker, Georgy Vasilevich can only think how hot he must be. The famous writer describes hero, villain, and woman pregnant with the symbolic baby of the future all with as much puzzlement as he describes the unexpected appearance of an elephant.

The famous writer finds answers to his questions only when Vinkich, the correspondent of the Russian Telegraphic Agency, begins to show him around the site. A famous writer would traditionally take on the role of mentor to an unknown journalist, but fame, talent, and writing experience have little meaning to Vinkich. Although he believes that Georgy Vasilevich's fame will bring attention and resources to the site, he does not attempt to seek advice or patronage from the novelist. Instead, he sets out to teach the famous writer about Soviet time and the writer's role in serving it. Vinkich draws his attention to the fact that in another city the previous cement-pouring record has been broken. On his own, he has failed to notice this, but when it is pointed out to him, Georgy Vasilevich recognizes and enthusiastically endorses "socialist competition." When Vinkich in turn welcomes his support in the fight, the famous writer stammers: "What do you mean fight? My opinion is—purely subjective . . . As you well know, I am not a specialist in concrete. I am, so to speak, an objective observer, nothing more" (306). His role as "objective observer" is to remove himself from the equation and to observe from a distance, as he does in the hotel through binoculars. But when he does so, he has only himself as a filter for reality; he thinks that the characters wandering around the site must be hot because he himself is hot. His assumed objectivity is in reality an extreme subjectivity. Therefore, when Vinkich introduces him to the opposing side of the debate about the cement-pouring record, he becomes increasingly confused, not knowing where to anchor his opinion, alternately agreeing first with one side and then the other. He has no connection to the workers and to the work site, and, although he can understand "socialist competition" intellectually, without physical connections to the workers and to the site itself, he cannot feel it.

Although Georgy Vasilevich has already been given the grand tour of the construction site suitable to a writer of his stature, only with Vinkich's guidance does he at last begin to understand the site:

> In half an hour Georgy Vasilevich learned more than during the entire three days of his life here. Now construction was no longer for him a generic Construction with a capital "C." Now people were no longer for him generic people, the steppe no longer a generic steppe, the mountains no longer generic mountains, machines no longer generic machines.
>
> Things and people acquired a tangible mutual connection. They stopped being nameless and mute. Vinkich generously gave them names and characteristics.

> And having received a name, a thing or person suddenly began to speak, to act with purpose, to exist consciously in the world, having lost the irritating charm of a rebus for Georgy Vasilevich. (332)

After coming down from his ivory tower—or in this case his Soviet hotel room—and after the narration of the site given by Vinkich on their tour, there is no longer a single person or object at the construction site that he can view without understanding. Things and people begin "to speak, to act with purpose, to exist consciously" because he has connected his intellectual understanding of Communism to the physical world and to the collective—he has achieved true consciousness, which requires a harmony of intellect and the extra-conscious. By achieving this harmony in the rapid pace customary to the construction site, he quickly forgets his own discomfort, and, like the other positive characters at the site, he directs his efforts not toward escaping the heat and the wind but toward beating the record. He works side by side with Vinkich and the others, covered with mud and cement. At one point Georgy Vasilevich has an idea that helps make the cement-pouring more efficient, but when Vinkich credits him with the idea, he insists that it is a joint effort; now he cannot conceive of his thoughts as separate from the collective.

THE WRITER AS TELEGRAPH OPERATOR

Just as in *Cement*, Georgy Vasilevich's newly acquired insight is described as the acquisition of a new language, a renaming of the world. Through Vinkich's fact-filled narration of the site, construction loses its capital "C"—its generic, abstract quality—and becomes real. With his newfound understanding of the "bird language of the machines" (333), the world begins to speak to the writer, supplying him with the words he needs. Therefore, when he writes a telegram about the production feat at the end of the novel, he does so quickly and easily. The writer's questions have vanished, replaced with informative answers:

> "What style!" exclaims Georgy Vasilevich, taking Vinkich by the arm. "Learn it, young man: 'Brigade concrete mixers have set a world record, having beat Kharkov, Kuznetsk, having completed 429 mixtures in a shift. Brigadier Ishchenko, Foreman Weinstein!' Homer! Iliad!" (518)

By participating in the construction feat, Georgy Vasilevich learns to see the connections among all things and people at the site, and having acquired a vision of "reality in its revolutionary development," he writes in a language the entire collective can understand. He thereby provides a new connection to other construction sites where people will be inspired by his writing to join the socialist competition and enter the cyclic transformative moment.

What does it mean to be a telegraph operator, writing in the starts and stops of socialist realism? First it requires an erasure of the writer's individual identity, expressed by the exclusion of Georgy Vasilevich's name from the telegram; the "famous novelist" is now only one of many and considers himself less important than those who organized this work effort, the brigadier and the foreman. Reduced to delivering just the facts, the famous writer has little creative input. He chooses only the starts and stops of the telegram, the empty white spaces that force the information into meaningful units, which can be seen as the tapping of the telegraph key falling into sync with the ticking of the collective clock. This act of telegram writing is echoed in the writing of *Time Forward!* itself by the insertion of a blank space in place of "Chapter 1," which is "omitted for the time being" (197). The narrator impatiently dives into chapter 2 and begins the novel with the ringing of the alarm clock that will also provide its conclusion. We are given chapter 1 only at the end of the book, right before the concluding chapter. Chapter 1 is in the form of a letter from V.K. (Valentin Kataev?), addressed to a special correspondent from the Telegraphic Agency concerning the earlier omission of chapter 1, which is now reinstated to provide the novel with the necessary "denouement," but without breaking the 24-hour period described in the book. Without proof that the cement poured was of high quality (possible only after seven days of drying), there can be no end to the novel—the test ensuring the success of the cement-pouring provides the denouement.

"Chapter 1" contains more than the stress test of a cube of concrete—"V.K." also discusses the writing of his novel, which he assures the special correspondent to be for the most part true: "I hope you will not reproach me a great deal for making some things up" (513). By 1932 a Soviet novel could no longer be sold as entirely fictional. In V.K.'s personal comments in "Chapter 1," he thanks the correspondent: "In a drop of rain you taught me to see a garden" (512), thereby hinting that the relationship between Georgy Vasilevich and the correspondent Vinkich was based on their "real" relationship and that he himself was transformed by the writing experience, brought into Soviet time in the same way that his character was. Chapter 1 is followed immediately by the final chapter of *Time Forward!* in which Georgy Vasilevich composes the telegram, a literary echo of Kataev's own writing—or at least the description of his writing contained in "Chapter 1." As in the telegram, the reader is supposedly given just the facts, punctuated by the starts and stops of the Soviet writer as telegraph operator, who times his creation to the beat of the Soviet clock—there is as little of "V.K." in *Time Forward!* as there is of Georgy Vasilevich in his Homeric telegram.

We see the same effacement of the writer in the perennial rewriting of *Cement,* as Gladkov bows to changing party policy in his continual reworking of the novel to make it less "fictional," that is, more in keeping with the contemporary party version of "reality in its revolutionary development." By 1932 it was becoming increasingly difficult for writers to publish texts that needed such correction. At the end of the First Five-Year Plan many of the early Soviet satirists and fantasists had grown silent, by choice or by force. The speculative nature of their open endings and uncured diagnoses required the active participation of the Soviet reader, which was increasingly viewed as risky in the mounting paranoia of the 1930s Soviet Union. As we have seen in texts such as *Shvambraniia* and *Time Forward!,* both published at the end of the First Five-Year Plan, Soviet writers were working overtime to ensure that the reader would reject the villainous voice and embrace Soviet time. The paranoia that would soon consume Soviet culture is apparent in the extreme satirical attacks by the narrator on the villains of *Time Forward!,* revealing an anxiety that, if they didn't have fangs dripping with spite and lilac ink, the reader might sympathize with these outcasts. Nevertheless, *Time Forward!* demonstrates that prior to the official adoption of socialist realism, selfish desire and fantastic hesitation had already found their socialist realist place in the toolbox of "engineers of the human soul," introduced in the villain so that they could be exposed as unnatural aberrations and expelled, translated by heroes into collective desire and confidence in the eternal repetition of "reality in its revolutionary development," an overlay of Communist utopia on the present that produces a transformative stasis, an ever-repeating and always identical moment of change. Through the strategies of exposure, expulsion, and transformation of villainous desire in a telegraphic message of collective power, the reader has presumably learned the compulsion to understand and ultimately enter Soviet time.

Conclusion

Writers Forward!

> Calm yourselves, Gentlemen! First of all, we are discussing party literature and its subordination to party control. Everyone is free to write and say whatever he likes, without any restrictions. But every voluntary association (including the party) is also free to expel members who use the name of the party to advocate anti-party views.
>
> —Vladimir Lenin, "Party Organization and Party Literature" (1905)

AS THE 1920S CAME TO AN END, proletarian groups increasingly touted Lenin's 1905 article on party literature as the definitive statement not only about *party* writers but about any writer in Soviet society: "Literature must become *part* of the common cause of the proletariat, 'a cog and screw' of one single great Social-Democratic mechanism set in motion by the entire politically-conscious vanguard of the entire working class."[1] As the 1920s progressed, satirists, who had occupied a prominent role in early Soviet literature, were forced to narrow their aim as systemic problems—party problems—became taboo targets; Richard Chapple in the closing lines of his study of 1920s Soviet satire writes that after 1934 satire met its "demise," acquiring "a monotonous tone that . . . overshadowed efforts to revitalize it."[2] And the fantastic, so prevalent in the 1920s, also fell under attack as doubt became tantamount to counterrevolution. A manifesto of the October literary group declared: "All *ideological* doubts are absolutely *inadmissible,* and we shall make a point of bringing them to light."[3] Literary utopias, journeys to other planets, and alternate realities were all seen to point to a lack here on present-day Earth, and as the 1920s drew to a close, proletarians became increasingly hostile to these devices, demanding instead a return to "everyday" proletarian life. Aleksandr Bezymensky wrote: "It's fine to toss the planets about as though they were little lumps of something, and in galvanic verse to celebrate the cosmos. But can you show us the dawn of the future in some chairman of a lumber commissariat. . . . Give up the heavens, forget about *things*, and give us instead the earth and living people."[4] By 1932 the time for dwelling on problems of the past and dreams of the future were over—the focus shifted to construction of the here and now. Richard Stites sees the publication of Jan Larri's *The Land of the Happy* (1931), the last communist utopia to be published during Stalin's lifetime,[5] as the official end of the 1920s: "The death of utopian science fiction in the early 1930s is the perfect metaphor of the death of the utopian revolution of the 1920s."[6] When Russian folklore was "rediscovered" in the 1930s it served only to support Soviet nationalism,[7] and the social and moral speculation found in Western science fiction was eschewed by socialist realist writers who won praise only for popularizing science or preparing the way for scientific innovation.[8]

It has been the thesis of this book, however, that satire and the fantastic did not just vanish or move underground with the official adoption of socialist realism. Instead their energies were channeled into the figure of the villain. Satirical exposure of the beast and the alien are the first step in a strategy that ends in the purging of textual hesitation, accomplished by cleansing the reactionary impulses of the villain and then translating them into a new collective voice. Although I have argued that satire and the fantastic constitute a vital part of socialist realism, satirical exposure and fantastic hesitation vanish before the concluding triumphal scene of a socialist realist text, thereby clearing the way for a conclusive vision of "reality in its revolutionary development." Through the use of fantastic hesitation, the hero rejects the villain and is cleansed of the villain's negative qualities; in theory at least, the reader would follow his example and through the act of reading move into that socialist realist land beyond doubt. I have also argued, however, that a dystopian fear accompanies this strategy, and that Soviet literary culture becomes increasingly centered on controlling the influence of the Soviet villain and conclusively silencing his toxic voice.

REALLY REAL MEN, OR APOLOGIES FOR THE ELEPHANT

Toward the end of *Time Forward!* a letter is inserted attesting that the novel was drawn from real life: "I hope that you will not reproach me especially for having made up some things. For example, the elephant. There really was no elephant. I made him up. But couldn't he have been? Of course, he could have been! More than that, he should have been!" (513). This apology for a fictional elephant typifies the insistence in socialist realist culture that the plot and heroes of every novel are in fact real; they may be overlaid with the ghost of future Communism, but they are echoes not of a time to come but of a cheerful here and now. Many of the classics of socialist realism contain such assertions or pick as their heroes historical figures such as those in Furmanov's *Chapaev* or Ostrovsky's *How the Steel Was Tempered.* Boris Polevoy's *Story of a Real Man,* based on the life of a real Soviet pilot, contains a postscript where the author recounts meeting his hero during the war; the concluding lines tell us that the hero of the novel continues his fight for the Soviet Union: "Life itself is writing the sequel to this story about Aleksey Maresyev—a Real, Soviet Man."[9] Life writes the story—the writer just chooses the metaphors. This insistence on the "real" in socialist realism is crucial to the suppression of fantastic hesitation, the goal of this genre. Socialist realism needs to control the reader's response in order to ensure that he or she is "ideologically remolded," purged of doubt during the reading process; this state of surety must continue long after the final page is turned. The speculative fictions of the early Soviet period—utopias, dystopias, fantastic journeys, and impossible transformations—have no place in a literature of real men and motivated elephants.

Socialist realism locks the present into a never-ending, very real moment of transformation. "Reality in its revolutionary development" is a liminal space, a hybrid of Zamyatin's entropy and revolution—constant transformation, but always into the same thing. The villain is a supernatural creature who exists outside this transformative stasis, an atavism, a throwback to an unsuitable past or a visitor from an unimaginable future. Silencing/expelling him—and along with him fantastic hesitation—is a necessary part of maintaining the purity of the transformative moment that constitutes socialist realism. By cleansing this space of the supernatural, the socialist realist text establishes "reality in its revolutionary development" with the intention that the reader carry this reality into the extra-textual world when the last page is turned. Therefore, every socialist realist assertion of reality must be so convincing that it silences any other voice.

Régine Robin argues that increasingly forceful campaigns for the "normalization" of language in the 1930s created the "mandatory monologism" of socialist realism.[10] This would indeed seem to be the case, since each field of Soviet scholarship describes the world with the same set of adjectives. Every branch of study from biology (Lysenko) to linguistics (Marr) was bent to grow in accordance with the ideas of class struggle and the Marxist stages of history—during the purges, Soviet astronomers were even accused of "non-Marxist" sunspot theories. And when Stalin undertook an intensive study of philosophy, the science of questioning the nature of reality, he was left with only one question: "What's all this got to do with the class struggle?"[11] Convinced that questioning voices had no utility in a society that had already discovered the final answers, Stalin set out to purge philosophers. Soviet society already knew the truth, and could without their help speak this truth in a unified voice, a "monologue," as Robin suggests.

Socialist realism is not, however, a true monologue, but rather one side of a never-ending debate, a perennial dialogue with the villain. In this debate the villain must always lose, but allowing him to speak in the first place constitutes a serious threat to the text's purported control of reader response. What if the reader sides with the wrong voice? How does the socialist realist writer keep that voice from echoing, even after it is silenced? To prevent this misidentification, as the Stalinist period progressed, positive heroes were made more positive and villains more villainous. Eventually the villain was removed altogether, which in the 1950s led to accusations that the socialist realist novel had become "conflictless." Narrating this "conflictlessness," however, is a relentlessly cheerful voice, loudly and stridently trying to convince anyone who would listen that life is indeed, as Stalin once declared, "better and more cheerful."

This attempt to muffle the villain's voice is evident in the piercing exclamations of the cheerful voice of Soviet culture. The ghostly echo of the villain calls out from the dark corners of brightly lit propaganda posters and the unfilled margins of enthusiastic accounts of overfulfilled quotas and record harvests. Socialist realism tries to drown out toxic voices and light up every dark corner with "reality in its revolutionary development," but every time socialist realism lets up its relentless shouting, the faint echoes of the villainous voice are heard from the remaining darkness. After Stalin's death, during the period of the so-called "thaws," the loud, happy voice of socialist realism once again gave way to the subversive sound of the fantastic and satire. In the late 1950s Andrey Sinyavsky famously called for the return of "a phantasmagoric art, with hypotheses instead of a Purpose" when he called for an end to socialist realism.[12] As we have seen in the preceding pages, however, satire and the fantastic were a vital part of socialist realism all along, just waiting, like Bulgakov's dog-man, for the chance to throw off their restraining collars and call out "bad words."

Notes

INTRODUCTION

The chapter epigraph is from Yury Olesha, *Envy*, in *The Portable Twentieth-Century Russian Reader* (New York: Penguin, 1985), 314.

1. For a discussion of the debate concerning Soviet literary heroes in this period see Robert A. Maguire, "Literary Conflicts in the 1920s," *Survey: A Journal of East and West Studies* 18, no. 1 (Winter 1972): 98–127.

2. Leon Trotsky, *Literature and Revolution*, trans. Rose Strunsky (Chicago: Haymarket Books, 2005), 207.

3. For example, see Geoffrey Hosking, *Beyond Socialist Realism: Soviet Fiction Since "Ivan Denisovich"* (London: Granada, 1980), 13–15; and Katerina Clark, *The Soviet Novel: History as Ritual* (Chicago: University of Chicago Press, 1981), 46–89. Marcia Morris places the socialist realist hero in a long line of Russian ascetic heroes, traced back to the Kievan saints' lives but heavily influenced by Nikolay Chernyshevsky's *What Is to Be Done*? (Marcia A. Morris, *Saints and Revolutionaries: The Ascetic Hero in Russian Literature* [New York: State University of New York Press, 1993]).

4. For a representative sampling of such studies, see Rufus W. Mathewson Jr., *The Positive Hero in Russian Literature*, 2nd ed. (Stanford, Calif.: Stanford University Press, 1975); Clark, *The Soviet Novel*; and Morris, *Saints and Revolutionaries*.

5. In Russian, the word for "spontaneity" (*stikhiinost'*) might better be translated as "elementalness," since it derives from the word for the "elements" (*stikhiia*). It is a primitive force that hearkens back to the basic elements of ancient Greek scientific thought: earth, wind, fire, and water. Although the term is often associated with Lenin, Leopold Haimson views it as informing the thought of the Russian intelligentsia throughout the nineteenth century; for example, in the 1860s Mikhail Bakunin viewed the Russian peasant as the elemental cleansing force that would scour away ancient, decaying civilizations. (Leopold Haimson, "Lenin's Revolutionary Career Revisited: Some Observations on Recent Discussions," *Kritika: Explorations in Russian and Eurasian History* 5, no. 1 [Winter 2004]: 57.)

6. Vladimir Il'ich Lenin, *What Is to Be Done? Burning Questions of Our Movement*, in *The Lenin Anthology* (New York: W.W. Norton, 1975), 29.

7. In her seminal book *The Soviet Novel: History as Ritual* (1981), Katerina Clark calls the spontaneity-consciousness paradigm "one of the key binary oppositions in Russian culture" and places it as central to the "master plot" of the socialist realist novel, in which the Soviet hero moves from "a state of relative 'spontaneity' to a higher degree of 'consciousness,' which he attains by some individual revolution" (Clark, *The Soviet Novel*, 20, 15, 16).

8. In February 2001 a conference was held in Essen, Germany, on the centennial of *What Is to Be Done?* (Lars T. Lih, "How a Founding Document Was Found, or One Hundred Years of Lenin's *What Is to Be Done?*" *Kritika: Explorations in Russian and Eurasian History* 4, no. 1 [Winter 2003]: 5). Anna Krylova was one of the participants, and, two years later, a special issue of *Slavic Review* was devoted to Krylova's article on instinct and two responses to the article by Igal Halfin and Reginald Zelnik.

9. Lih, "How a Founding Document Was Found," 27.

10. Anna Krylova, "Beyond the Spontaneity-Consciousness Paradigm: 'Class Instinct' as a Promising Category of Historical Analysis," *Slavic Review* 62, no. 1 (Spring 2003): 2. Krylova focuses on the term "instinct," which she has revealed to be prominent in Bolshevik discourse of the first thirty years of the twentieth century; she argues that this term arose after the 1905 uprisings, when Bolsheviks needed to explain how workers who had not yet achieved the consciousness necessary for revolution nevertheless took positive steps in that direction. Bolsheviks found an explanation in "class instinct" (*klassovyi instinkt, klassovoe chut'e*) or "revolutionary instinct" (*revoliutsionnyi instinkt*); workers "felt" (*pochuvstvovali*) what would further the movement to Communism before they consciously understood where they were headed. Therefore, Krylova suggests that feeling was as crucial as thought to the Bolshevik concept of the New Person, and she demonstrates the pervasive use of instinct in writings from the major figures of the Bolshevik movement, Anatoly Lunacharsky, Aleksandra Kollontai, Aleksandr Bogdanov, Lev Kamenev, Grigory Zinoviev, Leon Trotsky, and Joseph Stalin (Krylova, 16–23). Reginald E. Zelnik, although agreeing with Krylova, stresses that the concept of instinct should be seen not to replace the spontaneity-consciousness paradigm but rather to "enrich" it (Reginald E. Zelnik, "A Paradigm Lost? Response to Anna Krylova," *Slavic Review* 62, no. 1 [Spring 2003]: 33). Igal Halfin notes that the Bolsheviks' use of instinct fits in well with Marx's view of history, in which the intelligentsia serves as brain and the proletariat as heart (Igal Halfin, "Between Instinct and Mind: The Bolshevik View of the Proletarian Self," *Slavic Review* 62, no. 1 [Spring 2003]: 35).

11. Irina Gutkin, for example, traces the socialist realist aesthetic to two avant-gardes, the political (the Bolsheviks) and the artistic (the symbolists and futurists) (Irina Gutkin, *The Cultural Origins of the Socialist Realist Aesthetic,*

1890–1934 [Evanston, Ill.: Northwestern University Press, 1999]). See also Boris Groys's analysis of socialist realism as the culmination of the avant-garde experiment in the visual arts (Boris Groys, *The Total Art of Stalinism: Avant-Garde, Aesthetic Dictatorship, and Beyond* [Princeton, N.J.: Princeton University Press, 1992]). For an example of scholars who trace socialist realism to the theories of proletarian literary groups see Herman Ermolaev, *Soviet Literary Theories 1917–1934: The Genesis of Socialist Realism*, University of California Publications in Modern Philology (Berkeley: University of California Press, 1963). For a recent evaluation of the influence of proletarian groups on socialist realism, see Evgeny Dobrenko, *Aesthetics of Alienation: Reassessment of Early Soviet Cultural Theories* (Evanston, Ill.: Northwestern University Press, 2005), 109–26.

12. Yury Olesha's speech to the first Congress of Soviet Writers reads like an extended apology for his most famous hero, Nikolay Kavalerov of his 1927 novel *Envy* (see chapter 3).

13. I will discuss these genres in more detail in the relevant chapters (satire in chapter 2 and the fantastic in chapter 3).

CHAPTER ONE

The chapter epigraph is from Karl Marx, "Capital," in *The Portable Karl Marx*, trans. and ed. Eugene Kamenka (New York: Penguin Books, 1983), 452.

1. Ilya Ilf and Yevgeny Petrov, "How the Soviet 'Robinson' Was Written," in *"The Fatal Eggs" and Other Soviet Satire* (New York: Macmillan, 1965), 226.

2. Mircea Eliade, *Images and Symbols: Studies in Religious Symbolism* (Princeton, N.J.: Princeton University Press, 1991), 35.

3. Ilf and Petrov, "How the Soviet 'Robinson' Was Written," 225.

4. Ibid., 226.

5. Ibid., 227.

6. For a complete history of the Proletkult, see Lynn Mally, *Culture of the Future: The Proletkult Movement in Revolutionary Russia* (Berkeley: University of California Press, 1990). For a recent reassessment, see Dobrenko, *Aesthetics of Alienation*, 10–30.

7. Aleksandr Bogdanov was the pseudonym of Aleksandr Aleksandrovich Malinovsky (1873–1928). Much scholarship has focused on Bogdanov's monist philosophy and especially on his tectology, a system of organization commonly seen as a precursor of cybernetics or systems thinking; for a discussion of tectology in *Red Star* see Georgii Gloveli, "Bogdanov as Scientist and Utopian," in *Bogdanov and His Work: A Guide to the Published and Unpublished Works of Alexander A. Bogdanov (Malinovsky) 1873–1928* (Aldershot: Ashgate, 1998), 44–46. For a more detailed discussion of Bogdanov's theories, see Kenneth Martin Jensen, *Beyond Marx and Mach: Aleksandr Bogdanov's "Philosophy*

of Living Experience" (London: D. Reidel, 1978). For a comparison of Bogdanov's theories with Lenin's, see Zenovia A. Sochor, *Revolution and Culture: The Bogdanov-Lenin Controversy* (Ithaca, N.Y.: Cornell University Press, 1988).

8. Aleksandr Bogdanov, "Proletariat i iskusstvo: Rezoliutsiia, predlozheniia A. Bogdanovym na Pervoi Vserossiiskoi Konferentsii Proletarskikh kul'turno-prosvetitel'nykh organizatsii," in *Literaturnye manifesty ot simvolizma k oktiabriu: Sbornik materialov* (Moscow: Federatsiia, 1929), 130. Translation is mine.

9. Bogdanov, "Proletariat i iskusstvo [doklad]," in *O proletarskoi kul'ture, 1904–1924* (Leningrad: Kniga, 1924), 121.

10. Although Proletkult writers viewed past literature as tainted by ruling ideas, they also asserted that its components could be salvaged. A resolution of the First All-Union Conference of Proletarian Writers states that it "is necessary not only to make use of the old culture, but, in Ilich's phrase, to 'rework' it" ("The Ideological Front and Literature (1925): Resolution of the First All-Union Conference of Proletarian Writers," in *Bolshevik Visions: First Phase of the Cultural Revolution in Soviet Russia,* ed. William G. Rosenberg [Ann Arbor, Mich.: Ardis, 1984], 472).

11. Bogdanov, "Proletariat i iskusstvo [doklad]," 119. Translation is mine.

12. Phillip E. Wegner, *Imaginary Communities: Utopia, the Nation, and the Spatial Histories of Modernity* (Berkeley: University of California Press, 2002), 149.

13. In Zamyatin's many essays from the late 1910s and early 1920s, he repeatedly accuses Soviet writers of abandoning revolution to write "useful" literature, thereby promoting the stagnation of human thought that occurs in entropy. The wild "Scythians" had become domesticated (Yevgeny Zamyatin, "Scythians?" in *A Soviet Heretic,* ed. and trans. Mirra Ginsburg [London: Quartet Books, 1991], 21–33). And the "Futurists" had transformed into "Presentists" (Yevgeny Zamyatin, "The Presentists," in *Zamyatin's "We": A Collection of Critical Essays,* ed. Gary Kern, trans. Joe Denny [Ann Arbor, Mich.: Ardis, 1988], 263–65). Zamyatin is especially dismissive of the proletarians: " 'The Proletcults have not produced anyone or anything.' And indeed they could not. Dogma, static positions, consonance—all these are obstacles to catching the disease of art" (Yevgeny Zamyatin, "The New Russian Prose," in *A Soviet Heretic,* 92–93). For a comparison of Zamyatin's *We* with the imagery of the Proletkult, see Harry Weber and Kathleen Lewis, "*Zamyatin's We,* the Proletarian Poets and Bogdanov's *Red Star,*" in *Zamyatin's "We": A Collection of Critical Essays,* 186–208.

14. For a comparison of *Red Star* to other European utopias, see Mark B. Adams, " 'Red Star': Another Look at Aleksandr Bogdanov," *Slavic Review* 48, no. 1 (Spring 1989): 1–15; and Wegner, *Imaginary Communities,* 99–146. *Red Star* had a considerable impact on Soviet fantastic literature of the 1920s, influencing many communist utopias, from Vivian Itin's *The Land of Gonguri* (1922) to Jan Larri's *The Land of the Happy* (1931); see Richard Stites, *Revolutionary*

Dreams: Utopian Vision and Experimental Life in the Russian Revolution (New York: Oxford University Press, 1989), 171–79. For a discussion of how *Red Star* fits into the tradition of Mars in literature, see Robert Markley, *Dying Planet: Mars in Science and the Imagination* (Durham, N.C.: Duke University Press, 2005), 134–46.

15. Ellen Chances, "The Superfluous Man in Russian Literature," in *The Routledge Companion to Russian Literature,* ed. Neil Cornwell (London: Routledge, 2001), 111.

16. Andrei Siniavsky, "On Socialist Realism," in *The Trial Begins and On Socialist Realism,* trans. Max Hayward (Berkeley: University of California Press, 1960), 189–90.

17. Aleksandr Bogdanov, *Krasnaia zvezda: Roman-utopiia* (Petrograd: Petrogradskogo Soveta Rabochikh i Krasnoarmeiskikh Deputatov, 1918), 108. All quotations are taken from this source and followed by page numbers in parentheses. Translations are mine.

18. Many commentators on *Red Star* focus on the novel and its allusions to the Bolshevik movement and its individual members, especially Lenin. See, for example, Wegner, *Imaginary Communities,* 113.

19. The idea of Russia as an immature, undeveloped youth was not new to the 1920s; in fact, it goes back to the eighteenth century (Stites, *Revolutionary Dreams,* 24). And by the early 1920s, such an image of the Soviet Union was common in war-ravaged Europe (Robert C. Williams, "'Changing Landmarks' in Russian Berlin, 1922–1924," *Slavic Review* 27, no. 4 [December 1968]: 581).

20. The Martians' vision of maturation echoes Ernst Haeckle's "Law of Recapitulation," by which embryos pass through the species' evolutionary development. Mark Adams suggests that Bogdanov based his scientific worldview on Haeckel's "monism," which asserts that all life has a common genetic basis (Adams, "'Red Star,'" 10–11). See also Wegner, *Imaginary Communities,* 105–6. For a study of Bogdanov as proletarian scientist, see Nikolai Krementsov, *A Martian Stranded on Earth: Alexander Bogdanov, Blood Transfusions, and Proletarian Science* (Chicago: University of Chicago Press, 2011).

21. This is how Phillip Wegner reads the ending (Wegner, *Imaginary Communities,* 106–7).

22. Other similarities suggest that *Red Star* draws on Mikhail Lermontov's archetypal superfluous man, Grigory Pechorin of *A Hero of Our Time* (*Geroi nashego vremeni,* 1841). Like Lermontov's *Hero, Red Star* uses the device of a found journal framed by the comments of an editor. Both chronicle the hero's travels in a strange land where he is an alien. Faced with a personal threat, each "hero" murders a hated romantic rival who threatens his life. And each novel ends with a prediction by the "editor" that the hero has gone off to battle seeking death, leaving only his journal as evidence of his quest for truth. The functions of the two journals are, however, diametrically opposed. Pechorin's jour-

nal serves to nurture his delusions; through writing, he remains or becomes even more superfluous. On its pages, he continually blames his habit of destroying lives on society. The conclusion of the novel, "The Fatalist," can be seen as Pechorin's final excuse; despite the final chapter's lament for a generation without purpose, a generation with nothing left to do but play the games of society, the final entry of his journal still suggests that he believes that he has had no choice in the events described previously. Douglas Greenfield also notes this resemblance in his study of vampirism in *Red Star,* noting Pechorin's comparison of himself to vampire (Douglas Greenfield, "Revenants and Revolutionaries: Body and Society in Bogdanov's Martian Novels," *Slavic and East European Journal* 50, no. 4 [Winter 2006]: 633).

23. Evgenii Zamiatin, *My: Roman, povesti, rasskazy, p'esy, stat'i i vospominaniia* (Kishinev: Literatura artistike, 1989), 10. All quotations are from this source and followed by page numbers in parentheses. Translations are mine. The publishing history of *We* is complex, appearing first in English in 1924 and finally in a Russian version in 1927 (publishers claimed that this version had been translated from the Czech). An authoritative Russian version appeared in 1952 (New York). *We* was published in the Soviet Union only in 1988. For a detailed discussion see Robert Russell, *Zamiatin's "We,"* Critical Studies in Russian Literature (London: Bristol Classical, 2000), 1–5. Russell also provides an excellent survey of scholarship on *We* (Russell, *Zamiatin's "We,"* 5–43).

24. See, for example, Stites, *Revolutionary Dreams,* 188–89.

25. Harry Weber and Kathleen Lewis have documented Zamyatin's parodic treatment of a series of symbols and images from Bogdanov's *Red Star* in Zamyatin's *We* (Weber and Lewis, "Zamyatin's *We,*" 196–205). See also Russell, *Zamiatin's "We,"* 40–42.

26. Yevgeny Zamyatin, "On Literature, Revolution, Entropy, and Other Matters," in *A Soviet Heretic,* trans. Mirra Ginsburg (London: Quartet Books, 1991), 107.

27. Zamyatin, "On Literature," 108.

28. For a discussion of the second law of thermodynamics in Zamyatin's *We,* see Bruce Clarke, *Energy Forms: Allegory and Science in the Era of Classical Thermodynamics* (Ann Arbor: University of Michigan Press, 2001), 137–51.

29. See, for example, D. J. Richards, *Zamyatin: A Soviet Heretic* (London: Bowes and Bowes, 1962), 56. I-330 has been seen to represent many things by scholars, often an aspect of D-503's own psyche. Christopher Collins, in a Jungian interpretation, suggests that she is a manifestation of D-503's anima and sets out to put him in touch with his unconscious (Christopher Collins, "Zamyatin's *We* as Myth," in *Zamyatin's "We": A Collection of Critical Essays,* ed. Gary Kern [Ann Arbor, Mich.: Ardis, 1988], 71). Margaret Wise Petrochenkov asserts that I-330 awakens castration anxiety in D-503 (Margaret Wise Petrochenkov, "Castration Anxiety and the Other in Zamyatin's *We,*" in *The Fantastic Other: An*

Interface of Perspectives, ed. Brett Cooke, Critical Studies, vol. 11 [Amsterdam: Rodopi, 1998], 245). For an overview of such approaches, see Brett Cooke, *Human Nature in Utopia: Zamyatin's "We"* (Evanston, Ill.: Northwestern University Press, 2002), 112–17.

30. Andrew Barratt has written that D-503's journal entries are "very much like daily sessions with an absent psychiatrist" (Andrew Barratt, "The X-Factor in Zamyatin's *We,*" *Modern Language Review* 80, no. 3 [July 1985]: 669).

31. This has been seen as a satire on Aleksey Gastev's machinism; for a discussion of Gastev's influence on *We,* see Patricia Carden, "Utopia and Anti-Utopia: Aleksei Gastev and Evgeny Zamyatin," *Russian Review* 46, no. 1 (January 1987): 1–18.

32. Ray Parrott writes that eyes "are the direct means by which the *real* selves of the rebellious citizenry of the Only State are revealed" (Ray Parrott, "The Eye in *We,*" in *Zamyatin's "We": A Collection of Critical Essays,* ed. Gary Kern [Ann Arbor, Mich.: Ardis, 1988], 108. When D-503 looks into the crystal-clear eyes of O, however, he sees only what he wants to see—the entropic self that is promised by the One State. By looking into the eyes of I-330, D-503 sees not *her* inner self, but a reflection of *his* gestating "new" self, lit by fire, a traditional image of revolution for Zamyatin.

33. Eliot Borenstein also equates the awakening of the "I" with D-503's writing (Eliot Borenstein, "The Plural Self: Zamjatin's *We* and the Logic of Synecdoche," *Slavic and East European Journal* 40, no. 4 [Winter 1996]: 668). Borenstein proceeds to examine D-503's awakening through the recurring device of synecdoche.

34. R-13's name, which incorporates the English letter "R," is an inverse of the Russian first-person singular pronoun. Just as I-330 speaks for the "I" outside the entropy of the One State, so too does the backward "I" of D-503's illogical friend. Like I-330 he asks disturbing questions and muddies D-503's clarity.

35. Christopher Collins views R-13 as the "male sexual drive" and the spraying saliva as representing semen (Collins, "Zamyatin's *We* as Myth," 74). R-13 has frequently been seen as an allusion to Pushkin, whose portrait appears at the ancient house (Russell, *Zamiatin's "We,"* 64).

36. The One State, like Bogdanov's Martians, has transformed language, obliterated meanings not compatible with communism, and unified its citizens under one tongue. Nevertheless, each of its citizens seems to be afflicted like R-13 with a speech defect. Even the simple O-90 is described as a defective machine when she speaks. In the opening march (entry 2), she speaks that for which there are no words in the language of the One State: proprietary love. She disrupts the orderly flow of people and thoughts with her "inappropriate" assertion to the newcomer I-330 that D-503 is registered to her. Her disruptive speech is destructive to the entropic clarity of the One State and D-503, but it is also fertile, as seen in her "illegal" repeated expressions of desire for a child,

despite the One State's assertion that she is below the "maternal norm." In her assertions of love and desire, the comfortable, familiar O-90 becomes a revolutionary poet through her defective speech. Even the machines D-503 idolizes have speech defects—his childhood teaching machine when first plugged in would always utter "Plia plia." The adult D-503, who finds the imperfections in himself and those around him so disturbing, remembers "Pliapa" with affection precisely because of this verbal tic. By writing, D-503 becomes like this flawed "father," endowed with a "speech defect," the increasing inability to speak for the One State.

37. Nadya Peterson, *Subversive Imaginations: Fantastic Prose and the End of Soviet Literature, 1970s–1990s* (Boulder, Colo.: Westview, 1997), 42.

CHAPTER TWO

The chapter epigraph is quoted in Tricia Starks, *The Body Soviet: Propaganda, Hygiene, and the Revolutionary State* (Madison: University of Wisconsin Press, 2008), 12.

1. Between January 1919 and June 1922, over thirteen million items of public health literature were published (Starks, *The Body Soviet,* 5).

2. S. A. Smith, "The Social Meanings of Swearing: Workers and Bad Language in Late Imperial and Early Soviet Russia," *Past and Present* 160 (August 1998): 173–78.

3. Quoted in S. A. Smith, "Social Meanings," 190.

4. Leon Trotsky, "The Struggle for Cultured Speech," in *Problems of Everyday Life and Other Writings on Culture & Science* (New York: Monad, 1973), 53.

5. Michael S. Gorham, "Mastering the Perverse: State Building and Language 'Purification' in Early Soviet Russia," *Slavic Review* 59, no. 1 (Spring 2000): 135.

6. S. A. Smith, "Social Meanings," 192–93.

7. Ibid., 196.

8. Katerina Clark has called efforts in the 1920s to change people by changing language "promethean linguistics" (Katerina Clark, *Petersburg, Crucible of Cultural Revolution* [Cambridge, Mass.: Harvard University Press, 1995], 201–23).

9. Pavel Kerzhentsev published a guide entitled *How to Read a Book* in 1925, in which he chronicles how and where to sit. For a discussion of such advice literature in the early Soviet period, see Catriona Kelly, *Refining Russia: Advice Literature, Polite Culture, and Gender from Catherine to Yeltsin* (Oxford: Oxford University Press, 2001), 230–311.

10. For a complete history of satire in the early Soviet period, see Richard L. Chapple, *Soviet Satire of the Twenties,* University of Florida Humanities Monograph, no. 47 (Gainesville: University Presses of Florida, 1980).

11. The original title of *Heart of a Dog* was *A Dog's Happiness: a Monster Story (Sobach'e schast'e: Chudovishchnaia istoriia)*. It was written in the first months of 1925 and was initially accepted for publication by the almanac *Nedra;* Bulgakov also contracted with MXAT to adapt the novel for the stage. However, in 1926 Bulgakov's manuscript was confiscated and publication and staging plans were canceled. Although the manuscript was returned to Bulgakov two years later due to the intervention of Maksim Gorky, it was not published in the Soviet Union during Bulgakov's lifetime. It appeared for the first time in Germany in *Grani,* no. 69 (1968): 3–85. However, in Russia the novel was not published until Gorbachev's glasnost' period, when it finally appeared in the journal *Znamia* in 1987. It has since been staged several times; for a discussion of these theatrical productions, see Nadine Natov, "Ot teksta k stsene: Povest' 'Sobach'e serdtse' Mikhaila Bulgakova i ee teatral'naia interpretatsiia," *Zapiski russkoi akademicheskoi gruppy v S.Sh.A.* 24 (1991): 89–131.

12. A version of the following discussion of *Heart of a Dog* was published separately as Eric Laursen, "Bad Words Are Not Allowed!: Language and Transformation in Mikhail Bulgakov's *Heart of a Dog," Slavic and East European Journal* 51, no. 3 (Fall 2007): 491–513.

13. Mikhail Bulgakov, *Sobach'e Serdtse* (London: Bristol Classical, 1994), 89–90. All quotations are taken from this source and are followed by page numbers in parentheses. Translations are mine.

14. See Diana L. Burgin, "Bulgakov's Early Tragedy of the Scientist-Creator: An Interpretation of *The Heart of a Dog," Slavic and East European Journal* 22, no. 4 (1978): 494, 501; Sheelagh Duffin Graham, "Bulgakov's 'Sobach'e serdtse': A Polemical Povest'," *Journal of Russian Studies* 33 (1977): 29; Helena Goscilo, "Point of View in Bulgakov's *Heart of a Dog," Russian Literature Triquarterly* 15 (1978): 289–90; Natov, "Ot teksta," 80; Ellendea Proffer, *Bulgakov, Life and Work* (Ann Arbor, Mich.: Ardis, 1984), 133; Christine Rydel, "Bulgakov and H.G. Wells," *Russian Literature Triquarterly* 15 (1978): 307. Edythe Haber takes another view, noting that in his defense of material things, the professor shares "spiritual underpinnings" with the dog-man (Edythe C. Haber, *Mikhail Bulgakov: The Early Years* [Cambridge, Mass.: Harvard University Press, 1998], 220), and that, in his eugenic work, "Preobrazhensky shares the radicals' readiness to subordinate the individual living creature and traditional ethics to the abstract goal of improving humanity" (Haber, *Mikhail Bulgakov,* 214). However, she sees the professor as redeeming himself through his relationship with Bormenthal and in dissuading him from crime (Haber, *Mikhail Bulgakov,* 221–24).

15. The name "Preobrazhenskii" also has religious significance, since "preobrazhenie" also means "transfiguration." In the operating room he is compared to a "priest" (35) and a "deity" (35). Moreover, when he operates, the room is filled with blinding bright white light reminiscent of the biblical transfiguration. Eugenics was commonly seen as a "civic religion" in the first decades of the twentieth century. The Soviet eugenicist Nikolay Konstantinovich Kol'tsov as-

serted: "Eugenics is the religion of the future and it awaits its prophets" (quoted in Mark B. Adams, *The Wellborn Science: Eugenics in Germany, France, Brazil, and Russia* [New York: Oxford University Press, 1990], 162). Haber discusses the many comparisons of religion and science in the novel (Haber, *Mikhail Bulgakov,* 215–16).

16. In her encyclopedic study of the mad scientist, Roslynn D. Haynes lists Preobrazhensky in a chapter entitled "The Amoral Scientist," an archetype who embraces science for its own sake (Roslynn D. Haynes, *From Faust to Strangelove: Representations of the Scientist in Western Literature* [Baltimore: Johns Hopkins University Press, 1994], 245).

17. It is tempting to equate Professor Preobrazhensky with Trotsky and his ideas of constructing the new person through culture and clean language. Edythe Haber has argued that Rokk, from Bulgakov's other mad-scientist story, *Fateful Eggs* (*Rokovye iaitsa,* 1925), represents Trotsky and his ideas of societal improvement through science and high art (Haber, *Mikhail Bulgakov,* 196–200).

18. Scholars who interpret Preobrazhensky positively draw on Bulgakov's nostalgia for his childhood home, which was very like the lovingly depicted Turbin home in *White Guard;* they view Preobrazhensky's apartment as a similar refuge from the vulgar world. Mariia Shneerson is perhaps the most ardent in this interpretation (Mariia Shneerson, "Chto mozhet vyiti iz etogo Sharikova?" *Grani* 42, no. 150 [1988]: 145). But in Bulgakov's work beautifully furnished apartments are not always a refuge for those who love home and family. In *The Master and Margarita,* Margarita is miserable in her luxurious penthouse. And Berlioz's coveted apartment does not make him a hero any more than Professor Preobrazhensky's sparkling dining room does. After Berlioz's death, his uncle displays a flawed human nature by caring more about claiming the apartment than claiming his nephew's body, and Aloisy Mogarych plays Judas in an attempt to acquire the Master's cozy retreat. If anything, a love for comfortable apartments and material luxury signals a worsening of the human character in much of Bulgakov's work. As Edythe Haber notes, the professor has no love of *family,* a crucial element of home for Bulgakov (Haber, *Mikhail Bulgakov,* 213). For a discussion of home in *The Master and Margarita,* see Amy C. Singleton, *No Place Like Home: The Literary Artist and Russia's Search for Cultural Identity* (Albany: State University of New York Press, 1997), 117–42.

19. Suzanne Fusso connects the repeated use of the word "ruin" (*razrukha*) in the novel with Mayakovsky's poster figure with the same name, a gremlin-like destroyer of property (Suzanne Fusso, "Failures of Transformation in 'Sobach'e serdtse,'" *Slavic and East European Journal* 33, no. 3 [Fall 1989]: 394).

20. The dog's submission is also signaled by the change from first-person narration (by the dog) before he enters the apartment to third-person after. Suzanne Fusso interprets the dog's first-person narration as a pose on the

part of the primary third-person narrator, "an *imitation* of a dog's-eye view—a kind of ventriloquism" (Fusso, "Failures," 390). Helena Goscilo argues that the first-person dog narration is used for several reasons: for comic effect, to make the reader like the dog, and to elevate Preobrazhensky (Goscilo, "Point of View," 286).

21. Henrietta Mondry views the professor's feeding the dog "human" food as "aimed at socializing and civilizing Sharik" (Henrietta Mondry, "Beyond Scientific Transformation in Bulgakov's *The Heart of a Dog*," *Australian Slavonic and East European Studies* 10, no. 2 [1996]: 5). Ronald LeBlanc attributes the dog's transformation in Professor Preobrazhensky's apartment to an abundance of food; the dog moves from the "realm of necessity" to the "domain of pleasure" (Ronald D. LeBlanc, "Feeding a Poor Dog a Bone: The Quest for Nourishment in Bulgakov's *Sobach'e serdtse*," *Russian Review* 52, no. 1 [January 1993]: 65). LeBlanc views the dog's acquisition of food as symbolic of the acquisition of culture (LeBlanc, "Feeding," 58).

22. Haber also notes the resemblance between dog and master, seeing the subordination of the professor as a result of the New Economic Policy (Haber, *Mikhail Bulgakov*, 214). I would argue, however, that *Heart of a Dog* makes a more universal statement about science and state power. Haber argues that dog and master bear only a passing resemblance because the professor is too "insubordinate" (Haber, *Mikhail Bulgakov*, 215).

23. Helena Goscilo argues that Bormenthal's journal "humanizes" the doctors and serves to distance the reader from the likeable Sharik as the negative Sharikov enters. She also argues that the journal serves to further elevate Preobrazhensky in the reader's estimation: "he earns the reader's unreserved respect" (Goscilo, "Point of View," 287–88).

24. Later, in the third dining-room scene, a volume of Engels is brought into the dining room, and the professor, in frustration, orders that it be burnt.

25. For a discussion of Professor Preobrazhensky's musical selections, see Natov, "Ot teksta," 81–87.

26. Suzanne Fusso and Sergei Shargorodskii link the name to one of Mayakovsky's clients, Mospoligraf, and therefore to Mayakovsky (Fusso, "Failures," 398n11 and Sergei Shargorodskii, "Sobach'e serdtse, ili Chudovishchnaia istoriia," *Literaturnoe Obozrenie* 5 [1991]: 87). Fusso reads the novel as a rejection of Soviet propagandists, especially Vladimir Mayakovsky, whose agitprop work sought to transform society with words (Fusso, "Failures," 392–94). Haber, on the other hand, reads the name as a "backward echo" of the professor's name; she argues extensively and convincingly that they are spiritually very much the same, but, in their opposing tastes (high vs. low culture), they embody two extremes resulting from the New Economic Policy (Haber, *Mikhail Bulgakov*, 219–20).

27. Sharikov chooses his name from the calendar entry for March 4. Per-

haps Bulgakov intended this as a reference to Lenin's final article "Better Fewer, but Better" ("Luchshe men'she, da luchshe"), which was printed in *Pravda* on March 4, 1923. The article, which discussed reorganized state apparatus, is often seen as an attack on Stalin. Sharikov has frequently been seen as a Stalin figure.

28. Printers were among the first professions to unionize; their union was particularly strong and active in the decade leading up to the 1917 revolutions, both in supporting workers' rights and in fighting censorship; see Charles A. Ruud, "The Printing Press as an Agent of Political Change in Early Twentieth-Century Russia," *Russian Review* 40, no. 4 (October 1981): 378–95.

29. Diana Burgin also notes that the journal takes place during the Christmas season, but uses the new calendar for her analysis of Sharikov as a "reverse Christ" (thus she finds the December 25 note that the dog's health has improved to be an indicator of "birth") (Burgin, "Bulgakov's Early Tragedy," 501–4).

30. Many scholars see the operation itself as an allegory for the revolution. See Peter Doyle, "Bulgakov's Satirical View of Revolution in 'Rokovye iaitsa' and *Sobach'e serdtse*," *Canadian Slavonic Papers* 20, no. 3 (September 1978): 467–82; Michael Glenny, "Introduction," in *Heart of a Dog: A Novel by Mikhail Bulgakov* (New York: Harcourt, Brace & World, 1968), viii; Proffer, *Bulgakov*. Most of these interpretations have in common the idea that Preobrazhensky represents Lenin; S. V. Nikol'skii supports this view by seeing "Il'ich" contained in the professor's first name and patronymic (S. V. Nikol'skii, "Na grani metafor i alliuzii [o nekotorykh zashifrovannykh motivakh v antiutopiiakh Bulgakova]," *Izvestiia Akademii Nauk, Seriia literatury i iazyka* 58, no. 1 [January–February 1999]: 12). The most detailed—and certainly the most entertaining—of these interpretations is by Solomon Ioffe, in which he assigns historical figures to each of the characters in the novel. Sharik, Klim Chugunkin, and Sharikov are all Stalin at different times after the revolution, Preobrazhensky is Lenin, Zina is Zinoviev, Darya is Dzerzhinsky, and the stuffed owl is Nadezhda Krupskaya, Lenin's wife (Solomon Ioffe, "Tainopis' v *Sobach'em serdtse* Bulgakova," *Novyi zhurnal* 168–69 [1987]: 260–74).

31. Julie Clarke, "The Human / Not Human in the Work of Orlan and Stelarc," in *The Cyborg Experiments: The Extensions of Body in the Media Age* (London: Continuum, 2002), 35.

32. Jeffrey Jerome Cohen, "Monster Culture (Seven Theses)," in *Monster Theory: Reading Culture* (Minneapolis: University of Minnesota Press, 1996), 6.

33. Early in the year 1925, Bulgakov published his satirical novella *Fateful Eggs* (*Rokovye iaitsa*) in the Soviet journal *Nedra*. In *Fateful Eggs* a Soviet official appropriates a scientist's "red ray" and hatches a swarm of malicious reptiles and ostriches that ravage the Soviet countryside. The novella can easily be read as an invective against the Bolshevik Revolution, and, although it was praised by many critics, proletarians predictably attacked it as anti-Soviet. M. Lirov, in

his review of *Fateful Eggs,* wondered how the novella had been published in a Soviet journal, since it was obviously "intended exclusively for the White Guard press" (quoted in Haber, *Mikhail Bulgakov,* 186). For a discussion of propaganda in *Fateful Eggs,* see Eric Laursen, "An Electrician's Utopia: Mikhail Bulgakov's *Fateful Eggs,*" *Slavic and East European Journal* 56, no. 1 (2012): 56–70.

34. Quoted in Haber, *Mikhail Bulgakov,* 207.

35. Chapple, *Soviet Satire,* 9.

36. Julie A. Cassiday explains the name "Prisypkin" is derived from *syp'* (rash) and *prisypka* (dusting powder): "Prisypkin will always be associated with itchy maladies of the skin that discomfort the Soviet body politic" (Julie A. Cassiday, "Flash Floods, Bedbugs, and Saunas: Social Hygiene in Mayakovsky's Theatrical Satires of the 1920s," in *Against the Grain: Parody, Satire and Intertextuality in Russian Literature,* ed. Janet Tucker [Bloomington, Ind.: Slavica, 2002], 138).

37. Vladimir Maiakovskii, *Klop* (Durham, N.C.: University of Durham, 1985), 111. All quotations are taken from this source. Translations are mine. Subsequent quotes will be followed by page numbers in parentheses.

38. The character Oleg Bayan was probably based in part on the poet Vladimir Sidorov, who wrote a book of speeches and rituals designed for new "soviet" ceremonies, including wedding feasts, under the pseudonym "Vadim Bayan"; Robert Russell argues that Oleg Bayan's speeches are parodies of those written by "Vadim Bayan" (Robert Russell, "Introduction," in *"Klop"* (Durham, N.C.: University of Durham, 1985), 28–29.

39. Mayakovsky said that he chose the poets Zharov and Utkin for the firemen's speech, because "they draw Tolstoyan conclusions and today no longer struggle" (quoted in Russell, "Introduction," 124–25n78).

40. The advertisement for the play sums up the expected reaction of the Soviet theatergoer to satire: "This is not about you, but about your friend" (Maiakovskii, *Klop,* 116; translation is mine).

41. In Meyerhold's production of Mayakovsky's *Mystery Bouffe,* based on the biblical story of Noah's ark, the "unclean," who are to start the world anew, appropriately all wear identical *prozodezhda* (Konstantin Rudnitsky, *Russian and Soviet Theater 1905–1932,* trans. Roxane Permar [New York: Harry N. Abrams, 1988], 43).

42. Rudnitsky, *Russian and Soviet Theater,* 258–59.

43. A frequent conclusion of scholars is that Mayakovsky, although detesting the values Prisypkin represents, nevertheless includes himself in Prisypkin's cage. For example, Edward Brown writes: "Into a play that was planned as a simple propaganda exercise Mayakovsky, characteristically, injected a moment of his own pain, and a muffled cry for help" (Edward J. Brown, *Mayakovsky: A Poet in the Revolution* [Princeton, N.J.: Princeton University Press, 1973], 332).

44. Chapple, *Soviet Satire,* 17. Peter Henry sees a similar fading away during the Stalinist period (Peter Henry, comp. and ed., *Classics of Soviet Satire,* vol. 1 of *Anthology of Soviet Satire* [London, 1972], xiv).

45. Quoted in Robert Russell, "Satire and Socialism: The Russian Debates 1925–1934," *Forum for Modern Language Studies* 30, no. 4 (1994): 344.

46. "On the Policy of the Party in the Field of Belles-Lettres: Resolution of the TSK RKP (b), July 1, 1925," in *The Proletarian Episode in Russian Literature, 1928–1932* (New York: Columbia University Press, 1953), 235–36.

47. Russell, "Satire and Socialism," 347.

48. Henry, *Classics of Soviet Satire,* xiii.

CHAPTER THREE

The chapter epigraph is from Maxim Gorky, *On Literature* (Seattle: University of Washington Press, 1973), 265–66.

1. Karl Marx, "Manifesto of the Communist Party," in *The Portable Karl Marx* (New York: Penguin Books, 1983), 225.

2. Igal Halfin, *Terror in My Soul: Communist Autobiographies on Trial* (Cambridge, Mass.: Harvard University Press, 2003), 103, 122.

3. N. Bukharin and E. Preobrazhensky, *The ABC of Communism: A Popular Explanation of the Program of the Communist Party of Russia,* trans. Eden Paul and Cedar Paul (Ann Arbor: University of Michigan Press, 1966), 237.

4. Peterson, *Subversive Imaginations,* 42.

5. Tzvetan Todorov, *The Fantastic: A Structural Approach to a Literary Genre,* trans. Richard Howard (Ithaca, N.Y.: Cornell University Press, 1975), 33.

6. Rosemary Jackson, *Fantasy: The Literature of Subversion* (London: Routledge, 2003), 32; Eric S. Rabkin, *The Fantastic in Literature* (Princeton, N.J.: Princeton University Press, 1976), 190.

7. Kathryn Hume, *Fantasy and Mimesis: Responses to Reality in Western Literature* (New York: Methuen, 1984), 25.

8. Todorov, *The Fantastic,* 33; Darko Suvin, "On the Poetics of the Science Fiction Genre," *College English* 34, no. 3 (December 1972): 375; Rabkin, *The Fantastic,* 5; Farah Mendlesohn, *Rhetorics of Fantasy* (Middletown, Conn.: Wesleyan University Press, 2008), xiv–xxiv.

9. For a discussion of the fantastic as subversive, see Jackson, *Fantasy,* 9.

10. For overviews on scholarly approaches to science fiction, see Carl Freedman, *Critical Theory and Science Fiction* (Hanover, N.H.: Wesleyan University Press, 2000), 13–23; James Gunn and Matthew Candelaria, eds., *Speculations on Speculation: Theories of Science Fiction* (Latham, Md.: Scarecrow, 2005); Adam Roberts, *Science Fiction* (London: Routledge, 2000), 1–30.

11. Suvin, "Poetics of the Science Fiction Genre," 372.

12. Joanna Russ, "Towards an Aesthetic of Science Fiction," in *To Write*

Like a Woman: Essays in Feminism and Science Fiction (Bloomington: Indiana University Press, 1995), 3–13.

13. The novel appeared first in serial form in the journal *Red Virgin Soil* (*Krasnaia Nov'*) in 1927. In 1928 it was published with minor changes in book form by the publishing house Land and Factory (Zemlia i fabrika). For a discussion of these changes and of critical reception, see Rimgaila Salys, "Understanding 'Envy,'" in *Olesha's "Envy": A Critical Companion* (Evanston, Ill.: Northwestern University Press, 1999), 13–19. Olesha reworked *Envy* into a play under the title *Conspiracy of Feelings* that was staged successfully in 1929; for a discussion of this adaptation, see Daniel Gerould, "Introduction to 'The Conspiracy of Feelings,'" in *The Conspiracy of Feelings / by Yurii Olesha and The Little Theatre of the Green Goose / by Konstanty Ildefons Galczynski* (London: Routledge, 2002), 1–9.

14. Iurii Olesha, *Zavist'*, in *Izbrannoe* (Moscow: Khudozhestvennaia literatura, 1974), 61. All quotations are taken from this source. Page numbers are given in parentheses. Translations are mine.

15. Since Kavalerov is by profession a writer, many scholars conclude that Kavalerov is a stand-in for Olesha himself. See Andrew Barratt, "*Envy,* Part 1: Kavalerov as Myth-Maker," in *Olesha's "Envy": A Critical Companion* (Evanston, Ill.: Northwestern University Press, 1999), 50.

16. Salys, "Understanding 'Envy,'" 20.

17. For a discussion of the term "vydumka" in Olesha's work, see Kazimiera Ingdahl, *The Artist and the Creative Act: A Study of Jurij Olesa's Novel "Zavist'"* (Stockholm: Almqvist & Wiksell International, 1984), 76–123. In her discussion of Ivan's inventions, Ingdahl concludes: "In this mockery of his own and other people's *vydumka* Ivan reveals a fundamental ambivalence toward his imagination, in whose truth he both does and does not believe" (Ingdahl, *The Artist and the Creative Act,* 123).

18. Ivan's newest invention, the machine Ophelia, even more clearly occupies the liminal space of the fantastic. After Ophelia's first appearance, Kavalerov, the only witness, rejects the machine as a trick of the afternoon heat. He demands to know why Ivan is deceiving him, and in answer is told another lie, the "Tale of the Meeting of Two Brothers," in which Ophelia appears for the second time in the book, wreaking vengeance on Ivan's brother Andrey and destroying the Quarter. But even in Ivan's own story, Ophelia is "illusive in form" (79)—only a piercing whistle and ray of orange light can be perceived. In her third and final appearance, at the "real" (?) opening of the Quarter, none of the New People see or hear Ophelia. Moreover, they now fail to notice Ivan and Kavalerov, who have become like Ophelia, invisible instruments of revenge that accomplish only self-destruction.

19. Many scholars have emphasized the Freudian underpinnings of *Envy.* For an intriguing treatment of this issue that also gives an overview of previous

discussions, see Eliot Borenstein, *Men Without Women: Masculinity & Revolution in Russian Fiction, 1917–1929* (Durham, N.C.: Duke University Press, 2000), 125–90.

20. Quoted in Andrew Barratt, *Yurii Olesha's "Envy,"* Birmingham Slavonic Monographs 12 (Birmingham, Eng.: Department of Russian Language and Literature, University of Birmingham, 1981), 1.

21. Quoted in Barratt, *Yurii Olesha's "Envy,"* 3.

22. Quoted in Salys, "Understanding 'Envy,'" 18.

23. Ibid., 19.

24. Lynn Mally, "Intellectuals in the Proletkult: Problems of Authority and Expertise," in *Party, State, and Society in the Russian Civil War* (Bloomington: Indiana University Press, 1989), 300–301.

25. Mally, "Intellectuals," 301.

26. Bukharin and Preobrazhensky, *The ABC of Communism,* 237.

27. Quoted in Halfin, *Terror,* 62.

28. Halfin, *Terror,* 46.

29. Lev Kassil', *Shvambraniia* (Moscow, 1934), 91. All quotations are from this source and are followed by page numbers in parentheses. Translations are mine.

30. Janet G. Tucker, *Revolution Betrayed: Jurij Olesa's "Envy"* (Columbus, Ohio: Slavic Publishers, 1996), 11.

31. Iurii Olesha, "Rech' na I vsesoiuznom s'ezde sovetskikh pisatelei," in *Izbrannoe: Zavist' i drugie,* Russian Study Series, vol. 72 (Pullman, Mich.: Russian Language Specialties, 1973), 234. Translation is mine.

32. Ibid., 234–35. Translation is mine.

33. Ibid., 237.

34. See, for example, Maurice Friedberg, "New Editions of Soviet Belles-Lettres: A Study in Politics and Palimpsests," *American Slavic and East European Review* 13 (February 1954): 72–88.

35. Siniavsky, "On Socialist Realism," 174.

CHAPTER FOUR

The chapter epigraph is from Maxim Gorky, *Mother* (New York: D. Appleton, 1935), 15–16.

1. Gorky, *Mother,* 497.

2. Marx, "Manifesto," 225.

3. Bukharin and Preobrazhensky, *The ABC of Communism,* 230.

4. For a detailed discussion of the influx of new words into Russian, see Michael S. Gorham, *Speaking in Soviet Tongues* (Dekalb: Northern Illinois University Press, 2003), 23–26; and Larissa Ryazanova-Clarke and Terence Wade, *The Russian Language Today* (London: Routledge, 1999), 3–18.

5. Ryazanova-Clarke and Wade, *The Russian Language,* 17.

6. Michael G. Smith, *Language and Power in the Creation of the USSR, 1917–1953,* Contributions to the Sociology of Language 80 (Berlin: Mouton de Gruyter, 1998), 104.

7. Velimir Khlebnikov, *Letters and Theoretical Writings,* vol. 1 of *Collected Works of Velimir Khlebnikov* (Cambridge, Mass.: Harvard University Press, 1987), 337.

8. Stites, *Revolutionary Dreams*, 55, 169–70.

9. Patrick L McGuire, *Red Stars: Political Aspects of Soviet Science Fiction* (Ann Arbor, Mich.: UMI Research Press, 1985), 31. Early Soviet science fiction novels were themselves often translated into Esperanto in the 1920s, for example, Aleksey Tolstoy's *Aelita,* Aleksandr Bogdanov's *Red Star,* and Aleksandr Belyaev's *The Battle in the Ether* (Stites, *Revolutionary Dreams,* 135).

10. Party critics liked the novel (Clark, *The Soviet Novel,* 72). See also L. N. Smirnova, "Kak sozdavalsia *Tsement,*" in *Tekstologiia proizvedenii sovetskoi literatury: Voprosy tekstologii 4* (Moscow: Nauka, 1967), 172–73. Commissar of Culture Anatoly Lunacharsky was enthusiastic: "On this cement foundation we can build further" (quoted in Smirnova, "Kak sozdavalsia *Tsement,*" 180; translation is mine). Proletarian critics almost uniformly liked Gleb. Gladkov was a member of Proletkult, Smithy (Kuznitsa), and VAPP (Vserossiiskaia assotsiatsiia proletarsikh pisatelei). The only group to uniformly condemn the novel and its hero were the members of Lef (Left Front of Art); Halina Stephan discusses their opposition in detail (Halina Stephan, "*Cement:* From Gladkov's Monumental Epos to Müller's Avant-Garde Drama," *Germano-Slavica* 3, no. 2 [Fall 1979]: 88–93). But even Osip Brik, who found *Cement*'s themes unconnected and heroes falsely heroic, notes how well received *Cement* was in the press (O. M. Brik, "Pochemu ponravilsia Tsement," *Na Literaturnom Postu* 2 [1926]: 30). Sergey Budantsev hailed the appearance of the first worker-hero: "The character of Gleb . . . is always growing, evolving, submissive to the influence of the masses, whose noble impulse he has tested and now trusts" (Sergei Budantsev, "O Tsemente F. Gladkova," *Zvezda* 5 [1925]: 270; translation is mine). V. Krasil'nikov called Gleb "the best representative of the leaders and organizers of the masses, who are building a socialist society" (V. Krasil'nikov, "Fedor Gladkov," *Oktiabr'* 9 [1926]: 134; translation is mine). I. S. Grossman-Roshchin hailed him as "the living force of an era" (I. S. Grossman-Roshchin, "Epokha i liudi [Fedor Gladkov-*Tsement*]," *Molodaia gvardiia* 9 [1926]: 154; translation is mine). Maksim Gorky, in a letter to Gladkov, wrote: "Gleb is finely crafted, and, even though he is romanticized, that is how it should be" (quoted in Smirnova, "Kak sozdavalsia *Tsement,*" 162; translation is mine). *Cement* had a major impact on the socialist realist period, providing a prototype for both the construction novel, a dominant genre in the Stalinist era, and for the positive hero, a mainstay of socialist realism. It was among the five most mentioned examples of socialist realism at the First Congress of Soviet Writers (Régine Robin, *Socialist Realism: An Impossible Aesthetic,* trans. Catherine Porter [Stanford, Calif.:

Stanford University Press, 1992], 49); among these, it was the only novel to describe reconstruction rather than revolution and civil war. The plot and positive heroes in *Cement* were imitated more than any other Soviet work (Clark, *The Soviet Novel,* 69). Moreover, Gladkov went on to great prestige in the Soviet Union. He became the director of the Gorky Literary Institute, which trained writers, and won the Stalin Prize in 1950 and 1951. There are many editions of the novel, including a beautifully illustrated volume issued after Gladkov's death in 1958.

11. For a discussion of the 1930s production novel, see Piotr Fast, *Ideology, Aesthetics, Literary History: Socialist Realism and Its Others,* Literary and Cultural Theory 3 (Frankfurt am Main: Peter Lang, 1999), 43–52.

12. C. Vaughan James, *Soviet Socialist Realism: Origins and Theory* (New York: St. Martin's, 1973), 104.

13. An extended version of the following discussion of *Cement* was published separately in Eric Laursen, "'A New Enigmatic Language': The Spontaneity-Consciousness Paradigm and the Case of Gladkov's *Cement,*" *Slavic Review* 65, no. 1 (Spring 2006): 66–89.

14. Irina Gutkin writes that people were divided into three groups in Soviet culture of the 1930s: "former people," who could not overcome the past, "simple people," who existed only in the present, and "the best people," who were leading the march into the future (Gutkin, *Cultural Origins,* 115–21). We can find in *Cement* a precursor for this tripartite model. Dasha and Gleb achieve consciousness and become the "best people," work to remove or transform the "former people" (Polya and Badin), and lead the "simple people," who have not yet achieved consciousness.

15. Fedor Gladkov, in "My Work on *Cement,*" writes: "The task of art is to depict not only that which is but also that which ought to be, that is, art ought to depict reality in its aggressive movement and evolution" (Fedor Gladkov, "Moia rabota nad *Tsementom,*" in *Sobranie sochinenii,* vol. 2 [Moscow: Khudozhestvennaia literatura, 1958], 419–20; translation is mine).

16. Fedor Gladkov, *Tsement,* vol. 2 of *Sobranie sochinenii* (Moscow: Zemlia i fabrika, 1927), 49. All quotes from the novel are from this source and are followed by page numbers in parentheses. Translations are mine. Originally, *Cement* was published serially in *Red Virgin Soil* (1925), but, according to L. N. Smirnova, many passages and one entire chapter were removed by Voronsky, the editor of *Red Virgin Soil;* these were restored in the 1927 book version (Smirnova, "Kak sozdavalsia *Tsement,*" 161).

17. Anne E. Gorsuch, "'A Woman Is Not a Man': The Culture of Gender and Generation in Soviet Russia, 1921–1928," *Slavic Review* 55, no. 3 (Fall 1996): 644.

18. Thea Durfee argues that Dasha regains her "softness" and feminine attractiveness in Gleb's eyes after he learns to accept her as an equal (Thea Margaret Durfee, "*Cement* and *How the Steel Was Tempered:* Variations on the New

Soviet Woman," in *A Plot of Her Own: The Female Protagonist in Russian Literature,* ed. Sonia Stephan Hoisington [Evanston, Ill.: Northwestern University Press, 1995], 93).

19. Whenever a character is attracted to the past, they are given such stereotypically feminine traits. The intellectual Sergey Ivagin, who also longs for the past, is, like Polya, described as "feminine"; when Gleb shakes Sergey's hand, he finds "in his fingers . . . softness and a feminine timidity" (48). Disputes at the factory committee bring tears to Sergey's eyes. Other factory bureaucrats who maintain the ways of the past are similarly described as effeminate or overly emotional. For a discussion of Sergey's transformation in the novel, see Laursen, "A New Enigmatic Language," 85–88.

20. Dasha Chumalova is usually seen as an emancipated woman who embraces the Bolshevik vilification of housework and traditional marriage (see Xenia Gasiorowska, *Women in Soviet Fiction: 1917–1964* [Madison: University of Wisconsin Press, 1968], 241–42; and Durfee, "*Cement,*" 89–94). Calling herself a "free Soviet citizen" (32) and her husband Gleb "comrade," she places her daughter in the Children's Home and sets off to work, asserting her independence. Dasha's actions reflect the Bolshevik view of the family as a capitalist institution, tainted by hierarchy and exploitation; as society developed Communist values of equality and selflessness, the family, a useless vestigial organ of an unhealthy past, would "wither away." In the 1920s decrees to speed along this process made divorce easier, granted legal equality to both legitimate and illegitimate children, legalized abortion, and decriminalized bigamy and adultery. Lenin, who famously despised domestic work, led other Bolsheviks in campaigning for its "industrialization," its transferal from private to public. By taking cooking, cleaning, and child care out of the hands of individuals and freeing women of the exploitation inherent in traditional marriage, Soviet women would be freed to take on an equal part in the workplace and in political life. Dasha's transformation into "free Soviet citizen" does not, however, resemble what a twenty-first-century reader would call an assertion of independence. Instead it constitutes a filtering of choice through the needs of the collective. The Bolshevik feminist Aleksandra Kollontai, although notorious for comparing sex to drinking a glass of water, rejected the individualism of Western flapper culture in her discussions of sexuality, viewing the female body only in relation to the collective: "The woman herself must observe all the requirements of hygiene during the period of pregnancy, remembering that during these months she does not belong to herself, that she is working for the collective, that from her own flesh and blood she is 'producing' a new unit of labor, a new member of the Workers Republic" (quoted in Barbara Evans Clements, "Emancipation Through Communism: The Ideology of A. M. Kollontai," *Slavic Review* 32, no. 2 [June 1973]: 335). In the newly formed worker's paradise, a woman's body was not her own. In accordance with this principle, Dasha shifts focus to a greatly expanded domestic sphere, leaving her own home and child to be-

come a collective mother for all children. When the revolutionaries appropriate the goods of the bourgeoisie, Dasha sorts them into piles destined for the children's homes and the maternity homes "with the knowing hand of a homemaker [*khoziaika*]" (178). She places her own daughter Nyurka into one of these homes and goes there not to care for her but rather to provide for all children—here too she is called a "homemaker [*khoziaika*]" (39). This rebirth into communal mother and homemaker is not easy: "Nyurka was her life's sacrifice, and her heart could not bear this sacrifice" (250). Nevertheless, at the Children's Home she spurns special treatment for her daughter, distributing caresses and protection equally among the group of starving waifs, despite her longing to save Nyurka, who she admits is fading away without her. Nyurka symbolizes Dasha's own nostalgic glance back, depicted as a childish desire to return to individualism and hierarchy.

21. Durfee concurs: "The rape she suffers at Badin's hands is not depicted so much as inappropriate behavior for a party leader as the consequence of her own political and moral weakness" (Durfee, "*Cement,*" 94).

22. Igal Halfin notes that the charge of childishness (*mal'chishestvo*) was given to at least one of the students purged at Leningrad Communist University in 1924 (Halfin, "Between Instinct and Mind," 39).

23. V. Poliansky suggests as much in a 1926 review of criticism on *Cement,* when he writes the following about Dasha's relationship with Badin: "Perhaps, in all this, the author wanted to show the battle between the new way of thinking with the old, strong instincts found in the relations between the sexes" (Valer'ian Polianskii, "*Tsement* i ego kritiki," *Na literaturnom postu* 5–6 [1926]: 50; translation is mine).

24. Gleb and Dasha embrace the pet projects of Lenin (electrification—Gleb's first project brings electricity back to the workers' settlement and the factory) and his wife Krupskaya (literacy—Dasha conducts a literacy class, and the children's home where Dasha works is called the Krupskaya Children's Home).

25. For a discussion of the Stalinist New Person as mature adult, see Jay Bergman, "Valerii Chkalov: Soviet Pilot as New Soviet Man," *Journal of Contemporary History* 33, no. 1 (January 1998): 145.

26. Polianskii, "*Tsement* i ego kritiki," 51.

27. Clark, *The Soviet Novel,* 80.

28. Thea Durfee quite rightly posits Dasha as Gleb's "mentor" in the socialist realist mentor-disciple tradition, but I believe that she is wrong in her claim that Dasha is fully conscious at the beginning of the novel (Durfee, "*Cement,*" 92).

29. Gorham, *Speaking,* 48.

30. Ibid., 216 n57.

31. For a discussion of the changes, see Robert L. Busch, "Gladkov's *Cement:* The Making of a Soviet Classic," *Slavic and East European Journal* 22,

no. 3 (Fall 1978): 348–61; and also Friedberg, "New Editions," 85–87; and Smirnova, "Kak sozdavalsia *Tsement.*"

32. Busch, "Gladkov's *Cement,*" 348.

33. Despite the praise of plot and character, many critics attacked *Cement*'s style, valuing it more for its content (Smirnova, "Kak sozdavalsia *Tsement,*" 173). According to Robert Maguire, Aleksandr Voronsky, who first published the novel in the journal *Red Virgin Soil,* found *Cement* "devoid of literary merit" (Robert A. Maguire, *Red Virgin Soil: Soviet Literature in the 1920s* [Princeton, N.J.: Princeton University Press, 1968], 321). In each of the later editions, he worked to eradicate lexicon and stylistic elements criticized in the early editions. For a discussion of these changes, see Smirnova, "Kak sozdavalsia *Tsement.*"

34. Smirnova, "Kak sozdavalsia *Tsement,*" 175–76. See also Friedberg, "New Editions," 85–87.

35. The first version to remove Dasha's extramarital sexual encounters was published in 1933 (Morris, *Saints and Revolutionaries,* 154). Morris interprets the changes as an attempt to make an ascetic out of Dasha's character, who lives an "atemporal existence," thus imparting an epic or mythic cast to the novel; Morris sees this as a return to the devices of medieval literature (Morris, *Saints and Revolutionaries,* 155–56). Morris claims that Dasha, as an ascetic, "is unable to effect a change in others" (Morris, *Saints and Revolutionaries,* 157). Morris bases her conclusions on the 1958 version of *Cement,* whereas I examine the original 1925 version—this undoubtedly explains our differing interpretations.

36. In her study of female characters of the Soviet period, Xenia Gasiorowska describes a Stalin-era heroine as one who works outside the home, but focuses her attention on being a model wife, mother, and homemaker, rather than playing a role in party policy or trying to improve her education or professional skills. In literary texts of this period, there is no competition between husband and wife, and, although they have equal rights, he is the "senior partner" (*starshii*). Husband and wife are faithful and very much in love (Gasiorowska, *Women,* 102–4).

37. Smirnova, "Kak sozdavalsia *Tsement,*" 175. Translation is mine.

38. Gladkov, "Moia rabota nad *Tsementom,*" 421–22.

39. My discussion of the changes in *Cement* come from my 1984 master's thesis (University of Iowa). For other discussions of changes in *Cement,* see the following: Busch, "Gladkov's *Cement,*" 348–61; Friedberg, "New Editions," 85–87; Smirnova, "Kak sozdavalsia *Tsement,*" 140–227.

40. For a more detailed discussion of the writer in the First Five-Year Plan, see Katerina Clark, "Little Heroes and Big Deeds: Literature Responds to the First Five-Year Plan," in *Cultural Revolution in Russia, 1928–1931* (Bloomington: Indiana University Press, 1978), 189–206.

41. Morris, *Saints and Revolutionaries,* 167. It is often considered the "lone masterpiece of Soviet construction fiction" (Richard C. Borden, *The Art of Writ-*

ing Badly: Valentin Kataev's Mauvism and the Rebirth of Russian Modernism [Evanston, Ill.: Northwestern University Press, 1999], 10).

42. For a discussion of the criticism of Kataev's 1920s satire, see Robert Russell, *Valentin Kataev* (Boston: Twayne, 1981), 70–72.

43. For a discussion of this journey and its impact on *Time Forward!* see Mary A. Nicholas, *Writers at Work: Russian Production Novels and the Construction of Soviet Culture* (Lewisburg: Bucknell University Press, 2010), 197–238.

44. Valentin Kataev, *Vremia vpered!* vol. 1 of *Sobranie sochinenii v piati tomakh* (Moscow: Khudozhestvennaia literatura, 1956), 402. All quotes from the novel are from this source and are followed by page numbers in parentheses. Translations are mine.

45. Morris reads Margulies as a Soviet ascetic, and *Time Forward!* as a novel that makes a complete return to the conventions of medieval literature, into myth, where everything is "either black or white"; as an ascetic hero, Margulies "masters both time and space" (Morris, *Saints and Revolutionaries,* 170, 172).

CONCLUSION

The chapter epigraph is from James, *Soviet Socialist Realism*, 105.

1. James, *Soviet Socialist Realism*, 104.

2. Chapple, *Soviet Satire*, 142.

3. Quoted in Edward J. Brown, *The Proletarian Episode in Russian Literature 1928–1932* (New York: Columbia University Press, 1953), 20.

4. Quoted in Brown, *The Proletarian Episode*, 15.

5. McGuire, *Red Stars*, 11.

6. Stites, *Revolutionary Dreams*, 189. Stites discusses a variety of Communist utopias from the 1920s (Stites, *Revolutionary Dreams*, 171–79).

7. Lynne Attwood and Catriona Kelly, "Programmes for Identity: The 'New Man' and the 'New Woman,'" in *Constructing Russian Culture in the Age of Revolution: 1881–1940* (New York: Oxford University Press, 1998), 285–86.

8. For an example, see Anatolii Fedorovich Britikov, *Russkii sovetskii nauchno-fantasticheskii roman* (Leningrad: Nauka, 1970).

9. Boris Polevoi, *A Story About a Real Man*, trans. Joe Fineberg (Moscow: Foreign Languages Publishing House), 223.

10. Robin, *Socialist Realism*, xxii, xxxii.

11. Quoted in Jonathan Glover, *Humanity: A Moral History of the Twentieth Century* (New Haven, Conn.: Yale University Press, 1999), 279.

12. Siniavsky, "On Socialist Realism," 218. Nadya Peterson, in her study of the fantastic in Soviet literature of the 1970s, 1980s, and 1990s, asserts that this flowering was "a reaction to and a departure from the socialist realist dogma" (Peterson, *Subversive Imaginations,* 3).

Bibliography

Adams, Mark B. "'Red Star': Another Look at Aleksandr Bogdanov." *Slavic Review* 48, no. 1 (Spring 1989): 1–15.

———. *The Wellborn Science: Eugenics in Germany, France, Brazil, and Russia.* New York: Oxford University Press, 1990.

Attwood, Lynne, and Catriona Kelly. "Programmes for Identity: The 'New Man' and the 'New Woman.'" In *Constructing Russian Culture in the Age of Revolution: 1881–1940.* New York: Oxford University Press, 1998.

Barratt, Andrew. "*Envy,* Part 1: Kavalerov as Myth-Maker." In *Olesha's "Envy": A Critical Companion,* 47–60. Evanston, Ill.: Northwestern University Press, 1999.

———. "The X-Factor in Zamyatin's *We.*" *Modern Language Review* 80, no. 3 (July 1985): 659–72.

———. *Yurii Olesha's "Envy."* Birmingham Slavonic Monographs 12. Birmingham, Eng.: Department of Russian Language and Literature, University of Birmingham, 1981.

Bergman, Jay. "Valerii Chkalov: Soviet Pilot as New Soviet Man." *Journal of Contemporary History* 33, no. 1 (January 1998): 135–52.

Bogdanov, Aleksandr. *Krasnaia zvezda: Roman-utopiia.* Petrograd: Petrogradskogo Soveta Rabochikh i Krasnoarmeiskikh Deputatov, 1918.

———. "Proletariat i iskusstvo [doklad]." In *O proletarskoi kul'ture, 1904–1924.* Leningrad: Kniga, 1924.

———. "Proletariat i iskusstvo: Rezoliutsiia, predlozheniia A. Bogdanovym na Pervoi Vserossiiskoi Konferentsii Proletarskikh kul'turno-prosvetitel'nykh organizatsii." In *Literaturnye manifesty ot simvolizma k oktiabriu: Sbornik materialov,* 130–31. Moscow: Federatsiia, 1929.

Borden, Richard C. *The Art of Writing Badly: Valentin Kataev's Mauvism and the Rebirth of Russian Modernism.* Evanston, Ill.: Northwestern University Press, 1999.

Borenstein, Eliot. *Men Without Women: Masculinity & Revolution in Russian Fiction, 1917–1929.* Durham, N.C.: Duke University Press, 2000.

———. "The Plural Self: Zamjatin's *We* and the Logic of Synecdoche." *Slavic and East European Journal* 40, no. 4 (Winter 1996): 667–83.

Brik, O. M. "Pochemu ponravilsia Tsement." *Na Literaturnom Postu* 2 (1926): 30–32.

Britikov, Anatolii Fedorovich. *Russkii sovetskii nauchno-fantasticheskii roman.* Leningrad: Nauka, 1970.

Brown, Edward J. *Mayakovsky: A Poet in the Revolution.* Princeton, N.J.: Princeton University Press, 1973.

———. *The Proletarian Episode in Russian Literature 1928–1932.* New York: Columbia University Press, 1953.

Budantsev, Sergei. "O Tsemente F. Gladkova." *Zvezda* 5 (1925): 268–73.

Bukharin, N., and E. Preobrazhensky. *The ABC of Communism: A Popular Explanation of the Program of the Communist Party of Russia.* Translated by Eden Paul and Cedar Paul. Ann Arbor: University of Michigan Press, 1966.

Bulgakov, Mikhail. *Sobach'e Serdtse.* London: Bristol Classical, 1994.

Burgin, Diana L. "Bulgakov's Early Tragedy of the Scientist-Creator: An Interpretation of *The Heart of a Dog.*" *Slavic and East European Journal* 22, no. 4 (1978): 494–508.

Busch, Robert L. "Gladkov's *Cement:* The Making of a Soviet Classic." *Slavic and East European Journal* 22, no. 3 (Fall 1978): 348–61.

Carden, Patricia. "Utopia and Anti-Utopia: Aleksei Gastev and Evgenii Zamyatin." *Russian Review* 46, no. 1 (January 1987): 1–18.

Cassiday, Julie A. "Flash Floods, Bedbugs, and Saunas: Social Hygiene in Mayakovsky's Theatrical Satires of the 1920s." In *Against the Grain: Parody, Satire and Intertextuality in Russian Literature,* edited by Janet Tucker, 131–48. Bloomington, Ind.: Slavica, 2002.

Chances, Ellen. "The Superfluous Man in Russian Literature." In *The Routledge Companion to Russian Literature,* edited by Neil Cornwell, 111–22. London: Routledge, 2001.

Chapple, Richard L. *Soviet Satire of the Twenties.* University of Florida Humanities Monograph, no. 47. Gainesville: University Presses of Florida, 1980.

Clark, Katerina. "Little Heroes and Big Deeds: Literature Responds to the First Five-Year Plan." In *Cultural Revolution in Russia, 1928–1931,* 189–206. Bloomington: Indiana University Press, 1978.

———. *Petersburg, Crucible of Cultural Revolution.* Cambridge, Mass.: Harvard University Press, 1995.

———. *The Soviet Novel: History as Ritual.* Chicago: University of Chicago Press, 1981.

Clarke, Bruce. *Energy Forms: Allegory and Science in the Era of Classical Thermodynamics.* Ann Arbor: University of Michigan Press, 2001.

Clarke, Julie. "The Human / Not Human in the Work of Orlan and Stelarc." In

The Cyborg Experiments: The Extensions of Body in the Media Age, 33–53. London: Continuum, 2002.

Clements, Barbara Evans. "Emancipation Through Communism: The Ideology of A. M. Kollontai." *Slavic Review* 32, no. 2 (June 1973): 323–38.

Cohen, Jeffrey Jerome. "Monster Culture (Seven Theses)." In *Monster Theory: Reading Culture,* 3–25. Minneapolis: University of Minnesota Press, 1996.

Collins, Christopher. "Zamyatin's *We* as Myth." In *Zamyatin's "We": A Collection of Critical Essays,* edited by Gary Kern, 70–79. Ann Arbor, Mich.: Ardis, 1988.

Cooke, Brette. *Human Nature in Utopia: Zamyatin's "We."* Evanston, Ill.: Northwestern University Press, 2002.

Dobrenko, Evgeny. *Aesthetics of Alienation: Reassessment of Early Soviet Cultural Theories.* Evanston, Ill.: Northwestern University Press, 2005.

Doyle, Peter. "Bulgakov's Satirical View of Revolution in 'Rokovye iaitsa' and *Sobach'e serdtse.*" *Canadian Slavonic Papers* 20, no. 3 (September 1978): 467–82.

Durfee, Thea Margaret. "*Cement* and *How the Steel Was Tempered:* Variations on the New Soviet Woman." In *A Plot of Her Own: The Female Protagonist in Russian Literature,* edited by Sonia Stephan Hoisington, 89–101. Evanston, Ill.: Northwestern University Press, 1995.

Eliade, Mircea. *Images and Symbols: Studies in Religious Symbolism.* Princeton, N.J.: Princeton University Press, 1991.

Ermolaev, Herman. *Soviet Literary Theories 1917–1934: The Genesis of Socialist Realism.* University of California Publications in Modern Philology. Berkeley: University of California Press, 1963.

Fast, Piotr. *Ideology, Aesthetics, Literary History: Socialist Realism and Its Others.* Literary and Cultural Theory 3. Frankfurt am Main: Peter Lang, 1999.

Freedman, Carl. *Critical Theory and Science Fiction.* Hanover, N.H.: Wesleyan University Press, 2000.

Friedberg, Maurice. "New Editions of Soviet Belles-Lettres: A Study in Politics and Palimpsests." *American Slavic and East European Review* 13 (February 1954): 72–88.

Fusso, Suzanne. "Failures of Transformation in 'Sobach'e serdtse.'" *Slavic and East European Journal* 33, no. 3 (Fall 1989): 386–99.

Gasiorowska, Xenia. *Women in Soviet Fiction: 1917–1964.* Madison: University of Wisconsin Press, 1968.

Gerould, Daniel. "Introduction to 'The Conspiracy of Feelings.'" In *The Conspiracy of Feelings / by Yurii Olesha and The Little Theatre of the Green Goose / by Konstanty Ildefons Galczynski,* 1–9. London: Routledge, 2002.

Gladkov, Fedor. "Moia rabota nad *Tsementom.*" In *Sobranie sochinenii,* vol. 2, 410–26. Moscow: Khudozhestvennaia literatura, 1958.

———. *Tsement.* Vol. 2 of *Sobranie sochinenii.* Moscow: Zemlia i fabrika, 1927.

Glenny, Michael. "Introduction." In *Heart of a Dog: A Novel by Mikhail Bulgakov.* New York: Harvest, 1968.

Gloveli, Georgii. "Bogdanov as Scientist and Utopian." In *Bogdanov and His Work: A Guide to the Published and Unpublished Works of Alexander A. Bogdanov (Malinovsky) 1873–1928,* 40–59. Aldershot, Eng.: Ashgate, 1998.

Glover, Jonathan. *Humanity: A Moral History of the Twentieth Century.* New Haven, Conn.: Yale University Press, 1999.

Gorham, Michael S. "Mastering the Perverse: State Building and Language 'Purification' in Early Soviet Russia." *Slavic Review* 59, no. 1 (Spring 2000): 133–53.

———. *Speaking in Soviet Tongues.* Dekalb: Northern Illinois University Press, 2003.

Gorky, Maxim. *On Literature.* Seattle: University of Washington Press, 1973.

———. *Mother.* New York: D. Appleton, 1935.

Gorsuch, Anne E. "'A Woman Is Not a Man': The Culture of Gender and Generation in Soviet Russia, 1921–1928." *Slavic Review* 55, no. 3 (Fall 1996): 636–60.

Goscilo, Helena. "Point of View in Bulgakov's *Heart of a Dog.*" *Russian Literature Triquarterly* 15 (1978): 281–91.

Graham, Sheelagh Duffin. "Bulgakov's 'Sobach'e serdtse': A Polemical Povest.'" *Journal of Russian Studies* 33 (1977): 27–31.

Greenfield, Douglas. "Revenants and Revolutionaries: Body and Society in Bogdanov's Martian Novels." *Slavic and East European Journal* 50, no. 4 (Winter 2006): 621–34.

Grossman-Roshchin, I. S. "Epokha i liudi (Fedor Gladkov-*Tsement*)." *Molodaia gvardiia* 9 (1926): 142–56.

Groys, Boris. *The Total Art of Stalinism: Avant-Garde, Aesthetic Dictatorship, and Beyond.* Princeton, N.J.: Princeton University Press, 1992.

Gunn, James, and Matthew Candelaria, eds. *Speculations on Speculation: Theories of Science Fiction.* Latham, Md.: Scarecrow, 2005.

Gutkin, Irina. *The Cultural Origins of the Socialist Realist Aesthetic, 1890–1934.* Evanston, Ill.: Northwestern University Press, 1999.

Haber, Edythe C. *Mikhail Bulgakov: The Early Years.* Cambridge, Mass.: Harvard University Press, 1998.

Haimson, Leopold. "Lenin's Revolutionary Career Revisited: Some Observations on Recent Discussions." *Kritika: Explorations in Russian and Eurasian History* 5, no. 1 (Winter 2004): 55–80.

Halfin, Igal. "Between Instinct and Mind: The Bolshevik View of the Proletarian Self." *Slavic Review* 62, no. 1 (Spring 2003): 34–40.

———. *Terror in My Soul: Communist Autobiographies on Trial.* Cambridge, Mass.: Harvard University Press, 2003.

Haynes, Roslynn D. *From Faust to Strangelove: Representations of the Scientist in Western Literature.* Baltimore: Johns Hopkins University Press, 1994.

Henry, Peter, comp. and ed. *Classics of Soviet Satire.* Vol. 1 of *Anthology of Soviet Satire.* London, 1972.

Hosking, Geoffrey. *Beyond Socialist Realism: Soviet Fiction Since "Ivan Denisovich."* London: Granada, 1980.

Hume, Kathryn. *Fantasy and Mimesis: Responses to Reality in Western Literature.* New York: Methuen, 1984.

"The Ideological Front and Literature (1925): Resolution of the First All-Union Conference of Proletarian Writers." In *Bolshevik Visions: First Phase of the Cultural Revolution in Soviet Russia,* edited by William G. Rosenberg, 469–74. Ann Arbor, Mich.: Ardis, 1984.

Ilf, Ilya, and Yevgeny Petrov. "How the Soviet 'Robinson' Was Written." In *"The Fatal Eggs" and Other Soviet Satire,* 223–27. New York: Macmillan, 1965.

Ingdahl, Kazimiera. *The Artist and the Creative Act: A Study of Jurij Olesa's Novel "Zavist'."* Stockholm: Almqvist & Wiksell International, 1984.

Ioffe, Solomon. "Tainopis' v *Sobach'em serdtse* Bulgakova." *Novyi zhurnal* 168–69 (1987): 260–74.

Jackson, Rosemary. *Fantasy: The Literature of Subversion.* London: Routledge, 2003.

James, C. Vaughan. *Soviet Socialist Realism: Origins and Theory.* New York: St. Martin's, 1973.

Jensen, Kenneth Martin. *Beyond Marx and Mach: Aleksandr Bogdanov's "Philosophy of Living Experience."* London: D. Reidel, 1978.

Kassil', Lev. *Shvambraniia.* Moscow, 1934.

Kataev, Valentin. *Vremia vpered!* Vol. 1 of *Sobranie sochinenii v piati tomakh,* 197–522. Moscow: Khudozhestvennaia literatura, 1956.

Kelly, Catriona. *Refining Russia: Advice Literature, Polite Culture, and Gender from Catherine to Yeltsin.* Oxford: Oxford University Press, 2001.

Khlebnikov, Velimir. *Letters and Theoretical Writings.* Vol. 1 of *Collected Works of Velimir Khlebnikov.* Cambridge, Mass.: Harvard University Press, 1987.

Krasil'nikov, V. "Fedor Gladkov." *Oktiabr'* 9 (1926): 129–38.

Krementsov, Nikolai. *A Martian Stranded on Earth: Alexander Bogdanov, Blood Transfusions, and Proletarian Science.* Chicago: University of Chicago Press, 2011.

Krylova, Anna. "Beyond the Spontaneity-Consciousness Paradigm: 'Class Instinct' as a Promising Category of Historical Analysis." *Slavic Review* 62, no. 1 (Spring 2003): 1–23.

Laursen, Eric. "Bad Words Are Not Allowed!: Language and Transformation in Mikhail Bulgakov's *Heart of a Dog.*" *Slavic and East European Journal* 51, no. 3 (Fall 2007): 491–513.

———. "An Electrician's Utopia: Mikhail Bulgakov's *Fateful Eggs*." *Slavic and East European Journal* 56, no. 1 (2012).

———. "'A New Enigmatic Language': The Spontaneity-Consciousness Paradigm and the Case of Gladkov's *Cement*." *Slavic Review* 65, no. 1 (Spring 2006): 66–89.

LeBlanc, Ronald D. "Feeding a Poor Dog a Bone: The Quest for Nourishment in Bulgakov's *Sobach'e serdtse*." *Russian Review* 52, no. 1 (January 1993): 58–78.

Lenin, Vladimir Il'ich. *What Is to Be Done? Burning Questions of Our Movement.* In *The Lenin Anthology,* 12–114. New York: W.W. Norton, 1975.

Lih, Lars T. "How a Founding Document Was Found, or One Hundred Years of Lenin's *What Is to Be Done?*" *Kritika: Explorations in Russian and Eurasian History* 4, no. 1 (Winter 2003): 5–49.

Maguire, Robert A. "Literary Conflicts in the 1920s." *Survey: A Journal of East and West Studies* 18, no. 1 (Winter 1972).

———. *Red Virgin Soil: Soviet Literature in the 1920s.* Princeton, N.J.: Princeton University Press, 1968.

Maiakovskii, Vladimir. *Klop.* Durham, N.C.: University of Durham, 1985.

Mally, Lynn. *Culture of the Future: The Proletkult Movement in Revolutionary Russia.* Berkeley: University of California Press, 1990.

———. "Intellectuals in the Proletkult: Problems of Authority and Expertise." In *Party, State, and Society in the Russian Civil War,* 296–311. Bloomington: Indiana University Press, 1989.

Markley, Robert. *Dying Planet: Mars in Science and the Imagination.* Durham, N.C.: Duke University Press, 2005.

Marx, Karl. "Capital." In *The Portable Karl Marx,* translated and edited by Eugene Kamenka, 432–503. New York: Penguin Books, 1983.

———. "Manifesto of the Communist Party." In *The Portable Karl Marx,* 203–42. New York: Penguin Books, 1983.

Mathewson Jr., Rufus W. *The Positive Hero in Russian Literature.* 2nd ed. Stanford, Calif.: Stanford University Press, 1975.

McGuire, Patrick L. *Red Stars: Political Aspects of Soviet Science Fiction.* Ann Arbor, Mich.: UMI Research Press, 1985.

Mendlesohn, Farah. *Rhetorics of Fantasy.* Middletown, Conn.: Wesleyan University Press, 2008.

Mondry, Henrietta. "Beyond Scientific Transformation in Bulgakov's *The Heart of a Dog*." *Australian Slavonic and East European Studies* 10, no. 2 (1996): 1–10.

Morris, Marcia A. *Saints and Revolutionaries: The Ascetic Hero in Russian Literature.* New York: State University of New York Press, 1993.

Natov, Nadine. "Ot teksta k stsene: Povest' 'Sobach'e serdtse' Mikhaila Bulgakova i ee teatral'naia interpretatsiia." *Zapiski russkoi akademicheskoi gruppy v S.Sh.A.* 24 (1991): 43–131.

Nicholas, Mary A. *Writers at Work: Russian Production Novels and the Construction of Soviet Culture.* Lewisburg, Pa.: Bucknell University Press, 2010.

Nikol'skii, S.V. "Na grani metafor i alliuzii (o nekotorykh zashifrovannykh motivakh v antiutopiiakh Bulgakova)." *Izvestiia Akademii Nauk, Seriia literatury i iazyka* 58, no. 1 (January–February 1999): 11–19.

Olesha, Yury [Iurii]. *Envy.* In *The Portable Twentieth-Century Russian Reader.* New York: Penguin, 1985.

———. "Rech' na I vsesoiuznom s'ezde sovetskikh pisatelei." In *Izbrannoe: Zavist' i drugie,* 233–38. Russian Study Series, vol. 72. Pullman, Mich.: Russian Language Specialties, 1973.

———. *Zavist'.* In *Izbrannoe,* 13–94. Moscow: Khudozhestvennaia literatura, 1974.

"On the Policy of the Party in the Field of Belles-Lettres: Resolution of the TSK RKP (b), July 1, 1925." In *The Proletarian Episode in Russian Literature, 1928–1932,* 235–40. New York: Columbia University Press, 1953.

Parrott, Ray. "The Eye in *We.*" In *Zamyatin's "We": A Collection of Critical Essays,* edited by Gary Kern, 106–17. Ann Arbor, Mich.: Ardis, 1988.

Peterson, Nadya. *Subversive Imaginations: Fantastic Prose and the End of Soviet Literature, 1970s–1990.* Boulder, Colo.: Westview, 1997.

Petrochenkov, Margaret Wise. "Castration Anxiety and the Other in Zamyatin's *We.*" In *The Fantastic Other: An Interface of Perspectives,* edited by Brett Cooke, 243–55. Critical Studies, vol. 11. Amsterdam: Rodopi, 1998.

Polevoi, Boris. *A Story About a Real Man.* Translated by Joe Fineberg. Moscow: Foreign Languages Publishing House.

Polianskii, Valer'ian. "*Tsement* i ego kritiki." *Na literaturnom postu* 5–6 (1926): 50–53.

Proffer, Ellendea. *Bulgakov, Life and Work.* Ann Arbor, Mich.: Ardis, 1984.

Rabkin, Eric S. *The Fantastic in Literature.* Princeton, N.J.: Princeton University Press, 1976.

Richards, D. J. *Zamyatin: A Soviet Heretic.* London: Bowes and Bowes, 1962.

Roberts, Adam. *Science Fiction.* London: Routledge, 2000.

Robin, Régine. *Socialist Realism: An Impossible Aesthetic.* Translated by Catherine Porter. Stanford, Calif.: Stanford University Press, 1992.

Rudnitsky, Konstantin. *Russian and Soviet Theater 1905–1932.* Translated by Roxane Permar. New York: Harry N. Abrams, 1988.

Russ, Joanna. "Towards an Aesthetic of Science Fiction." In *To Write Like a Woman: Essays in Feminism and Science Fiction,* 3–14. Bloomington: Indiana University Press, 1995.

Russell, Robert. "Introduction." In *"Klop,"* 7–48. Durham, N.C.: University of Durham, 1985.

———. "Satire and Socialism: The Russian Debates 1925–1934." *Forum for Modern Language Studies* 30, no. 4 (1994): 341–52.

———. *Valentin Kataev.* Boston: Twayne, 1981.

———. *Zamiatin's "We."* Critical Studies in Russian Literature. London: Bristol Classical, 2000.

Ruud, Charles A. "The Printing Press as an Agent of Political Change in Early Twentieth-Century Russia." *Russian Review* 40, no. 4 (October 1981): 378–95.

Ryazanova-Clarke, Larissa, and Terence Wade. *The Russian Language Today.* London: Routledge, 1999.

Rydel, Christine. "Bulgakov and H.G. Wells." *Russian Literature Triquarterly* 15 (1978): 293–311.

Salys, Rimgaila. "Understanding 'Envy.'" In *Olesha's "Envy": A Critical Companion,* 3–43. Evanston, Ill.: Northwestern University Press, 1999.

Shargorodskii, Sergei. "Sobach'e serdtse, ili Chudovishchnaia istoriia." *Literaturnoe Obozrenie* 5 (1991): 87–92.

Shneerson, Mariia. "Chto mozhet vyiti iz etogo Sharikova?" *Grani* 42, no. 150 (1988): 136–62.

Singleton, Amy C. *No Place Like Home: The Literary Artist and Russia's Search for Cultural Identity.* Albany: State University of New York Press, 1997.

Siniavsky, Andrei. "On Socialist Realism." In *The Trial Begins and On Socialist Realism,* translated by Max Hayward. Berkeley, Calif.: University of California Press, 1960.

Smirnova, L. N. "Kak sozdavalsia *Tsement.*" In *Tekstologiia proizvedenii sovetskoi literatury: Voprosy tekstologii 4,* 140–227. Moscow: Nauka, 1967.

Smith, Michael G. *Language and Power in the Creation of the USSR, 1917–1953.* Contributions to the Sociology of Language 80. Berlin: Mouton de Gruyter, 1998.

Smith, S. A. "The Social Meanings of Swearing: Workers and Bad Language in Late Imperial and Early Soviet Russia." *Past and Present* 160 (August 1998): 167–202.

Sochor, Zenovia A. *Revolution and Culture: The Bogdanov-Lenin Controversy.* Ithaca, N.Y: Cornell University Press, 1988.

Starks, Patricia. *The Body Soviet: Propaganda, Hygiene, and the Revolutionary State.* Madison: University of Wisconsin Press, 2008.

Stephan, Halina. "*Cement:* From Gladkov's Monumental Epos to Müller's Avant-Garde Drama." *Germano-Slavica* 3, no. 2 (Fall 1979): 85–103.

Stites, Richard. "Fantasy and Revolution: Alexander Bogdanov and the Origins of Bolshevik Science Fiction." In *Red Star: The First Bolshevik Utopia.* Bloomington: Indiana University Press, 1984.

———. *Revolutionary Dreams: Utopian Vision and Experimental Life in the Russian Revolution.* New York: Oxford University Press, 1989.

Suvin, Darko. "On the Poetics of the Science Fiction Genre." *College English* 34, no. 3 (December 1972): 372–82.

Todorov, Tzvetan. *The Fantastic: A Structural Approach to a Literary Genre.* Translated by Richard Howard. Ithaca, N.Y.: Cornell University Press, 1975.

Tolstoi, Alexei. *Aelita or the Decline of Mars.* Translated by Leland Fetzer. Ann Arbor, Mich.: Ardis, 1985.

Trotsky, Leon. *Literature and Revolution.* Translated by Rose Strunsky. Chicago: Haymarket Books, 2005.

———. "The Struggle for Cultured Speech." In *Problems of Everyday Life and Other Writings on Culture & Science,* 53–56. New York: Monad, 1973.

Tucker, Janet G. *Revolution Betrayed: Jurij Olesa's "Envy."* Columbus, Ohio: Slavic, 1996.

Weber, Harry, and Kathleen Lewis. "Zamyatin's *We,* the Proletarian Poets and Bogdanov's *Red Star.*" In *Zamyatin's "We": A Collection of Critical Essays.* Ann Arbor, Mich.: Ardis, 1988.

Wegner, Phillip E. *Imaginary Communities: Utopia, the Nation, and the Spatial Histories of Modernity.* Berkeley: University of California Press, 2002.

Williams, Robert C. "'Changing Landmarks' in Russian Berlin, 1922–1924." *Slavic Review* 27, no. 4 (December 1968): 581–93.

Zamyatin, Yevgeny [Evgenii Zamiatin]. *My: Roman, povesti, rasskazy, p'esy, stat'i i vospominaniia.* Kishinev: Literaturnoe artistike, 1989.

———. "The New Russian Prose." In *A Soviet Heretic,* edited and translated by Mirra Ginsburg, 92–106. London: Quartet Books, 1991.

———. "On Literature, Revolution, Entropy, and Other Matters." In *A Soviet Heretic,* translated by Mirra Ginsburg, 107–13. London: Quartet Books, 1991.

———. "The Presentists." In *Zamyatin's "We": A Collection of Critical Essays,* edited by Gary Kern, translated by Joe Denny, 263–65. Ann Arbor, Mich.: Ardis, 1988.

———. "Scythians?" In *A Soviet Heretic,* edited and translated by Mirra Ginsburg, 21–33. London: Quartet Books, 1991.

Zelnik, Reginald E. "A Paradigm Lost? Response to Anna Krylova." *Slavic Review* 62, no. 1 (Spring 2003): 24–33.

Index

About the Author

Eric Laursen is an associate professor in the Department of Languages and Literature at the University of Utah.